THE

REAGAN
YEARS
A to Z

THE
REAGAN
YEARS
A to Z

An Alphabetical History of Ronald Reagan's Presidency

by

Kenneth Franklin Kurz

Lowell House
Los Angeles

Contemporary Books
Chicago

Library of Congress Cataloging-in-Publication Data

Kurz, Kenneth Franklin.
    The Reagan years Ato Z: an alphabetical history of Ronald Reagan's
presidency / by Kenneth Franklin Kurz.
       p.   cm.
    Includes bibliographical references and index.
    ISBN 1-56565-462-5
    1. United States—Politics and government—1981-1989-
-Dictionaries.   I. Title.
E876.K87   1996
973.927'03—dc20   96-30537
                                                CIP

Requests for such permissions should be addressed to:
Lowell House
2029 Century Park East, Suite 3290
Los Angeles, CA 90067

Lowell House books can be purchased at special discounts when ordered
in bulk for premiums and special sales. Contact Department TC at the
address above.

Publisher: Jack Artenstein
Associate Publisher, Lowell House Adult: Bud Sperry
Managing Editor: Maria Magallanes
Text design: Laurie Young

Manufactured in the United States of America
10 9 8 7 6 5 4 3 2 1

CONTENTS

To my parents.

ACKNOWLEDGMENTS

First of all, I want to thank Bud Sperry, who is both general manager of Lowell House and the editor of this book. I have more to thank Bud for than general managing and editing; this book was his idea, and he invited me to write it. It was nice of him to entrust his brain-child to me. Maria Magallanes, managing editor, guided me through the mysteries of proofing and final edits with diligence, patience, and understanding.

Karin Portman, who has seen me through so much in life, saw me through this. I can never thank her enough for the love, encouragement, support, comfort, and sheer joy she mustered on those endless nights she spent watching me lurch between the living-room couch and the computer. She never chided me as our Coca-Cola budget edged into deficit spending.

At UCLA, Professors Ruth Bloch and Muriel McClendon gave wise counsel about this project. Professor Robert Dallek, also at UCLA, offered advice and encouragement, and Professor Paul Boyer, of the University of Wisconsin, as always, contributed a humorous letter or two, and good counsel as well.

Paul Goyne and Bruce LaForse helped in countless ways, particularly as delegates from Earth during some of the more labor-intensive phases. My sister, Meredith, lent a good deal of companionship and empathy to the proceedings, as she has in so many contexts throughout my life.

Finally, I gratefully acknowledge Barbara Bernstein, assistant graduate adviser in history at UCLA, for all she did to help this project get started. Barbara helps a lot of people, and it's good to be able to thank her in print.

AUTHOR'S NOTE

Writing a general history of any given subject entails certain problems, and a history in dictionary form poses its own particular kind. The main questions, always, are what to include and what to leave out. That is true for any sort of history; in an alphabetical format, you must decide if an issue, event, or person merits its own entry, or should go under another topic's heading.

By and large, I tried to base those decisions on an item's larger historical significance or, in some instances, a singularity or peculiarity that made it stand out somehow, such as David Stockman's public apostasy against Reaganomics. The Iran-Iraq War, as another example, is included in a general Persian Gulf entry, rather than having its own. The war was significant indeed, but I believed it more useful to describe its importance in the context of the region. On the other hand, the Grenada invasion has a separate entry, because that event illustrates, or highlights, some particularly critical aspects of Ronald Reagan's foreign policy.

For individuals like Gerald Ford, Jimmy Carter, David Stockman, George Bush, William Casey, and others—I decided to concentrate on how their careers intersected with Ronald Reagan's or pertained to his presidency. So their biographical entries are not full biographies per se but rather part of the history of the administration—except for the biographical entries on Ronald Reagan and Nancy Reagan. It would be difficult to understand Reagan's presidency without trying, at least to some extent, to understand Reagan. There is no attempt at a major analysis of the man here, but I thought it appropriate to write fairly extensive individual entries about the president and first lady.

Still other individuals have separate biographical entries because their impact extended beyond Reagan and his presidency. That is why Barry Goldwater has a separate entry but Edwin Meese does not. On the other hand, some people who played major roles in the Reagan administration do not have their own entries because other entries chronicle their careers cumulatively.

This book is a history of Ronald Reagan's presidency rather than a general study of, say, the 1980s. All the material herein pertains directly to Reagan and his presidency in an overview of what I believe to be some of the more important aspects of the Reagan administration's history. Since a single author chose the material, I expect there will be some differences of opinion on how appropriate my choices were.

Other historians, no doubt, would make some different choices as well as some of the same ones. There is no definitive historical approach to any subject. My primary hope for this study is that readers will find it interesting, informative, and useful as a reference for a fascinating aspect of our recent history.

THE

REAGAN
YEARS
A to Z

A

AIR-TRAFFIC CONTROLLERS' STRIKE

The August 1981 strike by the Professional Air Traffic Controllers' Organization (PATCO) posed an early challenge for the new president. Thirteen thousand union members walked off their jobs, and President Reagan, acting on Transportation Secretary Drew Lewis's advice, threatened to fire strikers who did not return to work within forty-eight hours. The president told the union that the strike was illegal, and he intended to enforce the law against strikes by government employees.

PATCO was one of the few national unions that endorsed Ronald Reagan's 1980 candidacy. Reagan was the only president who had been a member of the AFL-CIO, and he later wrote that by "instinct and experience" he supported workers' rights to unionization and collective bargaining. But air-traffic controllers were government employees, and Reagan quoted one of his favorite predecessors, Calvin Coolidge: "There is no right to strike against the public safety by anybody, anywhere, at any time."

The union held firm, and so did the president; he fired the strikers en masse and initiated legal action against the union leaders. The political benefits for Reagan were considerable, as his decisive action impressed much of the public, and many observers contrasted his resolution with the alleged indecisiveness of his immediate predecessor, Jimmy Carter.

At the same time, many critics noted how far the conservative president had traveled from his younger, more liberal self, when he was a founding member and an early president of the Screen Actors Guild. In any case, Reagan's reaction to the PATCO strike was a clear indication of the sort of presidency he would conduct in the coming years.

YURI ANDROPOV

Leonid Brezhnev's immediate successor as leader of the Soviet Union was in power only a short time before his own death. Yuri Andropov was a former head of the KGB, and his ascension caused some nervousness in the West, but his early public statements suggested an interest in stabilizing relations with the United States and maybe even reviving the détente of the Nixon-Brezhnev years.

Possibly trying to make the new leader appear more attractive and less threatening to the West, Soviet sources spread stories that Andropov spoke fluent English and owned an extensive collection of jazz recordings. American journalists and diplomats found nothing to substantiate these rumors, and some American intelligence officers publicly expressed their doubts that Andropov knew English. It stood to reason, they asserted, that if a major Soviet political figure spoke our language and collected jazz records, the international intelligence community would know about it.

That these rumors even circulated, however, suggested that the Soviet leader at least sought some common ground with his adversaries. But Andropov, who served only from November 1982 to February 1984, never developed any particular relationship with Ronald Reagan and never met him. The communications between the two leaders were always at best distant and often chilly; this was a low point in U.S.-Soviet relations, the interim period between Brezhnev's death and the start of the Gorbachev era. During this period, Soviet fighter planes shot down Korean Airlines Flight 007, occasioning an international outcry and dealing yet another serious blow to any chance of improving relations between the two superpowers.

Andropov did make one memorable unofficial gesture to the West. Samantha Smith, an eleven-year-old American girl, wrote directly to Andropov, asking why there could not be peace between the United States and the Soviet Union. Andropov responded by inviting Samantha to visit the Soviet Union, and the little girl went there as Andropov's guest. The Soviets received Samantha as a state visitor, although she did not meet Andropov himself. The visit garnered heavy media coverage, and Ted Koppel interviewed Samantha on ABC's *Nightline*.

The invitation and visit were a public-relations coup for Andropov and the Soviet Union, but superpower relations did not thaw and, shortly thereafter, took a turn for the worse when the Soviets downed the South Korean airliner. Samantha Smith, however, became a heroine to the Soviet Union. When, two years later, she died at age thirteen in a plane crash, the Soviet government issued a commemorative stamp in her honor.

Reagan, for his part, took an unabashedly hard line in his dealings with Andropov. In a speech delivered on March 8, 1983, at Disney's EPCOT Center in Florida, he broadcast a direct message to the Soviet leader. Reagan reaffirmed his anticommunist stance, reminded his audience that the Soviets still seemed intent on world domination, and proposed a "50 percent cut in strategic ballistic missiles and the elimination of an entire class of land-based intermediate-range nuclear missiles."

But the United States would not accept a nuclear freeze, Reagan noted, and he described such a freeze as a "dangerous fraud." A freeze, Reagan maintained, would "reward the Soviet Union" for its recent massive arms buildup; the president decried some protesters' desire for "simple-minded appeasement or wishful thinking."

Andropov's reactions to these and similar pronouncements by Reagan were surprisingly mild, although he maintained the Soviet Union's refusal to discuss Soviet involvement in various Third World insurgencies and continued to demand that the United States not deploy new Pershing II and cruise missiles in Western Europe. Also, Andropov tried to minimize the USSR's military programs and called for internal changes in his country's economic policies.

Andropov in some ways outdid Reagan in presenting his case to the international community. Historian Robert Dallek has pointed out that Andropov, after only about two months in office, had designed "a coherent arms control policy towards the United States and Western Europe which encouraged the impression that Moscow was more eager than Washington to negotiate a treaty." This was, Dallek notes, largely Soviet propaganda, but "Washington's quick rejection of the proposals enhanced the view" that Reagan was "so rigidly anticommunist" that he would thwart any serious prospects for fruitful arms-control negotiations.

The downing of Flight 007, in September of 1983, destroyed the impression of a new Soviet reasonableness and entirely derailed the cool but steady cordiality that had been developing between the superpowers. Andropov answered Western expressions of outrage with traditional Russian defensiveness and recrimination. As Reagan had been reviving earlier American Cold War rhetoric, so Andropov now revived the old-time language of Soviet hard-liners. Andropov denounced America's "imperialist" policies and military aggression and seemed to agree with other Soviet officials that Reagan was unreasonable and dangerous and that it would be fruitless to enter into negotiations with him.

The climate worsened when Andropov deployed Soviet submarines, armed with nuclear weapons, closer than ever to the continental United States and then pulled out of the arms-control talks in Geneva. Formally, Andropov's actions were meant to protest the Pershing II deployments, but the talks had been going nowhere in any case.

The winter of 1983–84 was a near nadir of postdétente Cold War tensions. In January, perhaps recognizing the danger of the situation as well as seeing the American advantage over the Soviets' tottering economy, Reagan moderated his public pronouncements and spoke of 1984 as a year of new opportunities for achieving peace, or at least a working relationship between the United States and the Soviet Union. The Soviets seemed to respond favorably, and Reagan received Soviet foreign minister Andrey Gromyko at the White House. Then, in February, Andropov suddenly died.

Andropov's death touched off a brief period of confusion about foreign policy in both Moscow and Washington. Andropov's successor, Konstantin Chernenko, was another elderly old-line Communist and represented something of an unknown factor in Soviet-American relations, as had Andropov when he first took office. In any case, even with a titular head, there now was a vacuum in Soviet power, and the Reagan administration became perplexed as to what sort of Soviet policy to follow.

Chernenko, like Andropov, died soon after taking office. He was the last old-time Communist Soviet leader, prior to the Gorbachev era. (*See also* Leonid Brezhnev; Brezhnev Doctrine; Cold War; Foreign Policy/Foreign Relations; Korean Airlines Flight 007; Reagan Doctrine.)

ANTICOMMUNISM

Ronald Reagan, as president, initially repudiated and opposed détente. In one speech, the president referred to the Soviet Union as the "evil empire." On another notorious occasion, the president joked that the United States had just outlawed the Soviet Union and that we would begin bombing in five minutes. Unfortunately, Reagan spoke into a live microphone that he thought was turned off. The Soviets were not amused. The president made his joke during a low ebb in American-Soviet relations, although the Soviets probably would have found the jest unamusing in the best of times. Besides being undiplomatic, it drove home Ronald Reagan's strident hostility to Communism and the Soviet Union.

In its early years, the Reagan administration took a diplomatic stance that many diplomats considered perilous. The president effectively reverted to the rhetoric of the 1950s, though two of his predecessors, Jimmy Carter and Richard Nixon, had attempted to thaw Cold War relations by opening arms-control negotiations with the Soviet Union and making diplomatic overtures to normalize relations with the People's Republic of China. Reagan considered restoring relations with Taiwan and reversing the normalization of relations with the People's Republic that Nixon, Ford, and Carter sought and achieved.

Reagan was unequivocally hostile to Communism, in a way that American foreign-policy leaders had not been, at least publicly, since Nixon visited China in 1972. While Nixon, himself an inveterate anticommunist, and Carter had not been entirely conciliatory in their Cold War policies, they had sought to restore some sort of diplomatic balance to world politics in the wake of the Vietnam War; the Soviet Union's longstanding rift with the Chinese also provided an opportunity to play the two Communist giants against each other—some observers called this situation America's "China card" in its dealings with the Soviet Union.

The 1979 Soviet invasion of Aghanistan, however, caused President Carter to take a harder anti-Soviet line while further cultivating China. Reagan's "evil empire" stance, therefore, did not occur in a vacuum, although his two-China policy caused bewilderment and worry among many State Department heads.

On examination, Reagan's hostility is not difficult to understand and is consistent with his pre-White House political inclinations. As president of the Screen Actors Guild during the late 1940s and early 1950s, Reagan, then still a fairly liberal Democrat, maintained a strict anticommunist policy and cooperated with the House Committee on Un-American Activities in its highly publicized attempts to purge Hollywood of real and imagined Communist influences.

Reagan met his future wife, SAG member Nancy Davis, when she contacted him in order to clear up her misidentification with another actress of the same name who had been accused of Communist sympathies. Reagan led SAG at a time when Hollywood was under siege, at the beginning of what would become the McCarthy era. (*See also* Nancy Davis Reagan.)

By Reagan's own account, at the end of World War II, he was still very much a New Deal Democrat and believed that government could solve all the nation's social ills, just as it had fought the Depression and won World War II. Reagan was, he later claimed, hostile to big business and believed in government ownership of public utilities and socialized medicine. But even with all this, the actor opposed Communism and was shocked and appalled at the extent of Communist influence he saw in the Screen Actors Guild. By his own account, he became an outspoken liberal opponent of the Hollywood Communists, and curtailing their power became one of his major concerns. (*See also* Ronald Wilson Reagan.)

As the 1950s progressed, Reagan grew more politically conservative; his movie career waned, and he became a spokesman for the General Electric Company. In 1960, he later wrote, he realized that he had come to agree with the conservative Republicans he had previously opposed, and proceeded to support Richard Nixon for president (he had also, as a Democrat, supported Republican Dwight Eisenhower for president in 1952 and 1956). Reagan did not change his party registration that year but instead posed as a Democrat for Nixon, and campaigned with a convert's zeal.

Perhaps Reagan's zealous conversion explains the stridently unreconstructed Cold War rhetoric that characterized his own presidency's first several years. Reagan's budding conservatism "matured" during the late 1940s and the early 1950s, an era of pronounced polarization in national politics. As a Democrat, Reagan was a New Dealer but hardly any sort of extremist—he was neither a Socialist nor a Communist but a standard-issue American liberal. As a converted Republican, however, he quickly gravitated to the party's right wing and in 1964 actively campaigned for the Republican presidential nominee, Arizona senator Barry Goldwater, the Republican far right's hero. Reagan's nationally televised campaign speech for the senator helped launch Reagan's own political career; he was elected governor of California two years later. (*See also* Barry Goldwater.)

So Ronald Reagan, as a conservative, adopted a worldview of sharp and absolute verities, thus differing little from Goldwater himself. The governor quickly displaced the senator as the right wing's main hero during the mid-1960s and so found himself obligated to keep the faith. Besides his no doubt genuine convert's zeal, Reagan also needed to keep up the rightist stance in order to maintain his original and most loyal constituency in the GOP's most conservative wing.

Conservative Republicans were appalled by President Nixon's "sell-out" policy of détente, and Reagan probably shared their sentiments. He also was a clever and realistic politician and knew that his Cold War hard line would go over with more diverse and general audiences as well; through the 1970s and during the 1980 campaign, Reagan was in the happy position of having it both ways, in that his conservatism appealed to many Americans who were not put off by his more extreme views, and his more extreme views played to his right-wing supporters.

Historian Robert Dallek points out that during Reagan's first term, his perceptions of the Soviets seemed to mirror his domestic politics. Reagan's anticommunist rhetoric closely resembled his antiliberal rhetoric in that he described Communism as fostering the evils of big government, atheism, and excessive moral permissiveness. That description was identical to how Reagan depicted American liberal ideas and policies. He also spoke of Soviet Communism's indifference to matters of personal freedom, the individual's dignity, and the devaluation of initiative under the Soviet system. Those terms precisely matched the conservative critique of liberal social policies.

Once Mikhail Gorbachev came to power in the Soviet Union, President Reagan moderated his pronouncements. During a state visit to Moscow in 1988, Western reporters asked Reagan if he still thought of the Soviet Union as an evil empire. The president replied that the term came from "another time, another era." Even so, the tough stance Reagan took in negotiations with the Soviets seemed to indicate the president's undying hostility to Communism, and while Reagan's tone changed, he remained unyielding on the issue of preserving American primacy. (*See also* Arms Control/Arms Race; Cold War.)

One cannot but wonder how a less ideological and more pragmatic president, such as Richard Nixon, might have handled issues with Gorbachev. Nixon, after all, had been even more actively anticommunist than Reagan, and for a longer time, as Representative Nixon served on the House Committee on Un-American Activities during the late 1940s, when Reagan was still ostensibly a liberal Democrat. Nixon made his national reputation by going after accused Communist Alger Hiss.

Interestingly, and ironically, when Nixon ran for the Senate from California in 1950, Reagan actively supported the Democratic nominee, the very liberal Helen Gahagan Douglas, and publicly expressed outrage when Nixon accused her of Communist sympathies (the infamous "Pink Lady" charge).

So Reagan stands as a sort of Johnny-come-lately to the practice of Red-baiting, and his energetic accommodation of the congressional Red-baiters during his SAG presidency anticipated his equally energetic anticommunism as an elected public official, which often crossed the line into McCarthy-like demagoguery. As president of the United States, Reagan awarded a posthumous Medal of Freedom to Whittaker Chambers, Alger Hiss's accuser in the late 1940s.

At the same time, Ronald Reagan was the president who concluded important arms-control treaties with the Soviets and formed a personal relationship with Mikhail Gorbachev. That may seem paradoxical, but many who have studied Reagan note that, with all his doctrinaire anticommunism, he believed that the Soviets could be led to see reason, if only he could establish personal contact with their leaders. He considered Communism an aberration in human affairs and assumed, correctly, that it was declining during the 1980s. He also believed that he could reason with Gorbachev in particular.

No doubt Reagan's ideas and feelings were indeed paradoxical, as human beings, including presidents, are often contradictory creatures. That Reagan presided over the beginning of the Cold War's end may be as ironic as the fact that it was Nixon who went to China. (*See also* Arms Control/Arms Race; China and Taiwan; Cold War; Foreign Policy/Foreign Relations; Reagan Doctrine.)

ARMS CONTROL/ARMS RACE

When Ronald Reagan took office, both the arms race and arms control had been central issues for every American president since Truman, particularly after the Soviet Union tested its first nuclear device in 1949. Through the Eisenhower and Kennedy administrations, the superpowers discussed nuclear arms control, and the concept got a large boost when the United States and the Soviet Union concluded the 1962 Test Ban Treaty, which forbade nuclear testing in the earth's atmosphere. Then, during the Vietnam War, the issue lost some prominence, until Richard Nixon ushered in détente during the early 1970s.

Leonid Brezhnev, who led the Soviet Union from 1964 until his death in 1982, conducted a dualist arms policy, beginning an intensive military buildup while expressing willingness to negotiate with the United States. Brezhnev negotiated a series of treaties with presidents Nixon, Ford, and Carter. SALT I, the first Strategic Arms Limitation Treaty, concluded in 1972, put a five-year limit on American and Soviet deployment of strategic weapons systems.

Also in 1972, Brezhnev and Nixon signed the Anti-Ballistic Missile (ABM) Treaty, which restricted the two nations' deployment of defensive systems. In 1979 Brezhnev and Carter signed the second Strategic Arms Limitation Treaty, which would have limited strategic launch vehicles and delivery craft and put limits on developing new missiles. The United States Senate never ratified SALT II. The two nations have been unofficially observing the treaty's terms, but the 1979 Soviet invasion of Afghanistan badly strained relations with the United States, and after the détente of the 1970s, the Cold War entered a newly frigid period. President Carter withdrew the SALT II treaty from Senate consideration and stepped up production of cruise missiles.

When Ronald Reagan's presidency began in 1981, many observers believed that the Soviet Union had achieved nuclear parity with the United States. Various commentators have written that the United States military suffered a post-Vietnam malaise during the 1970s; morale and capability, critics argued, lagged among conventional troops, and the Soviets had caught up with America's nuclear capacity.

In speeches and writings, Reagan declared it a primary principle of his foreign policy to maintain military, particularly nuclear, superiority over the Soviet Union. Reagan intended to spend virtually unlimited amounts of money to outdo the Soviets in the arms race, and he declared that the United States "would never accept second place." Reagan believed that Communist Russia could not outspend or outproduce capitalist America and thus could not win the arms race. The successful capitalist system guaranteed a permanent industrial and technological advantage over the Soviets.

During Reagan's early years in office, he chose to continue Jimmy Carter's massive, and massively funded, arms buildup, although

Reagan appeared reluctant to credit his predecessor and often presented the buildup as his own original policy. The buildup produced some results, since an already shaky Soviet economy could scarcely maintain a matching buildup, and the war in Afghanistan proved a considerable drain on Soviet money, resources, and manpower.

Further, the Soviet arms buildup of the previous decade, combined with Soviet financing of localized foreign insurgencies and the bottomless pit for Soviet rubles in Cuba, proved a tremendous strain and may well have hastened the Soviet Union's collapse and demise after Reagan left office. Such difficulties probably made the Soviets more amenable to negotiation, although it did not seem so during the last years of Brezhnev's life, nor during the brief tenures of his immediate successors, Yuri Andropov and Konstantin Chernenko. It took a new generation of Soviet leadership, headed by Mikhail Gorbachev, to renew U.S.-Soviet arms-control negotiations in the mid-1980s.

Carter and Reagan's revival of the arms race may not have been the only crucial factors in bringing the Soviets to the bargaining table. The Soviet economic crisis slowed the USSR's arms buildup even before Reagan took office. After 1976, according to historian Walter LaFeber, the Soviet military budget increased only about 2 percent per year, and the Soviets seemed interested in achieving parity, rather than superiority. To attempt such a feat would have been pure fantasy, as Gorbachev's primary economic adviser estimated during the 1980s that Soviet labor productivity would have to increase 50 percent per year, in order just to keep up with American economic growth, and this could not be done.

Even in this tense atmosphere, the superpowers managed to sign the 1982 Strategic Arms Reduction Treaty (START), which provided for a 50 percent reduction of the American and Soviet nuclear arsenals. But this still did not promote harmony, and relations between the two nations remained dangerously cold.

The Reagan administration had not been breathlessly awaiting an opportunity for negotiations, however—at least the administration showed little interest in negotiating on equal terms. Reagan was aiming for superiority as a tool for forcing fundamental changes in Soviet foreign policy and military strategy. In his postpresidential memoirs, he wrote that the American buildup represented a new "realism" in America's Soviet policy. At the same time, he wished to inform the Soviet leaders that "the nuclear standoff was futile and dangerous," and the Soviets "had nothing to fear from us if they behaved themselves."

That was not an invitation to reason but rather a thinly veiled threat, and Reagan's continuing aggressive anti-Soviet rhetoric, as well as his earlier repudiation of détente prior to Gorbachev's ascension, helped perpetuate a hostile atmosphere. Additionally, under Andropov and Chernenko, the Soviets seemed in no mood to negotiate, and often objected publicly to the president's denunciations.

Arms-control negotiations, of course, hinged upon the overall state of U.S.-Soviet relations, and despite private and limited diplomacy, the two nations had barely been speaking to each other in any meaningful way since the Soviet invasion of Afghanistan in 1979. Worse, the Reagan administration pursued its military build-up and resisted arms-control negotiations. In July 1982, at the Geneva arms talks, a top Soviet negotiator and his American counter-part suggested that America not deploy the proposed Pershing II missiles in Western Europe, in return for the Soviets' reducing their SS-20s in Eastern Europe. Neither government accepted the idea, and Reagan went ahead with plans to deploy the Pershing II missiles. This episode clearly signaled the administration's stance on arms control during the early 1980s.

By the mid-1980s, Reagan's advisers realized that America's economy, too, would soon be unable to sustain a massive, ongoing military buildup. Thus arose a more favorable environment for arms-control negotiations. During the early and middle 1980s, U.S.-Soviet relations reached a low point, and the Soviet's downing of Korean Airlines Flight 007 in 1983 sorely aggravated the strain between the two superpowers. But new Kremlin leadership, the severe economic imperatives faced by the Soviet Union, and America's own economic difficulties were all conducive to opening renewed negotiations.

At the December 1985 Geneva summit, Gorbachev expressed definite interest in arms control, but Reagan upped the ante by proclaiming the United States' intention to develop the Strategic Defense Initiative (SDI), popularly known as Star Wars. SDI became a sticking point for the Soviets; going into the summit, Gorbachev hoped, according to LaFeber, to limit space weaponry, stop all nuclear testing, and keep alive the SALT II treaty, which the Carter administration had negotiated with Brezhnev and then renounced in 1979. The Geneva summit ended without any breakthrough on arms control, and Reagan came away angry and empty-handed.

Gorbachev continued to insist that SDI manifested a critical obstacle to achieving any effective arms-control treaties. The Soviet leader had a point, as the Reagan administration seemed to insist on strategic advantage while claiming to negotiate in good faith for nuclear balance. The Soviets found America's paradoxical stance unacceptable.

Reagan and his advisers believed that the crumbling Soviet economy held Gorbachev, and indeed the entire Soviet system, over a barrel. The Soviets, though veteran hardball negotiators themselves, traditionally reacted adversely to American hardball negotiating, and Gorbachev, to Reagan's great annoyance, reacted in that tradition at the next summit.

At Geneva Gorbachev accepted Reagan's invitation to visit the United States during 1986, and the two pursued the arms-control issue anew during that visit. Earlier, in January of 1986, the Soviets offered a proposal that both sides remove their intermediate nuclear missiles from Europe over the next several years. This was actually Reagan's old Zero-Zero Option idea that Brezhnev revealed several years earlier.

At the summit in Reykjavik, Iceland, in October 1986, Reagan reaffirmed the Zero-Zero Option and included in the bargain the removal of shorter-ranged missiles. Gorbachev, however, shocked Reagan once again by linking the deal to SDI.

Gorbachev seemed amenable to any number of American proposals, as long as Reagan would agree not to move forward with SDI. Reagan just as stubbornly insisted on developing SDI and claimed that, once the system was operational, the United States would share the technology with the Soviet Union. But Gorbachev and other Soviet officials still suspected that SDI was essentially a way for America to neutralize Soviet nuclear weapons while maintaining first-strike capability for itself.

Whatever Reagan's motives for pursuing the apparently unattainable SDI, he tried to assure the Soviets that their suspicions were groundless. Although Gorbachev offered to cut strategic weapons by half if the United States would give up SDI, Reagan continued to resist.

For several months, the arms-control issue stagnated, until Gorbachev suddenly became quite agreeable and in April offered to dismantle all shorter-range intermediate missiles in Europe. In 1987 negotiators for the United States and the Soviet Union finally agreed on a treaty to remove 2,500 American and Soviet missiles from Europe. That December Reagan and Gorbachev sealed this agreement by signing the Intermediate Nuclear Forces (INF) Treaty. The treaty provided for on-site inspections by both sides to verify compliance. (*See also* Leonid Brezhnev; Brezhnev Doctrine; Foreign Policy/Foreign Relations; Korean Airlines Flight 007; Reagan Doctrine; Strategic Defense Initiative; Zero-Zero Option.)

ASSASSINATION ATTEMPT

John W. Hinckley, Jr., shot President Reagan on March 30, 1981, after Reagan had been in office only seventy days. The attempted assassination jolted the nation and raised serious questions about issues of security, personnel, and politics, as well as the president's age and ongoing medical condition. The events that occurred immediately after the shootings (the White House press secretary, a Secret Service agent, and a Washington police officer also were hit by gunfire) revealed some of the rivalries and animosities that already plagued the new administration, and the disposition of the criminal case against Hinckley aggravated the already bitter controversy over criminal justice.

Hinckley began shooting just after 2:30 P.M. as Reagan was about to enter a car outside the Washington Hilton Hotel; the weapon was a cheap handgun, loaded with explosive-tipped Devastator bullets. As the shots rang out, Secret Service agents pushed the president into the car, and agent Tim McCarthy took a bullet in the abdomen when he turned to face Hinckley. Washington police officer Tom Delehanty was shot in the neck, and Press Secretary James Brady received the worst wound of all; a bullet traveled through his brain, leaving him partially paralyzed and permanently disabled.

The Secret Service at first ordered the driver to the White House, but when the president began to cough up blood, he was taken instead to a local hospital. Reagan did not realize he had been shot and thought that agent Jerry Parr inadvertently broke his rib when he pushed him into the car. Doctors discovered the bullet hole as they examined the president in the emergency room of George Washington University Hospital. Reagan's blood pressure was dangerously low, and he showed symptoms of going into shock.

The president was wounded in the chest; the bullet entered through the left armpit, struck a rib, glanced off the bone, pierced a lung, and stopped near the heart. Despite public-relations efforts that day, and in the days following, to play down his condition's seriousness, Reagan was in fact gravely wounded, and his medical condition, particularly on that first day, was dangerous indeed. His chest cavity was filling with blood, and he was showing signs of incipient shock as he was placed in the hospital's trauma unit.

Reagan's sense of humor and irony stood him in good stead even in this potentially deadly situation. He later admitted how frightened he was in that emergency room, but that did not keep him from entertaining the medical staff even before his condition stabilized. As he lay on a gurney, he felt, through his grogginess, a female hand holding his and assumed it was a nurse. He later wrote that he felt reassured and deeply touched, but he could not focus to see who his comforter might be. He asked and got no answer. Then he said, "Does Nancy know about us?"

Just before undergoing surgery, Reagan quipped to the surgical team that he hoped they were Republicans, whereupon one of the doctors assured him that, at that moment, everyone was a Republican. According to the medical personnel present, the president remained in strong spirits, and in the recovery room, a very groggy Ronald Reagan joked with the hospital staff and told stories to an enthralled bedside audience until one of the surgeons chased everyone away.

The would-be assassin had a long record of unstable behavior and had apparently convinced himself that actress Jodie Foster, an undergraduate at Yale University, was his girlfriend. He bombarded Foster with obsessive letters, telling her to maintain her virginity for him, to wait for him, and assuring her of his undying love. It has been suggested that his attempt to kill the president was really an attempt to impress the object of his obsession; Hinckley appears to have been essentially apolitical. Foster testified at Hinckley's trial about his communications with her and told her questioner that she herself had no relationship with the defendant. Upon hearing this, Hinckley left the courtroom in tears. From that day to this, Foster has declined to comment publicly on John Hinckley, except for an article she wrote for *Esquire* magazine after the trial.

Hinckley was found not guilty on grounds of insanity and confined indefinitely to a mental hospital in Washington, D.C., where he remains. His case is controversial; many people believe that he should have been convicted and sentenced to prison. However, as a mental patient, Hinckley may possibly be confined for life, whereas his sentence might have been limited if he were a federal prisoner. In any case, he has never been released from the hospital, even though his case comes up periodically for review.

In the wake of the shootings, events back at the White House raised questions as to who was in charge of what. Under the Twenty-fifth Amendment to the Constitution, adopted in 1967, when a president is disabled and transmits to the president pro tempore of the Senate and the speaker of the House of Representatives a "written declaration that he is unable to discharge the powers and duties of his office, and until he transmits to them a written declaration to the contrary, such powers and duties shall be discharged by the Vice President as Acting President." But no such notification was forthcoming from President Reagan. As he bled in the emergency room of a local hospital, he retained the full authority and power of the presidency.

Vice President George Bush, having heard of the shootings, was en route to Washington from Texas when Secretary of State Alexander Haig announced to the press that, pending the vice president's arrival, "I am in control. . . ." According to Haig's memoirs, he rushed to the White House after the shooting and almost immediately got into an argument with Defense Secretary Caspar Weinberger over the status of the armed forces.

Weinberger, new to the job and new to the military, could not give Haig a satisfactory explanation of whether he had raised the alert status of the armed forces. The two argued about the meaning of various terms and actions, and Haig grew ever more alarmed and anxious, for it seemed to him that the Defense Department, under the new secretary, did not know how to respond to this. Haig feared that raising our alert status might frighten the Soviets into raising theirs.

Whatever was said during that clash (there are conflicting accounts), a fairly unnerved Alexander Haig faced the news cameras and asserted that he was in control, meaning, probably, that he had restored some coherence to the confusion in the White House. Haig has claimed that he never meant to imply that he was commanding the government and thereby usurping the vice-president's duty to assume acting presidential authority.

Reagan was back on the job before mid-April. Although his full recovery took somewhat longer, the president showed remarkable resilience and spirit in bouncing back from such a serious wound. He impressed the nation on the day he was shot by repeating to his wife the famous words of Jack Dempsey, "Honey, I forgot to duck," and by slightly misquoting W.C. Fields's proposed epitaph, "All in all, I'd rather be in Philadelphia." (Fields actually said, "On the whole, I'd rather be in Philadelphia.")

That April Reagan impressed the nation with his will to recover and return to work. His standing in the polls escalated accordingly. Shortly after the assassination attempt, the president said, "God must have been sitting on my shoulder. Now, whatever time I have left, it belongs to someone else." (*See also* George Bush; Cabinet; Twenty-fifth Amendment.)

ASTROLOGY

During the last year of Ronald Reagan's presidency, word reached the public that Nancy Reagan had for years consulted an astrologer about matters concerning the president's scheduling, travel, and various other things. There was immediate widespread worry and speculation that the pseudoscience may have had an actual effect on White House decisions. While never escalating into a major controversy, the news, first revealed by former White House Chief of Staff Donald T. Regan in his memoirs, still proved significantly embarrassing.

Regan thought that Mrs. Reagan's beliefs may have caused the president to mishandle some situations, most notably press relations during the Iran-Contra scandal. According to Regan, when the scandal broke, Mrs. Reagan decided that the president should not talk to the press because her "friend" (probably astrologer Joan Quigley) advised against it. Regan wondered what other decisions may have ridden on the friend's reading of the stars.

Nancy Reagan always denied that her astrological beliefs had any bearing on policy decisions and later wrote that she turned to her astrologer friend for comfort after the assassination attempt in 1981. Astrology, claimed Mrs. Reagan, was a way for her to cope with her fears after the president was nearly assassinated. For the next few years, the first lady consulted astrologer Joan Quigley (paying her for her services on a monthly basis) about such matters as whether or not certain days might be dangerous for the president to travel, speak publicly, make certain decisions, and so on.

Long before Nancy Reagan's penchant became public, various administration officials, such as Regan and Michael Deaver, among others, found her zodiacal inclinations inconvenient, sometimes irritating, and potentially embarrassing. Regan wrote that Mrs. Reagan saw to it that important surgery for the president was rescheduled because the heavens seemed unfavorable to the original date.

How seriously the first lady took astrology and whether or not Ronald Reagan paid any heed remain undetermined, and the entire episode constitutes a quirky bit of White House history. But it is worth noting that Nancy Reagan also consulted an astrologer years earlier, when her husband was elected governor of California; some local reporters in Sacramento claimed that Reagan's first gubernatorial inauguration was held just past midnight, instead of during the day for astrological reasons. In her autobiography, Mrs. Reagan refers to her husband as fitting an Aquarian personality's astrological profile. She describes herself as a "classic Cancer."

Patti Davis, the Reagans' daughter, attests to her parents' earlier adherence to astrology. Davis wrote in her autobiography, *The Way I See It*, that Mrs. Reagan scheduled redecorating the governor's mansion in Sacramento around astrologically propitious forecasts. Both Mrs. Reagan and the governor, according to Davis, paid careful attention to newspaper horoscopes, and often read them aloud to each other at breakfast. She also claimed that her parents altered their schedules, travel plans, and other activities according to astrological advice.

Quigley became a minor celebrity for a time, and such authors as Kitty Kelley made much of her supposed influence in the Reagan administration. Quigley did little if anything to dispel this impression, and, in fact, wrote her own book on her career as the "White House astrologer." (*See also* Nancy Davis Reagan.)

B

BALANCED-BUDGET AMENDMENT

A Constitutional amendment to mandate a balanced federal budget has long been a feature of the conservative agenda, supported by most Republicans and some Democrats. The Reagan administration wanted a balanced-budget amendment but never seriously pursued the amendment process. According to Donald T. Regan, who was secretary of the Treasury and then White House chief of staff, the political climate never permitted such an effort during Reagan's two terms. Congress was not receptive, although the measure had significant popular support, particularly during the second term, but it was overshadowed by other, more pressing political and social issues.

Still, the administration won some portion of its goal by helping to pass the Gramm-Rudman-Hollings Act in December 1985. The act, popularly known as Gramm-Rudman, established a schedule of deficit reductions, to commence the following year.

The call for a balanced-budget amendment remained controversial but largely symbolic through the Bush administration. With the Republican seizure of Congress in 1994, however, the issue was revived as part of the so-called "Contract With America." In 1995 the House of Representatives passed a constitutional amendment that required a balanced budget by the year 2002. The amendment provided that this goal could be suspended in wartime and that it could be overridden by a three-fifths vote of Congress.

Even with those exceptions, public support for such an amendment remained doubtful, and the House amendment failed in the Senate by one vote. So, to the present day, the balanced-budget amendment remains an elusive goal to its supporters and a worrisome threat to its opponents. (*See also* Congress; Deficit; Grace Commission; Reaganomics; David Stockman.)

BEIRUT MARINE BOMBING

One of the worst disasters to befall the American military during Reagan's presidency occurred when 241 marines died after a truck bomb exploded in their barracks near the airport in Beirut, Lebanon, in October 1983. Besides being a tragic loss of life, the incident also represented a severe setback in American policy in Lebanon.

President Reagan learned of the disaster at a strange moment in history; the previous day, an armed intruder had broken into the country club where Reagan and Secretary of State George Shultz were playing golf. The gunman held several people hostage in the pro shop, including two White House staffers, and demanded to see the president. The incident ended with no injury or loss of life, but Reagan did not leave the club and even tried to speak to the gunman on the telephone, although the gunman refused to take Reagan's calls and demanded a face-to-face meeting.

On that same day, Reagan and his advisers decided to take military action in Grenada and planned the invasion for a few days hence. So, after a full and strange day, the president and first lady had dinner with friends and retired for the night, but at approximately 2:30 A.M., National Security Adviser Robert "Bud" McFarlane called the president and informed him that a suicide bomber had hit a marine barracks near the Beirut airport. A dynamite-laden truck drove past the guards and crashed into the barracks, killing, according to the first reports, at least one-hundred marines.

Reagan, Shultz, and McFarlane flew back to Washington shortly after dawn and received the latest reports. The next day, rescue workers found more bodies and eventually determined that 241 marines had died in the bombing. Many of them died as they slept. Reagan also found out that only minutes after the barracks bombing, another car bomb killed fifty-eight soldiers in a French complex only two miles away from the airport.

Early reports indicated both bombers were Shiite radical fundamentalists bent on martyrdom and on driving the Americans and the other members of the multinational peacekeeping force out of Lebanon. But for weeks, American intelligence agencies could not be sure exactly what group had carried out the bombings. Reagan therefore decided not to launch air strikes against several suspected organizations, since no one claimed responsibility for the bombings and no one could ascertain the culprits' identities.

Only a few months later, in 1984, the United States withdrew its forces from Lebanon, and some of the Middle East states assumed, perhaps correctly, that the Americans left because they had taken such heavy casualties. Whatever the case, the perception proved consequential, since friendly nations, such as Saudi Arabia and Kuwait, and hostile nations, such as Libya and Iran, doubted American fortitude. The Saudis and Kuwaitis grew unsure whether they could rely on American pledges of support, and the Libyans and Iranians were emboldened.

In the United States, meanwhile, Reagan attended memorial services for the slain marines and for American soldiers killed in Grenada, and his public-opinion ratings remained high. Relatively few people saw the Beirut bombing as a debacle that reflected poorly on the president.

In the months following the Beirut disaster, Reagan resolved not to commit military forces overseas unless the situation clearly involved American national interests. While the Middle East has continually been a foreign-policy priority for the United States, many concluded in 1984 that staying in Lebanon was a questionable proposition.

The United States pulled out of Lebanon, the civil war continued, and over the years terrorists in Lebanon took a number of Americans and Europeans hostage. The United States faced unresolved problems and crises in the region for the remainder of Ronald Reagan's presidency. (*See also* Hostages and Terrorists; Middle East; Persian Gulf; Muammar Qaddafi.)

BITBURG

Ronald Reagan's visit to the Bitburg cemetery in West Germany was one of the most controversial events of his presidency. The visit evinced a good deal of anger and disappointment among many Americans, among survivors of both World War II combat and the Nazi death camps, and among many Germans who either could not or would not understand why feelings about Bitburg ran so high in the United States.

The controversy began shortly after Reagan accepted Chancellor Helmut Kohl's invitation to make a state visit to West Germany in April 1985, after the economic summit scheduled for that spring. Reagan and Kohl decided to observe the fortieth anniversary of the end of World War II; as a gesture of postwar friendship, Kohl invited Reagan also to visit the military cemetery at Bitburg.

Almost immediately, there was a public outcry in the United States, for not only did the cemetery contain the graves of soldiers in Hitler's army, but forty-eight members of the notorious Waffen SS were buried there. The SS was the agency that had direct responsibility for carrying out the Holocaust. The SS dead buried at Bitburg mostly belonged to the Second SS Panzer Division, which had participated in the massacre at Oradour-sur-Glane in France, where both SS and regular German Army troops murdered all 642 village residents. Two hundred and seven children were among the dead.

The media covered the controversy intensely. The West German government insisted that Reagan honor his pledge to visit Bitburg. In the United States, public-opinion polls showed that most Americans opposed the visit. Even the American Legion criticized President Reagan's resolve to go to Bitburg. The first lady told her husband she was against it, and the prominent Jewish writer, Holocaust survivor, and future Nobel Prize winner Elie Wiesel publicly asked the president not to go. "That place, Mr. President, is not your place," said Wiesel. "Your place is with the victims of the SS."

Reagan determined not to cancel the visit and thereby embarrass Kohl; whether or not Reagan himself was embarrassed to visit Bitburg cannot be determined. At any rate, Kohl let the president know that to cancel the visit would be a diplomatic faux pas. The West German chancellor attempted to alleviate the pressure and appease Reagan's critics (who now included *Pravda*, which called the impending visit a slight to Jews) by also inviting Reagan to visit the site of the Dachau concentration camp, near Munich.

Ultimately, Reagan went to the Bergen-Belsen concentration camp after a brief visit to Bitburg, and delivered a memorial address for the victims of the Holocaust, amid the mass grave mounds that covered thousands of unidentified bodies.

In his memoirs, White House Chief of Staff Donald T. Regan called the decision to visit the Bitburg cemetery "an almost inconceivable blunder," though Regan himself accepted partial responsibility. The incident was one of the few times that American public opinion went largely against President Reagan. Reagan assuaged the bad feeling somewhat by not speaking at Bitburg, spending only a few minutes there, and then speaking at Bergen-Belsen, the place where many thousands of victims, including Anne Frank, lost their lives. (*See also* National Security Advisers.)

BOLAND AMENDMENTS

The House of Representatives passed the first of the so-called Boland Amendments in 1983. Sponsored by Massachusetts Democrat Edward Boland, chairman of the House Select Committee on Intelligence, the amendment forbade American covert action to overthrow the Sandanista government in Nicaragua. It also limited CIA financial aid to the Nicaraguan Contras to a cap of $24 million, with a proviso that such funds not be used to overthrow the Sandanistas.

Late in 1984, the House passed the second Boland Amendment (sometimes known as Boland II), which cut all funding for the Contras in Nicaragua and specifically forbade any United States government agency, including the CIA, to aid the Contras in any way whatsoever.

The reactions of several key administration officials to these amendments resulted in the Iran-Contra scandal, as, according to

Fawn Hall, they had to find a way to get "above" the written law in order to continue supporting the Contras in Nicaragua. One solution was to "privatize" aid to the Contras, and National Security Adviser Robert McFarlane and his deputy, Admiral John Poindexter, set Marine Lieutenant Colonel Oliver North about the task of raising funds for the Contras among private citizens and foreign governments.

This course of action put the administration on the path to the worst scandal of the Reagan presidency. Certain administration officials, such as Poindexter and North, saw the Boland Amendments as obstacles to be surmounted, rather than the law of the land. The report of the independent counsel on the Iran-Contra affair identified the attempts to circumvent the Boland Amendments in particular as a sign of the utter contempt that some Reagan administration officials had for Congress.

Constitutionally, Congress was well within its rights and prerogatives in passing the Boland Amendments, for it is Congress's duty to allocate funds to the executive branch and to mandate limitations on how those funds may be used. (*See also* William Casey and the CIA; Central America; Iran-Contra; National Security Advisers.)

BOLL WEEVILS

The Boll Weevils were the congressional Democrats who supported the Reagan administration's fiscal and economic policies and who could usually be relied upon to vote with the Reagan Republicans on these issues. David Stockman, who headed the Office of Management and Budget during Reagan's first term, called the Boll Weevil Democrats the "mainstay" of the administration's congressional coalition in the fiscal fights during Reagan's first term.

During Reagan's presidency, the House retained its Democratic majority, although a narrow Republican majority held sway in the Senate from 1981 to 1987. Since economic legislation must originate in the House, the Boll Weevils were crucial to the president's legislative success, much to the ongoing dismay of House Speaker Thomas P. "Tip" O'Neill.

O'Neill noted in his autobiography, *Man of the House,* that the Reagan administration's fiscal policies appealed to conservative southern Democrats. The more prominent Boll Weevils were Bill Tauzin of Louisiana, Ralph Hall of Texas, Kenneth Holland of South Carolina, Kent Hance of Texas, Charles Stenholm of Texas, G.V. Montgomery of Mississippi, Bo Ginn of Georgia, James Jones of Oklahoma, and some other fiscally conservative Democrats. (*See also* Congress; Democrats; Gypsy Moths; Thomas "Tip" O'Neill.)

ROBERT H. BORK

Robert Bork's battle for confirmation as an associate justice of the Supreme Court was one of the Reagan administration's rare public-relations reversals. It was a badly mismanaged campaign to get a controversial conservative nominee past a hostile Democratic Senate. At the same time, the Democrats on the Senate Judiciary Committee resorted to low-blow tactics in their fight to keep a conservative off the Court. Neither side emerged from the fray looking very good or honorable.

Before Judge Bork's Supreme Court nomination, Americans primarily remembered him as the third ranking Justice Department officer who fired Watergate special prosecutor Archibald Cox after Attorney General Elliot Richardson and Deputy Attorney General Dennis Ruckelshaus refused President Richard Nixon's order to do so. That was the infamous "Saturday Night Massacre" of 1972, at the Watergate scandal's height; Bork's obedience to Nixon endeared him to many Republicans and probably antagonized even more Democrats.

Bork served as solicitor general of the United States under President Gerald Ford, but left that post when Jimmy Carter took office in 1977. Among lawyers and legal scholars, Bork was primarily known for his prodigious and closely argued works of legal and constitutional scholarship—particularly his conservative, strictly constructionist views on how the Constitution's framers' "original intent" pertained to modern-day lawmaking—and for his distinctly conservative rulings as a judge on the United States Court of

Appeals for Washington, D.C. At the time of his nomination, Bork had sat on the Court of Appeals since 1982.

Bork's nomination was highly controversial from the outset. Liberals feared he would vote to overturn *Roe v. Wade* (the abortion-rights decision), as well as affirmative-action and civil-rights legislation and court decisions. Judge Bork was, in short, the liberal's nightmare: a militant conservative, up for a lifetime appointment to the nation's highest court. In 1987 the newly installed Democratic majority in the Senate mustered a formidable resistance to the president's choice and blocked Bork's judicial ascendency.

The ensuing fight was uncommon in the Reagan years: The Reagan White House mounted an uncharacteristically clumsy and incompetent effort, and the usually clumsy Democrats masterfully branded Bork as something approaching a judicial Antichrist. To add to the White House's woes, Bork himself was combative and sour tempered during the confirmation hearings, and this did not play at all well in the media; most of the proceedings were televised, and Bork came across as angry and quarrelsome. However, in fairness, it must be noted that his Democratic opponents did not turn in sterling performances, either. The entire affair played itself out in a very nasty manner, and neither side emerged with much credit.

While Bork was unabashedly conservative, his opponents nevertheless distorted his views and misrepresented his scholarship in order to demonize him before the public. However one may feel about Bork as a potential justice, the Democrats on the Senate Judicial Committee resorted to a sort of liberal McCarthyism in their attack. Senator Edward Kennedy even went so far as to raise questions about Bork's youthful flirtation with socialism, during his college years, as if that somehow undermined the judge's integrity. It was ironic, indeed, for a liberal Democrat to cast doubt on a Republican's conservative credentials.

Kennedy indulged freely in inflammatory rhetoric, claiming that Bork's confirmation would drive women back into dark alleys for dangerous, illegal abortions, would drive science out of the nation's classrooms in favor of creationism, would release police from any legal restraints in harassing innocent citizens in short, Robert Bork, as a Supreme Court justice, would work the ruin of the United States of America.

Kennedy's outspoken attacks were in keeping with the overall tone of the Democrats' campaign against Bork's confirmation. Not since the Republicans shredded the reputation of Abe Fortas, Lyndon Johnson's nominee to replace Earl Warren as chief justice in 1967, had a Supreme Court nominee sustained such concentrated, highly personal attacks. Bork's very character went on trial in the court of public opinion, even though not one accusation of misconduct or wrongdoing ever emerged. Bork's character was assassinated because of his views (which were by no means the most extreme in the conservative range), in nearly the same way liberals were pilloried during the McCarthy years simply for being liberals. Now the liberals went to similar excess in order to pillory Reagan's nominee.

That, no doubt, was the crux of the matter; the Democrats had just retaken the Senate after six years of Republican majority and were out to bloody the administration. Bork supplied a very obliging target. In contrast to the liberal Democratic practice of judicial activism, Bork advocated judicial restraint, which went hand in glove with the idea of original intent.

The position of original intent—or, as Bork himself called it, original understanding—holds that the Constitution's framers had certain principles in mind when creating the American judiciary; therefore, modern judges must base their legal rulings on those principles. The classically conservative interpretation of this view holds, further, that since the framers generally operated within the Jeffersonian view of a laissez-faire republic, judicial activism violates original intent, as it necessarily introduces politics into jurisprudence.

This view of original intent presupposes that liberal rulings, in effect, are political, whereas conservative rulings, in effect, adhere to original intent, as the framers envisioned a federal government that would not do much active governing; the states, according to this view, are primarily responsible for the day-to-day governing of the nation. By extension, Bork saw recent liberal jurisprudence as virtual nullification of constitutional law itself.

Liberal activist jurists, in Bork's view, were setting aside the Constitution and its principles in favor of their own political agenda. The liberal view held that the Constitution was intended as a flexible document, which is why the judiciary was given the power to interpret it and why the amendment process exists in the first place. Bork argued that those principles were true only inasmuch as they held to the framers' original principles.

In Bork's view, any number of recent federal actions—particularly various pieces of civil-rights legislation, affirmative action, and various federal regulations—fell beyond the scope of the framers' original intent for the Constitution's areas of concern, and so did any judicial decisions that upheld them. According to Bork's constructionist view, judicial lawmaking—such as *Roe v. Wade* and the decisions that mandated busing—absolutely flew in the face of original intent, as the courts were never meant to legislate.

Bork did not argue that original understanding necessarily precluded liberal judicial rulings, but he did quarrel with the notion that judicial rulings may reinterpret the Constitution. Rather, he believed that the original intentions of the document, as set forth by the framers, must guide interpretation, and that subsequent rulings should apply the original principles rather than attempt to remold the Constitution to fit the ruling judge's idea of modern necessity.

Bork cautioned that for either liberal or conservatives to rely on judicial activism to advance a particular political or social agenda risks a great deal. Judicial rulings can be simply overturned by future rulings, and once established, the power of judicial activism to reward one group may not only punish an opposing group but also eventually rebound and punish the original activist group.

The foregoing, like everything else in public affairs, is highly debatable, but this conservative orientation guided the Reagan administration's judicial philosophy. A distinguished conservative judge, scholar, and legal thinker like Robert Bork seemed an ideal nominee to help swing the formerly liberal and activist Supreme Court even farther to the right and thus more in line with Reaganistic jurisprudence.

At the outset, the administration had no reason to think that

Bork might not win confirmation; even with a Democratic Senate, presidential appointees were confirmed more often than not, except in the case of flagrant lapses, such as President Nixon's attempt to place Harold Carswell and Clement Hanesworth on the Supreme Court—two barely reputable and highly political lawyers. Johnson's debacle with Fortas also was highly unusual, especially considering Fortas's distinguished legal career and his honorable tenure as an associate justice. In 1987 hardly any observer seriously doubted that Bork would, in due course, take his place among the nine justices of the nation's highest court. The observers, and the administration, underestimated the ferocity of the Democrats on the Senate Judiciary Committee, and they underestimated the liberals' commitment to preserving the civil-rights decisions and *Roe v. Wade.*

As the confirmation hearings began to go badly, the struggle between the administration and the Senate captured the nation's attention, and this seemed to embarrass the administration. Bork, however, dug in for the siege and continued to trade punches with the Senate Judiciary Committee long after Reagan tried to distance himself from his own beleaguered nominee. Late in the game, Bork called a press conference to announce that he would not withdraw himself from consideration and vowed to fight it out to the finish, even though the finish would be almost certain defeat.

The administration made the necessary sounds of standing by its man, but Bork clearly was on his own. Bork was the first Supreme Court nominee not to be confirmed since 1970, when the Senate rejected Carswell. (*See also* Sandra Day O'Connor; Supreme Court and Federal Judiciary.)

LEONID BREZHNEV

Having become first secretary of the Communist party after helping to oust Nikita Krushchev in 1964, Brezhnev ruled as part of a troika with Prime Minister Alexei Kosygin and old-time party politico Mikhail Suslov. After 1971 Brezhnev emerged as the top Soviet leader. In 1977 he assumed the Soviet presidency while retaining his party post.

Brezhnev presided over the Soviet side of détente during the Nixon and Ford years and negotiated the Strategic Arms Limitation Treaties (SALT I and SALT II) with Nixon and Carter. When Ronald Reagan took office in 1981, U.S.-Soviet relations had been declining since Brezhnev's ill-advised and ill-fated invasion of Afghanistan in 1979. President Jimmy Carter responded to the invasion by refusing to press for SALT II's ratification or to send the American team to the 1980 Moscow Olympics. Additionally, Reagan's long-standing, virulent anticommunism was well known to the Soviet leadership. With all the foregoing, Brezhnev and Reagan's relationship got off to a rocky start.

Also unhelpful to the new relationship was the fact that Brezhnev had ushered in the rapid Soviet military buildup of the 1970s, while at the same time negotiating arms control. Brezhnev also ordered the invasion of Czechoslovakia in 1968 as part of the Brezhnev Doctrine, which claimed the direct right of Soviet intervention in the internal affairs of Eastern bloc countries. A skilled negotiator on one hand and a hard-line Soviet Communist on the other, Brezhnev determined to maintain Russian hegemony in its sphere of influence, and to match America's military capacity —in short, to negotiate from a position of strength. But the old party secretary could not see that he was squandering with his overseas adventurism the very strength he strove so forcefully to build and maintain.

Relations between the Soviet and American presidents were decidedly cold, and the two exchanged a long series of angry, barely civil letters during Brezhnev's last years. Even so, the initial correspondence was not out of the ordinary; the letters grew more acrimonious as relations deteriorated during the early years of Reagan's presidency. Shortly after Reagan took office, he struck a sour note when he wrote to Brezhnev that the United States would no longer "accept" the Brezhnev Doctrine. Reagan stated unequivocally that the United States regarded the doctrine as counter to the spirit of the United Nations charter, and that the Soviets had no right to intervene in the internal affairs of any other nation—a disingenuous bit of reasoning, considering major aspects of Reagan's own foreign policies. Reagan concluded on a more diplomatic note, suggesting a summit in the near future.

Brezhnev's reply to the president's message was, by Reagan's own description, "icy." Brezhnev took strong issue with Reagan's criticisms and objected to being scolded about the Brezhnev Doctrine, stating that the Soviet Union's foreign policies were its own affair.

Relations never really thawed between the two presidents, even though each man diplomatically expressed wishes for continued and improved communication and hope for a summit meeting someday. Brezhnev's last few years in office were plagued by troubles in Poland, competing American interests in the Middle East, and the ongoing and debilitating Afghan War, all of which contributed heavily to bad relations with the United States and made it virtually impossible for Brezhnev and Reagan to develop any sort of working relationship.

Leonid Brezhnev died of a heart attack on November 10, 1982, leaving behind a declining Soviet Union, an empire on the verge of rapidly waning international influence. In his old age, Brezhnev had led his country into near ruin with his infeasible foreign policies, his incompetent economic planning, and his antagonistic attitude toward the West. (*See also* Arms Control/Arms Race; Brezhnev Doctrine; Cold War; Foreign Policy/Foreign Relations; Mikhail Gorbachev.)

BREZHNEV DOCTRINE

In this 1968 proclamation, the Soviet Union claimed the right to intervene in any Eastern bloc nation that it considered "threatened" by internal or external forces seeking to restore or establish "a capitalist regime." The Soviets used the doctrine, promulgated under First Party Secretary Leonid Brezhnev, to justify invading Czechoslovakia in 1968 and to threaten intervention in other socialist countries where unrest manifested, such as Poland during the 1970s and 1980s—although the Soviets never invaded that nation.

President Reagan took direct issue with the Brezhnev Doctrine by publicly denouncing it and announcing the Reagan Doctrine.

The latter promised to go beyond the old American containment policy and revert to the even older policy of "rollback," that is, directly working to destabilize pro-Soviet regimes in the Third World. In response (particularly to the administration's energetic and effective aiding of the Contras in Nicaragua), Mikhail Gorbachev resurrected the Brezhnev Doctrine in 1986, although he was careful not to apply it directly to Central America.

The Brezhnev Doctrine was in essence an assertion of Soviet intentions to maintain hegemony in the Eastern Bloc and to aid friendly Third World governments (and try to thwart American efforts to destabilize them). It was also an answer of sorts to the seemingly endless string of American "doctrines" that had issued forth from nearly every presidency since Harry Truman's. (*See also* Reagan Doctrine; Leonid Brezhnev; Foreign Policy/Foreign Relations; Mikhail Gorbachev.)

GEORGE BUSH

Vice president under Ronald Reagan, and then forty-first president of the United States, George Herbert Prescott Bush had been one of the main rivals for the Republican presidential nomination in 1980. During that primary campaign, Bush used the memorable phrase, "voodoo economics" to describe Reagan's proposal to adopt supply-side economic policies and cut federal income taxes by at least 30 percent.

The son of a Republican United States senator from Connecticut, Bush was born into an aristocratic family. During World War II, he was for a time the youngest combat pilot in the navy; he was shot down in the Atlantic and rescued by an American submarine. After the war, the young Bush moved his wife and children to Texas, where he spent some years in the oil business and established his political base.

Bush's national political experience began with a brief stint in the House and an unsuccessful bid for the United States Senate against Lloyd Bentson (the 1988 Democratic vice presidential nominee). After his time in the House of Representatives, he served in a series of appointed posts, including chairman of the Republican National Committee, ambassador to mainland China, director of the Central Intelligence Agency, and ambassador to the United Nations.

Early in the 1980 campaign season, Bush was Reagan's main competitor for the Republican presidential nomination, and he dealt Reagan a setback by winning a narrow victory in the Iowa caucus. But Reagan outfoxed Bush at the infamous Nashua debate before the New Hampshire primary. Since Bush had temporarily displaced Reagan as the front-runner, the two opposing camps agreed to a debate at Nashua High School; only Bush and Reagan would participate. The two candidates paid for the school auditorium and for the personnel involved, including the moderator, local journalist Jon Breen.

At the last minute, Reagan proposed that the other major Republican candidates be included in the debate, but the Bush camp refused. Nevertheless, Reagan showed up at the high school with the other candidates in tow and invited them on stage with him. When an annoyed Breen instructed that Reagan's microphone be cut off, Reagan angrily replied, "I am paying for this microphone, Mr. Green!" (Reagan had misheard Breen's name earlier.) The incident became one of the campaign's defining moments, and Bush came out on the short end of it. Reagan looked decisive and seemed to take an inclusive attitude toward his Republican opponents, while Bush seemed petulant and exclusive. It was a coup for Reagan, who was in no real danger of losing the nomination, anyway, despite Bush's Iowa victory.

After being nominated at the 1980 convention, and after briefly flirting with the idea of asking former president Gerald Ford to be his running mate, Reagan announced that Bush would be his vice presidential candidate. Reagan's choice was an ingenious bit of political fence-mending, as Reagan appealed most strongly to the party's right wing and Bush would attract some of the more moderate Republicans. Voodoo economics vanished from Bush's vocabulary, as he got loyally in line behind the standard-bearer.

Bush had to deemphasize his moderate views in order to fit into the administration he would serve as, nominally, the number-two man. The party's right wing mistrusted him, and so did Reagan loyalists in general for his previous opposition to Ronald Reagan, for his moderate politics, and because of the Reaganites' suspicions that he would not fully support the so-called Reagan revolution. Further, many Reaganites considered Vice President Bush too moderate on Cold War issues.

Bush's presence in the administration may have caused some confusion in Moscow. As a former ambassador and CIA director, Bush was well known in diplomatic circles, and the Soviets may have regarded him as a moderating element in American foreign policy. That a cold warrior like Reagan chose a man like Bush for vice president could indicate either that the administration was likely to be more reasonable than its rhetoric indicated or that American politics were in a confused state.

Privately, according to historians Michael R. Beschloss and Strobe Talbott, Bush expressed his discomfort with the president's hard-line stance toward the Soviets. During the early part of Reagan's first term, Bush encouraged his boss to attend summits with the Soviet leadership. After Yuri Andropov died, and as the 1984 presidential election drew near, Reagan became more agreeable to a summit with Konstantin Chernenko. He followed Bush's suggestion to send a top aide to Moscow with a letter from the president to the Soviet leader, but the Soviets proved unreceptive.

Bush was the first American high official to meet Mikhail Gorbachev after Chernenko died in 1985. Bush quickly assessed the young Soviet leader as a man who would work for rapid and drastic change in the Soviet Union, and he told the press that many of Gorbachev's future actions might well depend on interactions with the United States.

During Reagan's second term, Bush was often displeased with the way the president conducted relations with Gorbachev. Even so, the vice president never gave any public hint of displeasure or dissent. As time went on, however, Gorbachev seemed to realize that Bush would likely succeed Reagan as president, and the Soviet leader sought to develop an independent relationship with him.

During Reagan's second term, there was a general softening of the administration's earlier anti-Soviet policies and rhetoric, and the president took some criticism within his own party. Vice President Bush now faced the problem of supporting the president while wanting to appear less favorable to Gorbachev than some thought Reagan had become. Mistrusted by the Republican right to begin with, Bush could not afford to appear "soft" on the Soviets.

Bush's solution was to harden his own Cold War rhetoric when talking to reporters and to limit public interactions with Gorbachev. At the same time, Bush directly told Gorbachev to ignore any anti-Soviet statements he might make to American audiences during the campaign. At first Gorbachev appreciated this lesson in American elective politics, but he later grew nervous as he sometimes wondered which of the vice president's statements were mere rhetoric and which had the strength of conviction.

During the 1988 campaign, Bush spoke of keeping up pressure on the Soviets, opposed defense cuts, and commented to reporters that the Cold War was not over. Bush could not afford the conservative Reagan's luxury of acting friendly to the Communists; any overly conciliatory words from the moderate Bush could be taken by hard-liners as weakness.

Domestically, Vice President Bush involved himself in the issue of deregulation during President Reagan's first term. Reagan appointed Bush to chair a special task force to look into federal regulations. A deregulatory trend began during the 1970s, when even President Carter, a Democrat, and the mostly Democratic Congress deregulated the airline and trucking industries. Bush's task force recommended getting rid of hundreds more federal regulations.

Bush's task force infuriated many public-interest groups, as the government ultimately lifted numerous regulations on pollutants, nuclear plants, food-products labeling, and other areas of concern to public health. Reagan was pleased with his vice president's performance, apparently, and wrote favorably of Bush's endeavors in his memoirs.

Bush was called upon for sober, calm leadership when President Reagan was shot in 1981. (Ironically, Bush himself had been the target of a single gunshot only a few weeks before; the shot grazed his limousine, and the sniper was never identified.) In 1985, when Reagan underwent several surgeries, Bush stepped in to assume his constitutional role as substitute chief executive, assuming presidential authority in the first transfer of power under the Twenty-fifth Amendment.

Bush's possible involvement in the Iran-Contra scandal plagued his bid for the presidency in 1988 and caused a famous shouting match with CBS News correspondent Dan Rather during a television interview. Despite persistent suspicions, Bush won the nomination and the election after waging a viciously negative campaign that practically portrayed the Democratic nominee, Massachusetts governor Michael Dukakis, as a dangerous coddler of criminals. The 1988 campaign, not noted for being particularly issue-driven, was one of the nastiest presidential contests in memory.

Bush ran on Reagan's record of peace and improved economic conditions. He played up patriotism (at the Republican convention, he led the delegates in the Pledge of Allegiance), promised not to impose any new taxes (the famous, "Read my lips: No new taxes" pledge), took a hard line on criminal justice (consisting mostly of a series of television ads that accused Governor Dukakis of responsibility for crimes committed by a furloughed convict named Willie Horton), and echoed Reagan's stand against liberal social programs. The electorate responded, and Bush overcame an initial seventeen-point deficit in the polls to win the election by a fairly large margin.

Bush was the first sitting vice president to win the presidency since Andrew Jackson's vice president, Martin Van Buren, won the election of 1836. Bush polled 47,946,422 popular votes and 426 electoral votes against Dukakis's 41,016,429 popular votes and 112 electoral votes. Bush took 54 percent of the popular vote to the Democrat's 46 percent. It was a convincing victory; even though Bush had called for a "kinder and gentler America," his election came on the coattails of his retiring predecessor. Many commentators wondered if Bush meant to be kinder and gentler than Reagan had been.

Kinder and gentler notwithstanding, President George Bush concentrated primarily on foreign policy, led the United States into the Persian Gulf War, and presided over the end of the Cold War.

Although Bush displayed impressive leadership qualities in handling the crisis that led to the Gulf War, he had worse luck with domestic issues, particularly the economy. One of the most common criticisms against Bush was his seeming indifference to domestic issues and his preoccupation with foreign affairs. Like the last incumbent vice president to win the presidency, Martin Van Buren, President Bush was undone mostly by the economy, although renewed doubts about his role in Iran-Contra may have contributed to his defeat as well.

Only days before the 1992 presidential election, Bush issued pardons for several Iran-Contra defendants, including former defense secretary Caspar Weinberger, and this registered poorly in the public-opinion polls. Bush lost his bid for a second term, and William Jefferson Clinton won the presidency.

The 1992 vote was interesting for more than just the defeat of an incumbent president (only the fifth such defeat in the twentieth century; the others were Taft in 1912, Hoover in 1932, Ford in 1976, and Carter in 1980). The campaign was enlivened by an independent challenger, Texas billionaire H. Ross Perot, who polled over 19 million votes, for 19 percent of the popular vote.

President Bush won 37.7 percent, or 38,167,416 popular votes, for 168 electoral votes. The victor, Bill Clinton, won 43,728,275 popular votes and 370 electoral votes; with only 43.2 percent of the popular vote, he took office as a minority president—that is, a president who has secured a plurality, but not a majority, of the popular vote.

George Bush retired into private life. (*See also* Debates; Deregulation; Grace Commission; Iran-Contra; Twenty-fifth Amendment.)

C

Since Ronald Reagan's presidency lasted eight years, his cabinet, as one might expect, changed considerably during that time. Besides the normal and more or less routine changes in cabinet personnel, scandals and indictments also affected the cabinet's composition. In one tragic instance, a fatal accident deprived President Reagan of an effective and experienced officer. Reagan's cabinet stands as one of the most curious mixtures in American history, with capable and honorable secretaries such as George Shultz, Terrel Bell, and Malcolm Baldridge serving alongside officials of highly questionable caliber and background, such as James Watt, Raymond Donovon, and Samuel Pierce.

Here is a summary, by department, of the cabinet's personnel history during Ronald Reagan's presidency, from 1981 to 1989.

STATE

Alexander Haig, Jr. (1981–1982), a former NATO commanding general and Richard Nixon's last White House chief of staff, attracted bad publicity with his famous "I am in control here" statement in the wake of the assassination attempt on President Reagan in 1981, although he most likely did not mean to imply that he was running the country. (*See also* Assassination Attempt.)

Haig resigned in June 1982, after a frustrating tenure during which he found himself at odds with presidential aides Edwin Meese and James Baker (himself a future secretary of state under President George Bush). Haig was a steadying force in the administration's conduct of foreign policy—for instance, he dissuaded President Reagan from reneging on the bargain that President Carter had made with the Iranians for the release of the Teheran hostages; Haig pointed out that an incoming administration could not legally or ethically abrogate an international agreement made by the previous administration.

However, Haig's actions on the day Reagan was shot antagonized key presidential advisers, and according to former White House spokesman Larry Speakes, within a year and a half, their "hazing" (such as scheduling the secretary's flights on windowless government airplanes) drove Haig from the cabinet. (*See also* Falklands War.)

Haig's successor, George P. Shultz, served until Reagan left office in 1989. Shultz participated in the major foreign-policy decisions and events of the Reagan years and emerged as one of Reagan's more capable and distinguished cabinet secretaries. Many analysts believe that Shultz had a steadying and stabilizing effect on the Reagan administration's foreign policy; in Shultz's own fascinating memoirs, he diplomatically outlines some of his differences with the president's thinking on many issues. He was a very mobile secretary of state, traveling widely, and was even the target of terrorist bombs. (*See also* Iran-Contra; Central America; China and Taiwan; Economic Summits; Hostages and Terrorists; Japan; Middle East; Persian Gulf; Philippines.)

TREASURY

Donald T. Regan (1981–1985), Treasury secretary during the first term, in a novel move switched jobs with White House chief of staff James A. Baker III (1985–1988). Baker resigned in 1988 to manage Vice President Bush's presidential campaign. Treasury Secretary Nicholas Brady (1988–1989) remained for the duration of the administration. (*See also* Astrology; Iran-Contra; National Security Advisers; Reagan Recession/Reagan Recovery; Reaganomics; Paul Volcker and the Fed.)

ATTORNEY GENERAL (DEPARTMENT OF JUSTICE)

William French Smith (1981–1985) resigned after the first term for unspecified reasons. In his posthumously published autobiography, Smith wrote that he wished to return to private life but did not explain why. Smith's successor, Edwin A. Meese III (1985–1989), ran into quite a bit of trouble as attorney general.

Meese seemed in many ways an odd choice to succeed Smith. As a White House adviser during the first term, he was one-third of the famous troika, along with Chief of Staff James Baker and long-time Reagan adviser and confidant Michael Deaver; the troika ran the Reagan White House and managed to keep the president from veering onto perilous extremist paths. Meese and his two associates, although mutually antagonistic, worked well together, but they incurred the wrath of the conservative faithful who expected President Reagan to promulgate a right-wing agenda.

Meese also caused the president and the administration considerable embarrassment with some very ill-considered comments. For instance, in 1983 Meese claimed that there were no hungry children in America. People went to soup kitchens, said Meese, because the food is free. Meese also attained significant notoriety for deciding not to awaken the president on the night of August 19, 1981, when U.S. Navy jets shot down two Libyan fighter jets in the Gulf of Sidra.

Attorney General Meese spent a good deal of his tenure as the nation's leading law-enforcement officer under criminal investigation for his possible role in the Wedtech scandal. Meese appeared before the grand jury five times and finally resigned during the summer of 1989. He was not charged with any crime; the independent prosecutor's report found insufficient grounds for indictment but criticized Meese for being insensitive to the appearance of impropriety, particularly in matters pertaining to Wedtech. (*See also* Wedtech Scandal.)

Meese further found himself criticized by all the agencies that investigated the Iran-Contra scandal. The Tower Board, the congressional joint committee, and the Office of the Independent Counsel all took the attorney general to task for slipshod investigating and giving politically motivated advice to the president.

Meese took the Wedtech report as a vindication and hit the lecture circuit. The next attorney general, Richard Thornburgh (1989), stayed on for the duration.

INTERIOR

One of the most visible and controversial figures in the Reagan administration was Secretary of the Interior James C. Watt (1981–1983), who was, overall, a conservationist's nightmare. Watts was so openly intent on opening up the national parks to corporate usage and so intemperate in his public remarks that he antagonized both conservatives and liberals and found himself under fire from both parties.

The secretary became a legend in his own time for saying foolish and nasty things, such as that, as a white man, he would be nervous about being treated by a black surgeon, since he would wonder if the doctor were some incompetent who got into medical school through a quota program.

Watt might be most widely remembered for his disparaging remarks about the musical group the Beach Boys and their audience; he decided against inviting the group to perform at a Fourth of July observance in Washington. The Beach Boys had performed at that function for years, but Watt told the press that the group attracted the wrong element to the celebrations.

Nancy Reagan publicly apologized to the Beach Boys (and to their maligned audience) and invited them to perform at another Fourth of July function, which the president and first lady attended.

Secretary Watt continued to utter inane and offensive public comments, such as referring to Indian reservations as examples of "the failures of socialism." The Senate seriously considered a bipartisan resolution calling for the secretary's ouster after Watt, with typical gracelessness, joked that he had set up an advisory commission consisting of "a black, a woman, two Jews, and a cripple." That was the biggest gaffe of its sort since 1976, when Earl Butz, President Gerald Ford's secretary of agriculture, made an insensitive and obscene remark about blacks. (Butz, too, was forced to resign.) Inevitable comparisons between Watt and Butz popped up in the media.

Watt had been on many hit lists for quite some time, but this latest foolishness was the final nail in his coffin, and he resigned with Congress howling for his blood. When the administration finally decided it would be better off without his services, President Reagan "reluctantly" accepted Watt's resignation.

After leaving the cabinet, Watt, like Edwin Meese, hit the lecture circuit, commanding a speaking fee of $15,000 per engagement. In 1995 Watt was indicted for alleged federal offenses committed while he was secretary of the interior.

William P. Clark, Jr. (1983–1985), a former associate justice of the California Supreme Court, also had been a national security adviser to President Reagan. Donald P. Hodel succeeded Clark in 1985 and remained until the president left office in 1989. (*See also* National Security Advisers.)

AGRICULTURE

John R. Block (1981–1986) and Richard Lyng (1986–1989) were Reagan's secretaries of agriculture.

COMMERCE

Secretary of Commerce Malcolm Baldridge (1981–1987), a canny, effective political operative, and an important adviser to President Reagan, had a lot to do with lobbying Congress on the president's behalf. A devoted amateur rodeo man, he was killed while practicing for a steer-roping competition in northern California on July 25, 1987. His death deprived the administration of a talented and experienced Washington operative.

Baldridge was succeeded by C. William Verity, Jr. (1987–1989).

LABOR

Labor Secretary Raymond J. Donovon (1981–1985) holds the dubious distinction of being the only sitting cabinet secretary ever to be indicted. Former presidential press spokesman Larry Speakes has written that he knew Donovon was a problematic appointment from the first; Fred Fielding, a counsel to President-elect Reagan, told Speakes that someone had called him and said that Donovon had some "unsavory connections" and would be troublesome for the new administration. According to Speakes, Fielding checked out Donovon's FBI file and found nothing irregular.

The caller, however, apparently knew something, for in 1984 Donovon came under investigation for labor fraud, links to organized crime, and other criminal activities. A New York grand jury indicted him for stealing $7 million from a subway construction project. Donovon resigned shortly after being indicted; he later stood trial and was acquitted of all charges.

Secretary William E. Brock (1985–1987) resigned to manage Senator Robert Dole's campaign for the 1988 Republican presidential nomination. Secretary Ann D. McLaughlin stayed on until 1989, when the president left office.

DEFENSE

Secretary of Defense Caspar Weinberger (1981–1987) served as secretary of Health, Education, and Welfare under Presidents Nixon and Ford. When Ronald Reagan was governor of California, Weinberger, one of Reagan's chief assistants, earned the nickname "Cap the Knife" for his support of massive budget cuts. But upon taking command in the Pentagon, he became an exponent of astronomical defense spending, causing at least one columnist to wonder in print, "What ever happened to Cap the Knife?"

During the Iran-Contra scandal, Weinberger came under fire for withholding information during his testimony to the Tower Board, the congressional investigating committee, and the independent counsel. The independent counsel's final report asserted that Weinberger knew of the arms-for-hostages deals nearly from the beginning and that he was kept informed by those who carried out the dealings with the Iranians.

Weinberger allegedly withheld evidence, which is a felony. The independent counsel reported that Weinberger made handwritten notes concerning the arms-for-hostages deals but deliberately withheld the notes from the Tower Board and Congress. The independent counsel discovered the notes in 1991, two years after the Reagan administration left office. The notes contained highly detailed and relevant evidence and showed that Weinberger was involved in meetings and discussions that concerned critical aspects of the Iran-Contra affair. Weinberger was indicted on perjury and other charges but was pardoned by President Bush. In 1987, when the investigations began, Weinberger resigned from the cabinet, citing personal reasons.

Weinberger's successor, Frank C. Carlucci (1987–1989), had briefly been Reagan's national security adviser. (*See also* George Bush; Iran-Contra.)

HEALTH AND HUMAN SERVICES

Secretary of Health and Human Services Richard S. Schweiker served from 1981 to 1983. He also was famous as the man Ronald Reagan chose for vice president when Reagan challenged President Gerald Ford for the Republican nomination in 1976.

Secretary Margaret Heckler, a former Gypsy Moth in the House of Representatives, ran afoul of Nancy Reagan and White House Chief of Staff Donald Regan during her tenure, although her private life may have been as much at issue as her alleged administrative deficiencies. Nancy Reagan apparently disliked Heckler's publicized divorce case, and Regan believed Heckler could not competently run her department. Regan thought that Heckler was too willing to compromise with her former colleagues in Congress and so undermine the president's programs when she met with congressional representatives.

Heckler resigned in 1985. President Reagan offered her the ambassadorship to Ireland; she initially turned it down, then accepted it. Her successor was Otis R. Bowen (1985–1989). (*See also* Gypsy Moths.)

HOUSING AND URBAN DEVELOPMENT

Samuel R. Pierce, Jr. (1981–1989), was the only cabinet secretary to serve for Ronald Reagan's entire presidency. The administration was not terribly interested in Pierce's department, nor in Pierce, and the secretary had very little contact with the president. On one occasion at a reception for mayors at the White House, the president did not recognize his own secretary of HUD and mistook him for one of the mayors.

Pierce was involved in several scandals at HUD, and, during George Bush's first term, the House Government Operations Subcommittee questioned Pierce about alleged wrongdoing at HUD during the past few years. Pierce claimed the Fifth Amendment privilege against self-incrimination. (*See also* HUD Scandal.)

TRANSPORTATION

Secretary of Transportation Andrew L. "Drew" Lewis (1981–1983) advised President Reagan to fire the striking air-traffic controllers in 1981. The president at various times considered Lewis for other posts, such as national security adviser. But Lewis stayed in the cabinet until he was succeeded by Elizabeth Hanford Dole in 1983. (*See also* Air-Traffic Controllers' Strike.)

In 1987 Secretary Dole resigned in order to help her husband, Senator Robert Dole, campaign for the 1988 Republican presidential nomination. Secretary Dole no doubt wished to avoid any appearance of conflict of interest, as Senator Dole's chief rival for the nomination was Vice President George Bush.

Secretary Dole was succeeded by James H. Burnley (1987–1989).

ENERGY

Secretary of Energy James B. Edwards (1981–1982) was appointed by President Reagan specifically to set about dismantling the Department of Energy; the department was a favorite target of conservatives. However, the administration's efforts met stiff opposition in Congress, and so in 1982, Secretary Edwards resigned to become president of the Medical University of South Carolina.

Edwards had two successors, Donald P. Hodel (1982–1985) and John S. Herrington (1985–1989).

EDUCATION

Secretary of Education Terrel Bell (1981–1985) found himself at odds with the White House early on, as Ronald Reagan had called for abolishing the Department of Education during the

1980 campaign. Unlike Energy Secretary James B. Edwards, Bell had no intention of trying to help wreck his department. He had served in the department during the Nixon administration and helped initiate a number of federal programs to aid education.

Bell attracted a good deal of publicity during Reagan's first term when his department published a study indicting the declining state of American education. The report drew a considerable public response, and the previously low-profile secretary suddenly found himself in the spotlight—so much so that he was given a highly visible and active role in the president's 1984 reelection campaign. In 1985, however, he resigned when the administration began to back away from its temporary concern with education and White House aides proposed large cuts in the department's budget. He died in 1996.

Secretary William J. Bennett (1985–1989) was very much in the public eye during his tenure. He toured the nation's schools and became a strong advocate of traditional educational values. Since leaving office, he has remained in the public eye by campaigning for old-fashioned "morality" in public education.

Secretary Lauro F. Cavazos (1989), a zoologist and physiologist, was the first Hispanic cabinet secretary. Unlike Bennett, Cavazos strongly advocated bilingual education. This stance was not favored by the conservative Reagan administration, but Cavazos took office during the administration's last months, so, presumably, his liberal views caused no particular stir among Reagan's advisers. (*See also* National Security Advisers.)

JIMMY CARTER

Thirty-ninth president of the United States (1977–1981), Jimmy Carter lost his bid for a second term in a landslide. Ronald Reagan swept into office on a wave of public animosity toward Carter, as frustration with both the economy and the Iran hostage crisis worked against the incumbent president.

Carter won a very narrow 3 percent victory over President Gerald Ford in 1976, even though he began that campaign with pollsters predicting he would win by a landslide in November. The margin diminished, and on election eve the race was too close to call. Democrat Jimmy Carter, the former peanut farmer and governor of Georgia, won the White House in a classic squeaker.

President Carter's term began well enough; he had high public-approval ratings, a Democratic Congress, and seemed destined to accomplish many good things. He appeared open and honest, in stark contrast to such recent predecessors as Lyndon Johnson and Richard Nixon. Carter took office when the presidency ranked low in public esteem. Vietnam and Watergate still haunted American politics. Even Gerald Ford seemed tainted; he was, after all, the man who pardoned Nixon. Carter, with his toothy smile and pleasant drawl, appeared fresh and promising, despite his victory's narrowness.

Unfortunately, Carter ran into trouble on two fronts during his first two years in office: First, the economy continued to decline, and second, Congress, though mostly Democratic, proved recalcitrant and even hostile to this Democratic president. The economy suffered both recession and inflation (the dreaded "stagflation" that contributed to Ford's defeat), and the president and Congress seemed unable, possibly unwilling, to get together and come up with workable solutions.

Carter declined in the polls despite such notable feats as brokering the Camp David peace accords. With the economy out of control, Carter appeared ineffectual, and he never could shake this image, even with his accomplishments. To voters, peace in the Middle East had little bearing on America's grocery bills.

Reagan's unofficial campaign for president began to gather steam during the second half of Carter's term. As the president's approval rating continued to decline, Reagan emerged as the front-runner for the 1980 Republican presidential nomination. There was widespread media speculation that Carter would prove to be a one-term president. By 1978 many pundits practically had Carter out of the White House already and figured that nearly any Republican could beat him in the coming election. The pundits usually called both Reagan and moderate Republican Howard Baker the GOP front-runners.

In 1979, Carter experienced a temporary upsurge in popularity when the Iran hostage crisis began, as the nation rallied around its leader in a time of trouble and anxiety. But the crisis wore on, and American actions seemed ineffective. A rescue attempt failed, and several servicemen were killed when one of the rescue aircraft crashed; Carter's stock with the public plummeted.

It was not Carter's fault that the rescue attempt went wrong. It was no fault of the would-be rescuers, either; the operation was well planned and well executed, and the crash was purely accidental. But the public was so disappointed and the media coverage so wrathful that hardly anyone noticed the rescue had actually penetrated deep into Iranian territory without ever being detected. It was a highly professional operation carried out by highly capable professionals, but the result disappointed the public, and the public blamed the president.

The sheer length of the crisis made it seem endless, and public resentment against the president mounted with every passing month. Through it all, Carter directed the negotiations that ultimately brought the hostages home safe and sound. The president also warned the Ayatollah Khomeini that the United States would respond militarily if even one hostage was harmed or killed. But these things were either ignored by the public, or unpublicized.

Meanwhile, in 1980, with the hostages still in Iran and the economy still in trouble, Carter faced a challenge for renomination from within his own party, as Massachusetts senator Edward M. Kennedy violated political custom and opposed the president. Carter and Kennedy waged a bitter slugfest in the Democratic primaries, and although Carter, in his own phrase, "kicked Kennedy's ass," the spectacle of an incumbent president fighting for his party's nomination could not have done much good for his reelection prospects.

Even so, midway through the 1980 campaign season, Carter's defeat still did not seem inevitable. Reagan's lead in the polls was not overwhelming, and Carter showed some of his old fire on the campaign trail, the fire that had enabled him to emerge from relative obscurity to win the 1976 nomination away from more famous and well-connected Democratic rivals.

But even Carter's renewed fire could not match his Republican opponent's performing savoir faire. The 1980 campaign's crucial moment came during the televised debate between Carter and Reagan, when Reagan, the old Hollywood actor, tapped all his aplomb and polish to outperform the visibly nervous and querulous-sounding Carter. After the debate, it became more and more apparent that the president would lose his bid for a second term.

Many observers consider the hostage crisis the prime liability that defeated Jimmy Carter, and that may well be so. In that case, it is also terribly ironic, since Carter did ultimately work out a plan for the hostages' release. The Iranians freed them on the day of Reagan's inauguration, possibly as a parting swipe at Carter—releasing them, that is, only after he was no longer president of the United States.

Carter worked on the hostages' release right up to and during Ronald Reagan's inaugural day; the president-elect commented to one of his subordinates on how bad Carter looked during Reagan's courtesy call to the White House that morning. Carter had been up all night ironing out the last-minute details of the agreement for the release, and he attended his successor's inauguration looking haggard and careworn. It was the new president, and not the outgoing one, who got to announce to the world that the hostages' plane had left Iranian air space that day.

As a former president, Jimmy Carter has overcome the public animosity toward him, and emerged as a respected, even revered, elder statesman. Some have called him our greatest former president, and he certainly has done much to earn that accolade. No other former president has remained so active on both the national and world stages. Carter's activities have included running the Carter Center at Georgia's Emory University and carrying out diplomatic missions for the United States (most notably in Haiti and Bosnia). He has authored and coauthored books on history, political analysis, and health, and has written two autobiographical volumes and a book of poems. (See also Arms Control/Arms Race; Debates; Elections—Presidential; October Surprise; Persian Gulf.)

WILLIAM CASEY AND THE CIA

As the director of the Central Intelligence Agency, William Casey figured as a significant and highly controversial participant in the events that led to the Iran-Contra scandal during President Reagan's second term. By the time the scandal broke, Casey was mortally ill with a brain tumor; he died shortly after the arms-for-hostages deal became public.

Many critics have charged that under Reagan and Casey, the CIA in effect carried on its own covert wars in Central America to support the Reagan administration's policy of trying to roll back leftist influences in the Western Hemisphere. Casey targeted the Nicaraguan Contras, in keeping with the president's intention to destabilize the Nicaraguan government and support the Contras in their war to overthrow it. Consequently, the agencies that investigated the Iran-Contra affair all had harsh words for Casey and his running of America's premier intelligence agency.

William J. Casey entered Ronald Reagan's life when he became Reagan's campaign manager after Reagan lost the 1980 Iowa caucus, and the candidate fired campaign manager John Sears and several political aides from California. During World War II, Casey served as an assistant to General William Donovan, head of the Office of Strategic Services, the forerunner of the Central Intelligence Agency. He was well known in both the intelligence community and the GOP, and several prominent East Coast conservative Republicans recommended Casey to Reagan. Under Casey's management, the Reagan forces mounted a successful campaign in New Hampshire, and put the front-runner back on track for the nomination.

Although he served as President Richard Nixon's chairman of the Securities and Exchange Commission, he was not an experienced politician, and despite the New Hampshire victory, his campaign inexperience showed. He had considerable trouble keeping Reagan from making public gaffes and misstatements, but subordinates in the campaign organization managed to impose some discipline and spin control. Many observers considered Casey an ideological figurehead, but he was nevertheless rewarded for his services when President

Reagan appointed him CIA director. According to some sources, Casey would have preferred to be secretary of state.

Casey quickly became an assertive and stubborn partisan in the often bitter infighting that plagued the Reagan administration, and he was frequently at odds with such officials as Secretary of State George Schultz and Secretary of Defense Caspar Weinberger. Like his opponents, Casey proved jealously territorial, and many of his fights were internecine turf wars. Casey quickly gained a reputation for combativeness that was richly deserved.

He also gained a reputation, fittingly enough, for secretiveness, and ran into difficulties with the Senate committee that oversaw the CIA. The CIA mining of Nicaraguan harbors, for instance, drew the bipartisan wrath of Republican Barry Goldwater and Democrat J. Patrick Moynihan, both prominent members of the Senate Select Committee on Intelligence. The CIA had not informed the committee in advance of the minings, and the senators learned about the operation from an article in the *Wall Street Journal*.

Moynihan threatened to resign from the committee, and eighty-four senators, evenly split between the two parties, condemned the agency's action. Casey apologized to Goldwater and promised, in writing, to abide by the law and notify Congress in advance when the CIA planned such actions. This agreement, known as the Casey Accords, was never entirely fulfilled.

By the time Iran-Contra broke in the press, Casey was terminally ill and had even lost the power of speech. Many commentators have wondered if Casey's brain tumor affected his thoughts and actions during the time he steered the CIA through the arms-for-hostages deals, but we will never know his side of the story. Both Ronald Reagan and Nancy Reagan, in their respective memoirs, lay some of the blame for Iran-Contra on Casey, but they both believed that the dying Casey was not thinking clearly.

Iran-Contra investigators concluded that significant evidence showed Casey participated extensively in the Iran-Contra affair from 1984 to 1986 and worked closely with National Security Adviser Robert McFarlane; McFarlane's deputy and successor, John Poindexter; Oliver North; and Richard Secord. Casey tried to distance himself from his associates' illegal activities although he participated in some of them. He also tried to help conceal those activities from Congress.

In 1984 it was the CIA's job to advise and train the Contras. By then the administration anticipated that Congress would soon take action to restrict or ban aid to the Contras, and in fact Congress passed the Boland Amendments shortly thereafter. During that summer, Oliver North and several CIA officials got together to coordinate their efforts to work around the congressional action and continue helping the Contras. CIA participation was essential; not only did the agency have resources and contacts in Central America but, being practiced in espionage and covert operations, it also had the experience and wherewithal to implement the clandestine plans to circumvent the written law.

According to North's later testimony, he recruited retired air force general Richard Secord on William Casey's directions. Casey knew Secord as an expert in clandestine operations, and he believed Secord could help North set up a secret network to supply the Contras with weapons. Later that summer, Casey personally took North to meet CIA senior field officers in a secret location in Central America.

Casey interceded with the president and presidential counselor Edwin Meese to keep North on the National Security Council staff when it came time for North to be assigned back to active duty with the marines. The ailing CIA director was alert enough to ensure that the system for the Contra-support scheme, including personnel, remained in place.

Casey advocated an opening to Iran early on. The director became particularly concerned that the administration set a new Iran policy when he received reports that the terrorists who held CIA agent William Buckley were torturing him. In the spring of 1985, Casey argued that the embargo on arms to Iran might be counterproductive to American interests in that the Iranians, desperate for weapons, might try to obtain from the Soviet Union what they could not get from the United States. Casey therefore concluded that the United States should at least encourage its allies to resume arms sales to Iran. It also occurred to Casey that easing the embargo might give moderates more solid footing in the Iranian government.

Not long afterward, National Security Adviser McFarlane began his dealing with the Iranian so-called moderates through Israeli middlemen. McFarlane later testified that he kept the president informed and also briefed Shultz, Weinberger, Casey, and Vice President Bush. McFarlane added that Casey advised him that Congress should not be told of the Iran opening.

The various investigative reports found that Casey involved himself in the arms-for-hostages deals and the diversion of the arms sales profits into funding for the Contras. While Casey denied that he knew about the diversion of funds, he at least helped make the diversions possible, whether or not he knew about North's activities past a certain point. Casey testified that the CIA merely provided transport for cargo from Israel to Iran without explaining whether he or his agency understood that the cargo was a shipment of missiles.

Casey also tried to leave the hostages out of his testimony about the arms-for-hostages deals. He explained the Iran opening by describing Iran's strategic location and its importance in geopolitical affairs. He also made misleading statements about the disposition of funds from the arms sales, claiming that the profits were deposited in an Israeli account, then transferred to a "sterile" CIA account. Actually, the funds went into a Swiss account controlled by Richard Secord.

Finally, Casey tried to throw Congress off the scent of the diversions altogether, claiming to the last that the funds went into a bank account and stayed there. He gave elusive answers about whether or not President Reagan knew of and authorized the activities of the officials involved in Iran-Contra.

The independent counsel concluded that Casey probably knew of the diversions, knew that he and his associates engaged in illegal activities, and actively sought to conceal those activities. Casey's actions, concluded the report, compromised the CIA's professionalism and integrity. The director utilized his agency's resources, contacts, and personnel to support actions and policies that were clearly illegal. (*See also* Central America; Foreign Policy/ Foreign Relations; Iran-Contra; Philippines.)

CENTRAL AMERICA

In a very real sense, Ronald Reagan aimed his foreign policy in Central America at counterrevolution. The Reagan administration was determined to undermine leftist insurgencies in several Central American nations (particularly El Salvador) and to destabilize and possibly overthrow the Sandanista government in Nicaragua. This policy involved considerable covert action by the CIA and other American intelligence agencies. It also involved the secret diplomatic initiatives that led to the Iran-Contra scandal.

The administration justified its actions in Central America by maintaining that under the Sandanistas, totalitarian repression was rampant in Nicaragua. It further maintained that the insurgencies in El Salvador were supported by the Sandanistas, possibly the Cubans, and so, by extension, the Soviet Union. Consequently, the administration spent a good deal of time and resources trying to isolate Nicaragua, diplomatically and economically, from the rest of the hemisphere. The administration trained, funded, and otherwise supported the rebel forces in Nicaragua, who were known in the United States as the Contras (from the Spanish "Contradores").

Historian Stephen Ambrose has written that President Reagan was personally obsessed with Central America and with the potential Communist threat to the region, which he believed a critical threat to American security. Reagan conducted a personal public-relations campaign against the Sandanistas and for the Contras, often speaking of the latter as freedom fighters and comparing them to the Minute Men of the American Revolution. He claimed that the Sandanistas actively attempted to subvert neighboring El Salvador. In one memorable remark, he noted that the Sandanistas, who maintained the largest army in Central America, were only a two-day drive from the American border with Mexico.

Early in Reagan's first term, CIA Director William J. Casey oversaw the drafting of a working plan to launch covert actions to support the Contras; Reagan later justified these actions by calling the insurgents (and probably the Sandanistas, as well—his language was not clear on this point) Marxist guerrillas who were funded by Leonid Brezhnev and Fidel Castro. Reagan bluntly asserted that the Soviet Union and Cuba were responsible for the troubles in Central America.

As time went on, Casey and the CIA oversaw protracted civil wars in Nicaragua and El Salvador. There were several public-relations setbacks; in one memorable and tragic instance, several American nuns were raped and murdered by government troops in El Salvador, and the administration refused to admit that the women had been killed by America's allies, despite conclusive evidence. In Nicaragua, the Contras committed many well-publicized atrocities, and these, too, were either ignored or rationalized by the administration.

This is not to say that the Sandanistas and the Salvadoran insurgents were good guys. The Sandanistas conducted a political dictatorship in Nicaragua, shut down opposition newspapers, controlled the mass media, and committed their own acts of terror, particularly against Indians in rural areas. The Sandanistas only agreed to hold free elections under intense international pressure and in the face of effective sabotage by the United States.

Reagan ultimately claimed triumph in his campaign to overthrow the Sandanistas, although it is difficult to assess the actual effects that the administration's overt policies and covert actions had. Among the more overt was the CIA mining of Nicaragua's principal harbor, although it was a while before the American public knew of that.

In autumn of 1985, a State Department report asserted that the Sandanistas had been supplying arms to the leftist guerrillas in El Salvador since 1981. The report is questionable in many aspects, but it served to justify, and ratify, Reagan's Central American policy, in that it portrayed Nicaragua as the region's prime troublemaker and exporter of Communist revolution.

Anti-Sandanista measures remained the cornerstone of Reagan's regional policy, as he extolled the virtues of the Contras and pledged not to "abandon" El Salvador, even though the State

Department never conclusively demonstrated an active link between the Salvadoran insurgents and the Sandanistas. The Salvadorans undoubtedly received funds and arms from foreign sources; it would be naive to assume otherwise. But the administration's anti-Nicaragua policy, in terms of public pronouncements, verged on hysteria, and it took on an ugly McCarthyistic tone as Reagan, and other administration spokespersons, questioned the intelligence and even the patriotism of any political opponents who dared question the administration's version of the Central American situation.

In El Salvador, particularly, the United States chose between unattractive alternatives. While José Napoleón Duarte held nominal power as El Salvador's president, the real political power belonged to the right-wing military, which received massive American aid to combat the leftist guerrillas. Much of this aid went to a military campaign to terrorize the Salvadoran civilian population with brutal army death squads, which became the shame of the Americas. They murdered perhaps 70,000 peasants in the countryside, as well as teachers, trade unionists, church workers, and anyone else the army deemed possibly subversive. A major international scandal erupted when one such death squad raped and murdered several American nuns (see above).

The Reagan administration continued to fund the Salvadoran government under the Reagan doctrine of aiding any nation facing a leftist insurgency. In 1988, finally, elections were held in El Salvador, but the outcome was questionable. Duarte and his civilian government were voted out, and the even further right-wing ARENA won national power. The civil war continued after President Reagan left office. (*See also* Cold War; Foreign Policy/Foreign Relations; Grenada; Reagan Doctrine.)

CHINA AND TAIWAN

The Communist People's Republic of China came into being in 1949, when the followers of Mao Zedong won their civil war against the Nationalists led by Chiang Kai-shek. The civil war erupted after the

Japanese were expelled when World War II ended, and the creation of a second Communist giant besides the Soviet Union inflicted a deep shock on American politics and energized the Cold War. The Nationalists, driven from the mainland, established a government on the island of Taiwan and claimed to be the legitimate rulers of China.

The United States recognized the Taiwanese capital at Taipei and refused to recognize the Communist government on the mainland. When, during the Korean War, the Americans drove the invading North Koreans out of South Korea and chased them close to the Chinese border, the Chinese entered the war on the North Korean side, and the conflict dragged on for three years. The Korean War set the tone of mutual distrust and hostility for American-Chinese relations over the next two decades.

During the early 1970s, the inveterate anticommunist Republican president Richard Nixon reestablished relations with China; he visited Beijing and met with the Chinese Communist leaders. Much to Taiwan's chagrin, Nixon and the mainland leaders issued the Shanghai Communiqué in 1972, which proclaimed, "The United States acknowledges that all Chinese on either side of the Taiwan Strait maintain there is but one China and that Taiwan is part of China. The United States does not challenge that position. It reaffirms its interest in a peaceful settlement of the Taiwan question by the Chinese themselves."

Once Nixon made his opening to the People's Republic of China, the relationship became centrally important to each nation. Both nations opposed the Soviet Union, and each wanted to enlist the other's aid militarily and economically. The United States now considered a strong, prosperous People's Republic good for American interests, and the People's Republic considered a strong ally like the United States a good trading partner and a counterbalance against Soviet influence in Southeast Asia.

Accordingly, in 1978 President Carter formally cut ties with Taiwan and established full and formal diplomatic relations with the People's Republic of China. Ronald Reagan, then a private citizen very much in the public eye as a possible presidential candidate in 1980, spoke out against Carter's China policy and indicated that if he became president, he might reverse Carter's policy and resume diplomatic relations with Taiwan. Further, Reagan said several times during the late 1970s and into 1980 that he favored weapons sales to Taiwan. This last evinced anger from the Chinese mainland.

But when Reagan took office as president in 1981, it was clear that the two nations needed each other, or at least considered each other useful. China was willing to help support the anti-Soviet guerrillas in Afghanistan, and the United States already was helping the Afghan mujaheddin with money, weapons, and supplies. China, in turn, needed American loans and trade. The Chinese wanted Western technology and money to help modernize their economy. But for the first year or so of Reagan's first term, the president continued to criticize Communist China and spoke of restoring recognition to the Taipei regime as China's legitimate government.

In 1982 the Chinese agreed in principle that the United States had the right to sell arms to Taiwan, as long as the Reagan administration pledged a gradual reduction of the sales. So, for a time, the Reagan administration conducted what in effect was a two-China policy, though only in part. The United States did not restore diplomatic recognition to the government in Taiwan and continued to consider the government in Beijing to be the legitimate one.

President Reagan let up on his anti–People's Republic rhetoric. Even as he called the Soviet Union the "evil empire," the president, as historian Michael Schaller points out, rarely even mentioned China during his second term. President and Mrs. Reagan paid a state visit to China in 1984, during which the two governments stressed harmony and good relations. Necessity had forced a thaw after the icy chill that gripped Sino-American relations when President Reagan first took office.

Relations between the United States and the People's Republic of China took a turn for the worse during the Bush administration, when the Chinese government shocked the world with the Tiananmen Square massacre of pro-democracy students in 1989. America's relationship with China hit rough waters, as Soviet-American relations were improving.

President Bush condemned the massacre and extended the visas of Chinese students in America who were afraid to return home. But the Bush administration was reluctant to antagonize the Chinese, and America's official reaction to the massacre was muted. With things so uncertain in the new world order, the United States still played the China card with the Soviets and the Soviet card with the Chinese.

CHRISTIAN RIGHT/NEW RIGHT

The Christian Right and the New Right are a collection of right-wing interest groups, many (perhaps most) of which are animated by evangelical Christianity. Although such interest groups are not new in and of themselves, their coalescence into a large political base during the 1960s and 1970s is a significant development in American politics, particularly since the New Right has exercised considerable power and influence. Since the 1970s, the New Right has contributed to the conservative consensus in American politics, and it was instrumental in electing Ronald Reagan president in 1980 and 1984 and the Republican Congress in 1994.

The very name *New Right* indicates the reactive nature of the movement, since it is at least in part a reaction against the New Left. But the genesis of the New Right is more complicated than a simple countermovement against the left-wing radicalism of the late 1960s. The New Right's roots go back farther in history, and if the movement was a pronounced reaction to anything, it would be New Deal liberalism rather than the sixties youth rebellion.

Many American rightists saw Franklin Roosevelt's New Deal as the introduction and entrenchment of socialism in American life, hence the 1952 Republican presidential campaign slogan Twenty Years of Treason. The onset of the Cold War abroad and the liberalization of American domestic policy helped to perpetuate a siege mentality among the ultraconservatives. In the late 1950s, after the waning of Joe McCarthy's career, beverage millionaire Robert Welch founded the John Birch Society, and conservative intellectual William F. Buckley started publishing his *National Review* as an organ for a newly militant right wing.

In 1960 Arizona senator Barry Goldwater published his book, *The Conscience of a Conservative*, which remains a sort of right-wing bible to this day. The title itself was reactive: Shortly before, John Kenneth Galbraith, a particular target of right-wing hatred, had published *The Conscience of a Liberal*. Goldwater's manifesto specifically attacked and rejected the New Deal and advocated returning to unregulated capitalism, along with an actively anticommunist foreign policy. On that last point, American foreign policy had been uniformly anticommunist since 1945, but liberals and conservatives took turns accusing each other of being soft on Communism.

The *New Right*, though not a monolithic movement, had a core set of beliefs and values. Gun control, abortion, affirmative action (prior to 1964, most conservatives opposed federal civil-rights legislation altogether), pornography, feminism (including the proposed Equal Rights Amendment), gay liberation, and other liberal tenets were all anathema to the "movement conservative" mindset. Movement conservatives saw society as too liberal and permissive, believed America was losing its moral compass, and sought to restore what they believed to be the proper moral order. The term New Right did not come into use until the 1970s, but the conservatives were conscious of participating in a social and political movement long before the New Right found its label. Ironically, after the Goldwater debacle of 1964, the next presidential candidate to attract the New Right's interest was Jimmy Carter in 1976.

Carter, a Democrat, was also an evangelical Christian, and he attracted many of the fundamentalist Christian voters of the New Right. The part of the movement based on religious affiliation (the Christian Right) abhorred the rise in divorce, unwed sex, tolerance of homosexuality, and general permissiveness in the 1970s that many believed Carter himself deplored. But President Carter disappointed them with his own tolerance of diversity and pluralism—he even publicly opposed an antigay initiative on the 1978 California ballot, and that same year, praised the assassinated San Francisco County supervisor Harvey Milk as a "gay leader." So the New Right, which had never tended toward the Democratic Party in any case, became almost exclusively Republican.

As the 1980 election approached, several Christian Right political organizations rose to prominence, most notably Jerry Falwell's Moral Majority. Falwell was one of the many famous "televangelists"—fundamentalist preachers who appeared regularly on religious television programs and who became the most visible leaders of the Christian Right. Fallwell, Jimmy Swaggert, Jim and Tammy Faye Bakker, and Oral Roberts (who had been on television for many years longer than his colleagues), among others, reached a viewing audience of perhaps 100 million. When the televangelists joined with other New Right political activists, the New Right became a force to be reckoned with, exerting power and influence in a way it never could in 1964, when its first national hero, Goldwater, succumbed to crushing defeat at the hands of Lyndon Johnson's Democrats.

Even before 1980, Ronald Reagan courted the New Right's support, particularly the Christian Right's. During the 1980 campaign, he described himself as a born-again Christian, called for prayer in schools, advocated teaching creationism along with evolutionary theory, and attacked liberalism and permissiveness in terms very pleasing to Christian fundamentalists. Reagan won the Republican nomination, and the New Right had its first bona fide movement-conservative hero since Barry Goldwater and its first viable presidential candidate ever.

Groups like the Moral Majority and the National Conservative Political Action Committee (NCPAC) issued "moral report cards" on various liberal Democratic (and some liberal Republican) candidates and officeholders targeted for defeat. New Right leaders marshaled fund-raising and vote-getting techniques in an orchestrated effort to win local, state, and federal offices nationwide, to defeat liberal incumbents, and to elect a president they found suitable. The effort was a resounding success on all levels.

Ronald Reagan won the presidency in a landslide victory over President Carter, and the Republicans won a majority in the Senate and made gains in the House of Representatives. The Republicans owed much of its national success to the New Right's efforts, and it was a debt the party freely acknowledged. For at least the first two years of the Reagan administration, the Moral Majority and other New Right groups enjoyed immense influence and prestige in party and administration circles. (*See also* Elections—Congressional; Elections—Presidential.)

As the 1980s wore on, the New Right focused on issues concerning the American family, thus sparking the family-values debate. New Right leaders often attributed all of the bugaboos listed above that can be lumped under "permissiveness" to some sort of breakdown of family life in America. Christian Right ministers, along with many eager Republican politicians, quickly tied the breakdown to liberal Democratic social policies—for example, the so-called "welfare state" that had dominated national life since the New Deal era. As the Reagan years progressed, the New Right's family-values, antipermissiveness crusade escalated.

The Christian Right was not alone in pursuing that agenda, as the New Right also had a secular, intellectual component. The neoconservatives originally were a group of Democrats who were born again as conservatives. Among the neoconservative movement's stars were Jeanne Kirkpatrick (who became President Reagan's ambassador to the United Nations); writers Norman Podhoretz, Midge Decter (who was married to Podhoretz), and Irving Kristol. Although they did not couch their arguments in religious terms, their agenda closely tallied with the Christian Right's; they opposed affirmative action and gay rights and also decried "permissiveness." They became latter-day Cold War hard-liners and supported Reagan's renewal of Cold War policy during his first term. (*See also* Cold War; Foreign Policy/Foreign Relations; Mikhail Gorbachev.)

The neoconservatives may have provided some secular ideological grounding for the New Right, but the New Right's Christian activists got out the vote. The Moral Majority and later the Christian Coalition reached millions of ultraconservative voters in a manner that the rarefied neoconservatives could not. Reagan and his people fully understood and appreciated the power of this grassroots evangelical populism and knew how to court its followers and keep their support. In this respect, Ronald Reagan himself had something approaching perfect pitch.

Reagan went out of his way to address conventions and rallies held by New Right Christian groups; during the 1980 campaign, he told one enthusiastic convention of fundamentalist ministers that they, as clergy, could not endorse him, but that "I can endorse you." Reagan's impeccable credentials as a movement conservative stood him in good stead with the extremists. He had, after all, been a visible and charismatic part of the Goldwater campaign in 1964; he had been a movie star in good, clean American movies (for the most part—*King's Row* actually concerned some seedy doings in a neurotic small town); and he built a conservative reputation during the 1950s and 1960s with his speaking tours on behalf of General Electric. Reagan barely had to court the New Right. It would be more accurate to say that in the New Right Reagan had a ready-made constituency: those who had kept the faith since Goldwater and who remembered Reagan's memorable, nationally televised speech on the Arizonan's behalf. (*See also* Anticommunism; Barry Goldwater; Ronald Wilson Reagan.)

Ironically, many New Rightists became disenchanted with Ronald Reagan during his years in office, although the president never entirely alienated his base of support in the New Right, particularly the Christian Right. Still, Reagan struck many as less enthusiastically committed to the New Right agenda than they had hoped. As extreme as some of candidate Reagan's rhetoric had been during the 1980 campaign, President Reagan by necessity had to moderate some of his goals and policies in order to govern. The Reagan presidency did not bring about the reactionary renaissance that many ultraconservatives so fervently sought through their support of Ronald Reagan.

The New Right was disappointed by any number of things, not the least of which was the improvement of relations with the Soviet Union during Reagan's second term, after the ascension of Mikhail Gorbachev. (*See also* Arms Control/Arms Race; Cold War; Foreign Policy/Foreign Relations; Mikhail Gorbachev.) But what may have drawn the most criticism was Reagan's failure, by Christian Rightist standards, to mount sufficiently effective opposition to such things as abortion, affirmative action, and the overall breakdown of American morality. The administration simply did not meet movement conservatives' expectations.

The New Right itself had its share of troubles during the Reagan years. Several of its most charismatic ministers were discredited in a series of financial and personal scandals. Jim Bakker, a cable television pastor, ended up serving a prison sentence after being convicted of fraud and conspiracy. Bakker and others stole about $3 million from his own Praise the Lord ministry, and embezzled millions from followers' investments in a planned religious theme park that was to be called Heritage USA. Bakker also was accused of forcing sex on a woman named Jessica Hahn and then attempting to bribe her into silence. Hahn became a minor celebrity for a time and more recently has appeared on infomercials for singles services and such things.

Other famous preachers got into trouble or, as in the case of Oral Roberts, simply came under ridicule. Roberts claimed that Jesus was going to "call him home" unless he raised $8 million for a new medical school at Oral Roberts University. Rival preacher Jimmy Swaggart summarized Roberts' dilemma with his dry comment that the "dear brother says that Jesus is gonna kill him if he doesn't raise" the money.

Jimmy Swaggart, for his part, was caught at least twice with prostitutes and thus lost his television show and his following. Jerry Falwell, the head of the Moral Majority, never got into legal trouble but lost political power as the Reagan years went on, and in 1988 he left the Moral Majority, the group he did so much to found and to empower.

After Reagan left office in 1989, the New Right continued its activities and has exerted a good deal of influence on the nation's politics, particularly at the local level. Newer groups, such as the Christian Coalition, have concentrated on local issues and on electing candidates to city councils, school boards, and other such institutions. But the coordinated activities of groups such as the Moral Majority have diminished or at least have been deemphasized in the years since Ronald Reagan left the White House.

On the other hand, many Christian Rightists refocused their attentions during the later Reagan years and afterward, turning them more militantly to the antiabortion movement. The antichoice factions since the late 1980s have manifested the Christian

Right's predominant activism in American politics in the post-Reagan years.

Although Reagan in his time proved disappointing to many New Rightists—both the religious and secular varieties—he is today revered as a former president by many of his old New Right supporters. Many of the more prominent New Right extremists, such as Patrick Buchanan, claim loyalty and adherence to the Reagan revolution. Buchanan, who unsuccessfully sought the Republican presidential nomination in 1992 and 1996, claimed to be Ronald Reagan's political heir, the Republican who had kept faith with Reaganism.

Mainstream Republicans, such as former Senator Robert Dole, also lay claim to the Reagan mantle, although they do not share the New Right's extremist views, and New Rightists usually view moderates like Dole with suspicion and mistrust.

CIVIL RIGHTS

The Reagan administration's reputation concerning civil rights suffered several serious blows, due mostly to clumsy administrative decisions that played to alienated whites and the movement conservative constituency. Civil-rights activists, members of Congress, and others often accused the administration of conducting racist policies.

Ronald Reagan was not a racist in any active or hateful sense of the word and claimed that his Democrat father raised him to abhor racism and believe in human equality. Reagan, when a college athlete, sometimes had a black football teammate as a houseguest in his family home in Dixon, Illinois; in that very segregated era, such a thing was unusual and perhaps even risky. But whatever the president's personal inclinations, he was conservative in his approach to civil rights, and his indifference to racial issues raised many eyebrows.

Reagan ran into trouble during his first term when the administration made it known that it might not request that Congress extend the 1965 Voting Rights Act, several clauses of which were about to expire. Close on that public-relations gaffe came the Internal Revenue Service's announcement that it would no longer deny tax exemptions to private schools that practiced racial discrimination in their admissions policies.

The administration staffed the Civil Rights Commission with conservatives who were openly hostile to such programs as affirmative action, and it appointed as the Equal Opportunity Commission's head Clarence Thomas, a conservative black attorney openly resented by many members of the black community. Thomas had previously served in the Education Department; he candidly stated that he regularly ignored court-ordered deadlines for processing discrimination complaints against various colleges and universities. When he moved over to the Equal Opportunity Commission, he displayed a decidedly passive attitude toward many cases before the commission, and his passivity accorded with the administration's stated policy.

Poor urban blacks suffered significantly from the Reagan administration's cutbacks in social spending, and during the Reagan era, federal spending for public works in the nation's cities also sustained severe cutbacks; ghetto dwellers were the chief losers as a result of these policies.

Despite Reagan's own protestations that he believed in equality, integration, and equal opportunity, during his presidency the federal government reversed nearly a generation's worth of social policies aimed at helping the mostly black urban poor. This went against executive policies of both Democratic and Republican presidents before him. Even during the Nixon era, social programs often were extended, and federal money remained available to help maintain the urban infrastructure. Under Reagan, this all was reversed. (*See also* Unemployment.)

COLD WAR

The Cold War entered its terminal phase during Ronald Reagan's presidency. The reasons for this are hotly debated, and no doubt will be for generations to come, with wide disagreement over how much credit is due to Reagan and how much to the policies of Mikhail Gorbachev, or the Soviet leadership's blunders during the Carter and Reagan years.

Several factors seem beyond question: The Soviet war in Afghanistan crippled the Soviet economy, drained resources and manpower, and tested the loyalty and endurance of the Soviet people; the massive Soviet arms buildup during the 1970s and early 1980s severely damaged the Soviet economy; the endless military and financial aid the Soviet Union gave Cuba played a large role in the Soviet collapse. The Soviet government weakened, and the Communists began to lose control of the union. When an outright war erupted between two Soviet republics, Armenia and Azerbaijan, Moscow could neither stop the fighting nor keep arms out of the war zone.

In retrospect, the accelerated decline seems to have begun during Leonid Brezhnev's last years; it continued through the brief reigns of his successors, Yuri Andropov and Konstantin Chernenko. The reforms of Mikhail Gorbachev seemed to inject new life into the USSR, but in time even this vigorous young leader proved unequal to the task of salvaging the decaying Soviet system. The Cold War subsided as the Soviet Union declined; the Soviets became less formidable adversaries as they increasingly had to turn to the West for help.

The United States and the Soviet Union had been on unfriendly terms since the Bolsheviks established the Communist regime in 1917. In 1934, however, President Franklin D. Roosevelt granted the Soviet Union diplomatic recognition, although this act did not create any sort of friendship between the two nations. During World War II, the United States and the USSR entered into an uneasy and mistrustful alliance against Nazi Germany. President Roosevelt and the Soviet leader, Josef Stalin, formed a personal working relationship, but the interests of the two emerging superpowers remained at odds. Also, Stalin and other hard-line Soviets harbored a traditional, even paranoiac Russian mistrust of the West.

Despite the wartime alliance, there were divisive controversies. Stalin wanted the United States and Great Britain to stage a cross-channel invasion to open a second front in Western Europe as early as possible; in 1942 he tried to persuade Roosevelt and British prime minister Winston Churchill to invade sooner rather than later.

Stalin was unmoved by his allies' arguments that a cross-channel invasion before 1943 would be premature, as America and Britain were not yet in a position to open an effective second front. Stalin suspected that Roosevelt and Churchill held back in the hope that the Soviets and the Germans would exhaust each other and the war would end with a defeated Germany and a greatly weakened Soviet Union. Stalin often grumbled that the allies were willing to fight to the last Russian.

It is unlikely that this was the Western leaders' strategic goal. There was ample reason for mistrust on the Anglo-American side, too, for in 1939 the Soviets had signed an alliance with Nazi Germany and seized part of eastern Poland when the Germans invaded that nation in November. Russia found itself allied with the West when Hitler betrayed the Nazi-Soviet pact by invading Russia in August 1941.

The Western allies also were mindful that the newborn Soviet Union had made a separate peace with Imperial Germany in 1918 and withdrawn from the First World War, thus allowing the Germans to take their troops from what had been the eastern front and concentrate on the war in France. The Germans launched a massive western offensive that very nearly succeeded; the Bolsheviks proved faithless allies to the West, and now the Americans and the British had no faith that Stalin would not repeat Lenin's desertion of a generation before.

Roosevelt and Churchill finally were ready to mount the Normandy invasion in June 1944, but the Soviets' lingering bitterness continued to be a signficant factor in relations between the allies. Additionally, Stalin was determined to form the Eastern European nations that bordered the Soviet Union into a series of buffers, thus revisiting the traditional Russian fear of invasion from the West. Considering Russia's experience during the Napoleonic wars and the two world wars, this was understandable. However, Stalin considered it necessary to impose repressive puppet governments in the eastern states, although Roosevelt and Churchill insisted on free elections in Poland and other border nations.

Just how insistent the Western leaders actually were, or to what extent their insistence was pro forma, is subject to debate. The Soviets were already in Eastern Europe in the war's waning days, and possession is nine-tenths of the law. It was fairly easy to oppose expansionism in principle, but it would have been quite another matter actually to try to drive the Soviets out of the occupied areas.

When the "Big Three" met at Yalta, in the Soviet Union in February 1945, Stalin, Roosevelt, and Churchill tried to hash out issues concerning the coming postwar world. The three made several key agreements: The United States and Britain promised concessions to the Soviet Union in Manchuria and pledged to return territories that Czarist Russia had lost in the Russo-Japanese War of 1905. The three leaders decided to partition Germany (in a manner to be decided later), and Stalin agreed to a United Nations conference in San Francisco, to be held the following April.

But Stalin insisted that the Soviet Union must dominate Eastern Europe, and he particularly did not want to relinquish control of Poland. Roosevelt and Churchill continued to demand free elections in Poland, and Stalin agreed in principle.

There was not much the Americans and the British could do, as the nearly 10 million-strong Red Army had overrun Eastern Europe, and by the spring of 1945 the Soviets had installed puppet governments in Bulgaria, Hungary, and Romania. There also were independent Communist insurgencies in Albania and Yugoslavia, as well as a civil war between Communists and Nationalists in Greece. The extent of Soviet support for the three insurgencies is debatable, but to Western eyes, the postwar balance of power in Europe was shaping up to be tricky and threatening, particularly when the Soviets never did allow free elections in Poland. By 1946 they had entrenched a puppet regime there as well.

When President Roosevelt died in April 1945, the relationship between the Soviet Union and the West altered drastically. The Truman administration pursued the policy of containment and set the basic tone of America's approach to the Cold War for the duration. Stalin, for his part, manifested more openly his paranoia about the threat from the West and proceeded to confiscate factories and manufacturing materials from the areas that the Red Army had occupied. Early in 1946, the Soviet leader declared that there could be no lasting peace with the capitalist world and announced his intention to enter into an arms race, to overcome the Western advantage in weapons technology.

Shortly thereafter, American chargé d'affaires in Moscow George Kennan told the Truman administration that the Soviet Union was committed to the idea that there could be no permanent peace with the Americans. Kennan added that the remedy for the situation would be for the United States to contain Russia's "expansive tendencies."

From that idea grew the containment policy, the American attempt to confine Communism and prevent its spread to countries outside the Soviet sphere of influence. Later that year, former British prime minister Winston Churchill drove the point home for Americans when he delivered his famous "iron curtain" speech at Westminster College in Truman's home state of Missouri. Stalin had drawn an iron curtain across Europe, said Churchill, and he warned that the West must stand firm against the Soviet challenge, for the Soviets respected strength and exploited weakness.

In the postwar world, the possibility of the rapid and widespread growth of international Communism did not seem farfetched to policymakers or the general public. Much of Europe teetered on the brink of starvation and social collapse, and in Asia and Africa, the collapse of the old European colonial empires left a power vacuum that seemed ripe for the Communists to fill. It was a terrifying world that loomed in the dark wake of World War II, and both the West and the East were uncertain of what was to come. The Soviets were as frightened as their Western counterparts.

After the war, the Cold War properly commenced. Over the next several decades, it varied in intensity. The Korean War, the quarrels over Berlin, and the Vietnam War all served to aggravate tensions between East and West. The Korean War lasted three years and brought the United States into combat with the Communist Chinese; the Soviets clearly supported the Chinese and North Koreans but did not directly intervene. The American response to the initial North Korean invasion of South Korea was the earliest major overt use of the containment policy. The United States went to war rather than allow a wholly Communist Korea.

The closest the Cold War ever came to becoming World War III was the 1962 Cuban Missile Crisis, when President John F. Kennedy blockaded Cuba and threatened war rather than permit the Soviets to maintain nuclear missiles in Cuba. The Soviets backed down, and that retreat led to the ouster of Soviet leader Nikita Krushchev nearly two years later. Before Krushchev's ouster, however, the United States and the Soviet Union negotiated the Nuclear Test Ban Treaty, which banned testing atomic weapons in the atmosphere. In 1963 the two leaders who nearly went to war concluded the first significant nuclear treaty between the two superpowers.

The Vietnam War was the last major invocation of containment, and it was disastrous. Even so, in the early 1970s, the notably anticommunist president Richard M. Nixon initiated the policy of détente, ushering in a new era of East-West relations. While the Vietnam War was still in progress, Nixon visited Communist China and the Soviet Union, entered into strategic arms-control talks with the Soviets, and, overall, worked to effectuate stable and peaceful relations with the two Communist giants.

Nixon's policy of détente with the Chinese continued through the Ford and Carter administrations, but relations with the Soviets were problematic. The 1979 Soviet invasion of Afghanistan was a particular irritant in U.S.-Soviet relations, and in the early eighties, many observers believed that the Cold War, after thawing during the seventies, had again reached a dangerous intensity. The military buildups in both America and Russia only served to worsen the mutual bad feeling.

Reagan and his supporters have claimed that the Cold War finally ended and the Soviet Union collapsed because the Russians could not withstand the strain of competing with the United States in the accelerated arms race. Reagan's policy, they say, forced the Soviets into bankruptcy, since a wobbly Communist economy could not sustain such a competition against a capitalist economy. No doubt there is truth to this, but many who subscribe to this idea tend to minimize Mikhail Gorbachev's role. Other observers give Gorbachev considerable credit for the ultimate Cold War thaw.

Gorbachev's leadership had two paradoxical effects: He loosened the Communist grip on the Soviet people but proved unable to solve the formidable economic problems he inherited from the previous generation of Soviet leaders. Surely, American policy toward the Soviets played an important part, but one must not underestimate the effects of both Gorbachev's administration and the Soviet Union's domestic problems, upon which American policies likely had little if any effect.

Ronald Reagan's own unreconstructed anticommunism helped to aggravate tensions, particularly during his first term. Reagan flirted with a two-China policy, thus irritating the mainland Chinese, and unhelpfully referred to the Soviet Union as an evil empire. Reagan and his administration maintained an overtly hostile attitude toward the two Communist states, particularly the Soviet Union, even as the USSR and People's Republic of China sought to normalize relations with the United States. After Brezhnev's death, Soviet leader Yuri Andropov expressed interest in reviving détente, but he met with American resistance.

The "new" Cold War intensified when the Soviets shot down Korean Airlines Flight 007 over Soviet airspace in 1983, and the situation remained tense and unpromising until Gorbachev took power in Moscow in 1984. The new leader's policies of glasnost and perestroika did a lot for creating a new climate of international relations, and because of Gorbachev, the Soviet Union found acceptance in the world community for the first time. To this day, Gorbachev's role in easing Cold War tensions often is underestimated by Americans. In his memoirs, Reagan described Gorbachev as a leader who was open to discussion and new ideas, but Reagan didn't entirely give credit where it was due.

Both leaders were willing to hold a number of summits, and despite Reagan's earlier stance against "the evil empire," both actively sought to improve superpower relations. The Cold War became untenable in the 1980s; besides the ongoing threat of mutually assured destruction, both superpower economies suffered serious strains in the competition for supremacy in armaments. The Soviet economy, particularly, faltered under the strain of the arms race.

The Soviet Union dissolved during President Bush's term of office in 1991, although by the end of Reagan's term, the Soviet grip on Eastern Europe had clearly loosened. In any case, with no Soviet Union, there was no longer a Cold War. Even China, though on uneasy terms with the West, eased its own anticapitalist ideologies as it, too, attempted to join the world community. (*See also* Yuri Andropov; Anticommunism; Arms Control/Arms Race; Brezhnev Doctrine; Leonid Brezhnev; Central America; Foreign Policy/ Foreign Relations; Mikhail Gorbachev; Korea Airlines Flight 007; Reagan Doctrine.)

CONGRESS

Ronald Reagan enjoyed such phenomenal popularity, especially during his first term, that he dominated Congress as few other presidents have. In the twentieth century, perhaps only Franklin Roosevelt managed his first-term relations with Congress more masterfully than did Reagan. He had amazing success getting a Democrat-controlled House of Representatives and a Senate that the Republicans held only by a thin majority to pass his military programs, ratify his massive social-spending cuts, go along with extensive deregulation, and pass his legislative packages. For the first four years, the Reagan administration had something approaching a free run on Capitol Hill, but Reagan encountered difficulty in his second term, especially after the Democrats took back the Senate in 1986 and the Iran-Contra scandal broke in 1987.

When Reagan won the presidency in 1980, and the Republicans won their majority of the Senate, the GOP made significant gains in the House of Representatives. With the new congressional balance, the Reagan administration won victory after victory during Reagan's first term. Reagan relied a good deal on the Boll Weevils, a group of conservative Democrats who usually supported the administration's economic and monetary policies, going against their own party in several key votes. As for the Senate, while the Republicans never had a commanding majority, party discipline and the Senate's Boll Weevils enabled them to frustrate the Democrats consistently.

More than one analyst has observed that the attempt on Reagan's life at the very beginning of his presidency gave him an almost-mystical public image that was not evident beforehand. To be sure, Reagan won a commanding majority in the 1980 election and was well liked by voters, but prior to the shooting, he was not the "Teflon president" and had yet to be tested by crisis. When Reagan rebounded from being shot and touched the country with his good humor in the face of personal anguish, his popularity verged on the mythic.

The members of both congressional houses knew this. Only three months after the shooting, Reagan addressed Congress and spoke for his legislative programs. Congress then passed, by impressive bipartisan margins, the president's proposed tax cuts and voted the funds for his massive defense buildup. Money bills by law have to originate in the House of Representatives, and this compliant House held a large Democratic majority. Reagan clearly was in command.

House Speaker Thomas "Tip" O'Neill led the opposition on Capitol Hill during most of Reagan's presidency. A formidable political tactician, O'Neill nonetheless suffered a string of defeats at the hands of his GOP adversaries, led by the Republican president. O'Neill often groused about the Boll Weevils, wondering how the Democrats could have "lost" these people. An old-time New Deal–Kennedy Democrat, O'Neill fit uncomfortably into the new political era of the 1980s; this solid Democratic liberal found himself swimming against the tide, in a more polarized environment than he was used to. After all, during the 1960s and 1970s, even Republican presidents could work with the liberals in Congress, and even the conservative Richard Nixon did not seek to reverse the trend of federal action in social welfare that had held sway since the days of Franklin Roosevelt.

In the Reagan era, however, many congressional Democrats found themselves very much at odds with the new regime in the White House, which was, if anything, even more conservative than the Senate majority—whose leader, Senator Howard Baker of

Tennessee, was fairly liberal for a southern Republican. But Baker proved a friend to the administration and helped win Senate approval for much of Reagan's more controversial legislation. This is less strange than it may seem, for Baker and many other moderate Republican Senators were fiscal conservatives.

The Reagan administration showed a good deal of know-how in dealing with Congress during Reagan's first term and a good portion of his second, even after the Republicans lost the Senate. Reagan was a capable legislative leader, and the administration during the first term set definite and limited goals for its legislative agenda: Primarily, the administration concentrated on shrinking the welfare state through major domestic spending cuts, and increasing defense spending. The administration also aimed for a major income-tax cut.

Reagan's contacts with Congress were significantly strengthened by his capable and savvy White House staff. Speaker O'Neill, not one to compliment Republicans easily, described Reagan's staff as the best-run political team he had seen in his career. Reagan and his team lobbied Congress heavily on behalf of the president's programs, and Reagan involved himself in extensive personal contacts with representatives and senators in a way that the Carter administration had not.

Congress approved some of Reagan's most drastic proposals: a $35 billion reduction in domestic-program spending; nearly $750 million in tax cuts over several years; an increase of 27 percent in defense spending over a three-year period. By the end of April 1981, Reagan had pushed through Congress his entire initial budget program.

Reagan ran into trouble over his Central American policies, and members of both parties sometimes were wary of Reagan's economic policies, but Congress stayed fairly compliant until the Iran-Contra affair visibly weakened Reagan in the public-opinion polls. It is common in American history for Congress to rebel against presidential leadership, particularly when a strong and effective president weakens. The Democrats regained the Senate and solidified their hold on the House in the 1986 midterm elections.

Even though Speaker O'Neill retired, the Democrats were now in a position to be considerably less cooperative and get away with it. Reagan remained popular and regained much of his prestige in the polls as Iran-Contra became old news, but from 1986 to the end of his term in 1989, Reagan never again had a docile and cooperative Congress upon which to work his will. (*See also* Boland Amendments; Boll Weevils; William Casey and the CIA; Central America; Democrats; Elections—Congressional; Gypsy Moths; Thomas "Tip" O'Neill.)

CALVIN COOLIDGE

Thirtieth president of the United States, John Calvin Coolidge was one of Ronald Reagan's favorite predecessors. Reagan considered Coolidge to be underrated, and he admired the fact that Coolidge had eliminated the First World War debt without raising taxes—according to Reagan, President Coolidge cut taxes and still increased federal revenues. To commemorate his predecessor, Reagan hung a painting of Coolidge in the Cabinet Room.

Besides admiring Coolidge's tax policy, Reagan likely respected his stand on the Boston police strike of 1919, when, as governor of Massachusetts, Coolidge called in the national guard to police the city and proclaimed that "there is no right to strike against the public safety by anybody, anywhere, any time." Reagan took this line against the air-traffic controllers' strike in 1981.

Vice President Coolidge became president on the death of Warren G. Harding in 1923 and won his own term in 1924. He was a very popular president, as his laissez-faire style of governing fit well with the voters' mood in the prosperous 1920s. Even so, he did not seek election to another term. When asked his intentions, he replied with his classic New England terseness, "I do not choose to run in 1928."

Some historians wonder if Coolidge in fact was playing a coy game and actually wanted the Republican party to draft him for another nomination. Had he run and won in 1928, he would have been the first president to serve for more than eight years, and that would have broken the two-term precedent. Possibly, under those circumstances, he thought it better politics to wait for his party to "ask" him to run. Franklin Roosevelt followed that strategy when he sought a third term in 1940 and succeeded. If that was Coolidge's game in 1928, it did not work.

Other historians, however, believe that Coolidge meant what he said and simply did not choose to run in 1928. Whatever the truth may be, Calvin Coolidge left office in 1929 and returned to Massachusetts. He died in 1932.

D

DANILOFF-ZAKHAROV AFFAIR

The Daniloff-Zahkarov affair was a tangled web of international horse-trading, agencies working at cross-purposes, shocking incompetence, residual Cold War animosities, and, in effect, hostage taking. The administration insisted that it refused to negotiate a prisoner swap when it was doing just that, and the affair very nearly derailed plans for a summit between President Reagan and Soviet leader Mikhail Gorbachev and came close to halting the ongoing improvement in American-Soviet relations.

Despite the fact it was headline news, the press and the public had no idea of the situation's intricacies until years later. It all happened at precisely the wrong moment, but the superpowers reached a resolution before the thaw in the Cold War iced over.

In New York on August 23, 1986, the FBI arrested Gennadi F. Zakharov, a Soviet science attaché to the United Nations Secretariat. Zakharov walked into an FBI sting and purchased supposedly classified documents that the FBI gave to a student whom Zakharov had contacted earlier. One week later in Moscow, the Soviets arrested Nicholas S. Daniloff, *U.S. News and World Report's* Moscow correspondent. In an old Cold War maneuver, the Soviets had grabbed an American to use as a bargaining chip, or hostage, in securing their spy's release. Evidently, they wanted to trade; there was ample precedent in the history of American-Soviet relations for such a thing.

An anonymous White House spokesman may have unwittingly added fuel to the Soviet's fire by telling the press that the United States might be receptive to trading Zakharov for Daniloff; to counter that impression, Secretary of State George Shultz stated, in a previously scheduled speech at Harvard University, that the United States would not agree to any trades, since Zakharov faced a legitimate espionage charge but Daniloff was an innocent man whom the Soviets decided to use as a pawn.

On September 5, President Reagan sent a message to Gorbachev informing him that Daniloff definitely was no spy and asking that the Soviets release the hapless reporter forthwith. The two governments were amid negotiations to set up a summit between Reagan and Gorbachev, and the twin arrests presented sticking points on both sides. The Soviets wanted their man back, and the Americans wanted theirs. That Daniloff had no CIA affiliations and was a genuine news correspondent encouraged the Americans to hope that the Soviets would see reason. Reagan and Shultz still insisted that a swap was unacceptable, since that would amount to admitting that Daniloff was a spy when he was not.

Then came a revelation that jolted the administration and escalated the situation's seriousness. A few years earlier, Daniloff had delivered to the American embassy in Moscow a letter from a Russian named Potemkin. The letter found its way into the CIA's possession, and CIA agents contacted Potemkin to try to develop a "relationship" with him. Worse, one agent spoke to Potemkin by telephone and mentioned Daniloff's name during the conversation. The KGB had been watching and listening to all these comings and goings and thus concluded that Daniloff was, if not a CIA agent, then at least informally affiliated with the agency.

Daniloff was neither an agent nor an affiliate, but the CIA's clumsy performance in this case compromised Daniloff and exposed him to great danger, all without his knowledge. Secretary Shultz later wrote that he believed the United States owed it to Daniloff to go all out for his release, since it was government stupidity that landed him in the fix.

As if that weren't bad enough, it turned out that Daniloff had in fact committed an illegal act in Moscow. The reporter managed to acquire some secret Soviet government documents and photographs connected to a story on which he was working. Acquisition and possession of such materials violated Soviet law, just as an equivalent act in the United States would violate American law, although in Washington reporters did that sort of thing all the time. The United States government often extended a grudging tolerance for such activities as long as national security was not involved, or unless the government decided to charge the reporter in question for some other reason. In any case, the Soviets seemed unlikely to be lenient unless, of course, the Reagan administration could see its way clear to a trade for Zakharov.

On September 7, the Soviets upped the stakes by formally charging Daniloff with espionage, a capital offense. Reagan responded with a hot-line message to the Soviets demanding Daniloff's release and threatening "serious and far-reaching consequences" if the Soviets continued holding him. Reagan's message used the word *hostage* to describe Daniloff's status. The Soviets probably were well aware what a loaded word that is in American political and diplomatic language.

But the Americans did offer a possible deal, despite their continued insistence that they would not trade Zakharov for Daniloff. Zakharov had been legitimately arrested and charged with an offense under federal law and so had to be tried. The president, of course, had the legal power to pardon him, but such an action would be unacceptable to the administration as it would be tantamount to equating Zakharov and Daniloff.

Still, Shultz proposed to the Soviets that the administration would ask the court to remand Zakharov into the custody of the Soviet embassy if the Soviets would first remand Daniloff to the American ambassador's custody and then simply expel Daniloff from their country. In return, Zakharov would go on trial almost immediately and, if convicted, the United States would expel him in turn.

The Soviets responded by turning Daniloff over to the American embassy in Moscow, but they did not want the United States to put Zakharov on trial. In a blunt threat, the Soviets informed the Reagan administration that it would have itself to blame for Daniloff's fate unless "mutually acceptable solutions can be found."

A series of meetings between Secretary of State Shultz and Soviet Foreign Minister Eduard Shevardnadze had previously been scheduled for late September to begin working out details for the summit meeting between Gorbachev and Reagan. When Shevardnadze and Shultz met, however, the Daniloff case took up most of the discussions. Shultz, while still denying that the United States would trade Daniloff for Zakharov, presented his Soviet counterpart with a proposal for exactly that.

Shultz reiterated that the United States would release Zakharov after his trial if the Soviets first released Daniloff. Then Shultz upped the stakes and asked that, after Zakharov's release, the Soviets allow certain Russian dissidents to leave the Soviet Union. Shultz stressed that he wanted the Soviets to release Daniloff first so that his release would seem unrelated to the other releases; in other words, the United States wanted to maintain the thin fiction that there had been no trade.

Shevardnadze was more blunt. He wanted a simple swap of Daniloff for Zakharov. He wanted the United States to release Zakharov without a trial. Confronted with the Soviet's no-frills counterproposal, Shultz flatly turned it down.

To the foreign minister's no doubt unpleasant surprise, he was next summoned to the White House to meet with President Reagan. In the Oval Office, Reagan, by White House chief of staff Donald Regan's account, gave Shevardnadze hell over the Daniloff situation. Unsmiling and clearly angry, Reagan unceremoniously demanded Daniloff's release and reiterated the American position that there would be no trade of one prisoner for the other. Reagan told the silent foreign minister that he wondered how the United States could trust the Soviets when they had leveled a false accusation at an innocent American citizen. Reagan bawled Shevardnadze out for forty-five minutes in a rare display of genuine fury.

Reagan told Shevardnadze that unless Daniloff was released, progress in improving American-Soviet relations would come to a standstill. After the president more or less subsided, Shevardnadze gave him a personal letter from Gorbachev and took his leave. The letter contained a message that would have seemed unlikely, given the circumstances. Gorbachev did not mention Zakharov or Daniloff, but formally proposed that he would like to meet with Reagan sometime soon in a summit preliminary to a second summit in Washington. Gorbachev suggested the first summit take place in London or Reykjavik. Reagan was interested almost despite himself.

The Gorbachev letter went on. The Soviet leader wanted to discuss completely eliminating both superpowers' intermediate-range nuclear missiles in Europe. In return, he wanted the United States not to try to activate any antiballistic missile systems such as the Strategic Defense Initiative, and he suggested that the two nations agree to extend the Anti-Ballistic Missile Treaty for another fifteen years. If all this was done, then they should next discuss reducing strategic nuclear arms and place a moratorium on testing nuclear weapons. These proposals were actual enlargements of similar but more limited proposals that President Reagan made during the previous July.

Shultz relayed to Shevardnadze that the president liked the idea for a summit meeting in Rekyavik but that the Daniloff case still obstructed everything. There will be no summit, Shultz told Shevardnadze, unless the Daniloff situation is resolved as quickly as possible. Shevardnadze was not entirely forthcoming, but Shultz began to regard him as fairly reasonable and reported to the White House that things were looking a bit better.

But the haggling continued. The following week, the Soviets indicated that they would put Daniloff on trial if the Americans tried Zakharov. On the other hand, Shevardnadze told Shultz, if the United States released Zakharov the Soviets, after releasing Daniloff, might then release some dissidents. The United States still balked, but the two foreign ministers agreed to meet again in a few days, and Shevardnadze told Shultz that Gorbachev wanted to hold the summit in Reykjavik that October, so he was eager to get the Daniloff case out of the way. Shevardnadze also told Shultz that Gorbachev wanted to move forward on negotiating the INF Treaty so that it would be ready for signing when he came to Washington.

In short, the Soviets had told the United States that they wanted to settle the Daniloff case quickly and were ready to be flexible.

Both sides had been stubborn up to this point, and it would be difficult to judge which one had been the more obstinate. The Soviets insisted on a straightforward trade, but the Americans insisted that they would not trade, while offering a trade in language meant to obscure the fact that they were offering a trade. The question arises, who would not recognize that a trade had taken place, no matter what it was called? The American proposals and counterproposals might remind one of the Nixon era, when a counterattack was a "protective reaction strike," a retreat was a "strategic withdrawal," and an invasion was an "incursion." At least Secretary Shultz did not attempt to substitute some tortured term for "trade."

In any case, at their next meeting, Shultz and Shevardnadze worked out a plan for the trade. On the first day, the Soviets would let Daniloff leave the Soviet Union. On the second day, Zakharov would be expelled from the United States after pleading no contest in court. On a future third day, then, the Soviets would allow certain designated dissidents to leave the country. On another day, the Soviets would reduce the number of personnel at their United Nations mission (this had been a sore point between the two powers for months; the United States maintained that the mission was overstaffed, probably with KGB agents). Then, on the last day of September, the two governments would announce that Reagan and Gorbachev would have their summit meeting in Reykjavik beginning October 10.

Things then went smoothly up to a point. The Soviets released Daniloff, but Zakharov's release hit a snag; apparently, no one thought to inform the judge and prosecutor what was going on. Attorney General Edwin Meese intervened; Zakharov pled no contest, got probation, and was promptly expelled from the United States, but not before the Soviets got the idea that the Americans were reneging on the deal. The Soviets roared their defiance in the world press, and there were fears that Daniloff, whose plane had not yet taken off, might be rearrested. None of that happened, however, and before long each former prisoner was in his home country.

The Soviets kept their part of the bargain and released the hostages. The summit came off as planned, although Reagan had been widely denounced in the American press and by various political rivals for caving in to the Soviets. Since the crucial details of the deal were not public, people outside the administration were not fully aware what was at stake and did not realize that future summits, and by extension the course of superpower relations, were riding on the outcome of the Daniloff-Zakharov case.

Mysteriously, both Reagan and Shultz continued, even after leaving office, to maintain that the United States had not agreed to nor participated in a trade of Zakharov for Daniloff. Reagan later wrote that the United States had stood firm, and "the Soviets blinked." Shultz wrote that the Americans secured Daniloff's release without letting him be labeled a spy and had secured the release of several Soviet dissidents. It was, wrote Shultz, a satisfactory conclusion.

Obviously, it was a satisfactory solution for both sides. But it was certainly a trade, and it is puzzling why some of the participants believe they can deny that fact credibly. (*See also* Arms Control/ Arms Race; Mikhail Gorbachev.)

DEBATES

The televised presidential candidates' debates, during both the primary campaigns and the general election campaign of 1980 greatly aided Ronald Reagan's prospects for victory. In 1984 Reagan's stumbling performance against Walter Mondale was eclipsed by his star turn in his second debate against the Democratic nominee. In both 1980 and 1984, Reagan, the old Hollywood actor, used television to his advantage in a way that his opponents, who lacked his Hollywood polish and savoir faire, could not match.

Reagan's masterful, assertive performance against George Bush in the fabled Nashua, New Hampshire, debate in 1980 ("I paid for this microphone, Mr. Green!") showed his telegenic prowess early on. Unsurprisingly, the debates were short on substantive issues and long on posturing. All of Reagan's showmanship and charm was brought to bear on the small screen, and his opponents often seemed hesitant, inarticulate, and shrill in comparison. (*See also* George Bush.)

It was not a fair comparison, by any means. Reagan resorted to rhetoric and even ridicule, as when he baited President Jimmy Carter with the line "There you go again," when Carter accused Reagan of opposing Medicare during their 1980 debate. Granted, Carter's performance left much to be desired, and Reagan effectively converted the Medicare clash into one of the 1980 campaign's defining moments. It was worth millions of votes.

Also worth millions of votes was Reagan's summation at the end of that debate, when he used a phrase that has remained fixed in popular memory. "Are you better off than you were four years ago?" the candidate asked the television audience. "Is it easier for you to go and buy things in the store than it was four years ago? Is America as respected throughout the world as it was? Do you feel that our security is as safe, that we're as strong as we were four years ago?"

Whatever the true answers to these rhetorical questions may or may not have been, the voters responded favorably to the Republican nominee. They seemed to like Reagan's way of appearing to talk directly to them, a talent he shared with his early idol, Franklin D. Roosevelt. Reagan played to citizens who felt themselves "suffering at the hands of impersonal government."

In 1984 Reagan faced the Democratic nominee, former Vice President Walter Mondale, twice. The first time, the president was uncharacteristically bumbling and hesitant, and Mondale clearly won the debate on points. However, the Democrat needed a knockout, and Reagan, the old pro, was savvy enough to stay off the ropes. Still, the president looked bad, and for the first time, there was speculation in the media as to how the campaign might go.

Reagan later claimed that he was overrehearsed and overcoached, and this may be true. In their second debate, Reagan was far more relaxed and took command of the proceedings early and, in terms of public relations, scored a knockout victory over the hapless Mondale. Reagan even revived his "There you go again" line of 1980. It was widely reported that the campaign managers had decided to ease off on the coaching and rehearsals, in order to "let Reagan be Reagan," in James Watt's memorable phrase.

Perhaps the key moment of the second debate, however, was one that had little, if anything, to do with issues or policies. Just as Reagan had scored a rhetorical victory over Carter with "There you go again," he trumped Mondale on the age issue. When one of the questioners raised it, President Reagan quickly responded, "I am not going to exploit, for political purposes, my opponent's youth and inexperience." It was a classic Reagan moment, the sort of showmanship that helped to define Reagan's public image. Like Franklin Roosevelt, Ronald Reagan always knew his constituency, as well as how to play to his strongest supporters. His liturgies of clichés, slogans, and rhapsodies of "morning in America" played extremely well, and the Democrats, particularly Carter and Mondale, could not compete with this one-man show of optimism and promise. Neither could Reagan's Republican rivals for the nomination in 1980.

Reagan offered a powerful combination of winning personality and conservative ideology. It vanquished all electoral opposition, and planted him firmly in the White House. The debates were not the only medium he used, but they contributed significantly to his landslide election victories.

DEFICIT

The predominant economic issue and primary economic news story of the Reagan years was the federal budget deficit. The federal deficit more than doubled during the 1980s, jumping from less than 3 percent of the gross national product in 1980 to 6.3 percent in 1983 and never falling below 5 percent for the remainder of Reagan's time in office.

During Reagan's presidency, the United States ceased being the world's greatest creditor nation and became the world's greatest debtor nation. The deficit reached the trillions of dollars, and all deficit-reduction policies since, whether put forth by Republicans or Democrats, have had to promise very gradual reductions over a period of many years. No one has claimed that the deficit can be drastically reduced or eliminated in the forseeable future. The deficit, by all accounts, is here to stay for a very long time, and perhaps forever.

Politically, the deficit presented (and continues to present) any sentient politician with a series of knotty problems. Reagan, who made a career of condemning "tax-and-spend" liberal Democrats, did not want to raise taxes or curtail tax breaks for the well-to-do in order to raise the revenues necessary to begin balancing the budget. At the same time, a balanced federal budget was (and is) a conservative Republican battle cry in the electoral wars. Further, the Reagan administration always sought some way to reduce the deficit while preserving its tax-reform legislation and maintaining its buildup of the armed forces. The conflicting desires and political imperatives made for a considerable quandary and plagued the Reagan administration throughout its eight years in the White House.

Though the deficit rose sharply during Reagan's first term, the administration reined in military spending after 1984, and especially after 1986. Also, following the recession of the early 1980s (the worst since the Great Depression of the 1930s), inflation stabilized to some degree, and by 1984 an unmistakable economic recovery was in progress. Politically, these developments overshadowed the deficit and aided considerably in Reagan's reelection. The Democrats accentuated the deficit, but Reagan could claim, with credibility, that the American people were nonetheless better off than they were in 1980.

The administration and Congress tried a number of measures to bring the deficit under control: The so-called Domenici Plan of 1981 called for cutting domestic spending by $40 billion, raising taxes by the same amount, and lopping $16 million off the defense budget. According to former budget director David Stockman, Treasury Secretary Donald Regan's opposition effectively scuttled the Domenici Plan, costing the administration an opportunity to effectuate a $100 billion deficit reduction by 1984. It was, according to Stockman, the $40 billion tax raise that excited Regan's ire.

More successful, politically at least, was the Gramm-Rudman-Hollings Act of 1985, which sought to require balancing the budget through a system of spending limits imposed on Congress. Gramm-Rudman, as it is more popularly known, mandates that when the budget falls short of specified limits, the president must propose spending cuts in accordance with the law. Social Security is exempted from Gramm-Rudman cuts, as are certain other social programs.

The functional success of Gramm-Rudman is difficult to determine at this early date; the law took effect in 1986, and it is hard to judge either its effectiveness or the level of compliance in Congress. It also must be noted that by the time the Reagan administration left office, the nation was more than $375 trillion deeper in debt, and many critics argue that this fact alone attests to the failure of the Gramm-Rudman-Hollings Act, and perhaps to the failure of Reaganomics as a whole.

The federal deficit has haunted each succeeding administration, and the goal of a balanced federal budget remains the grand objective of Republican economic policy. Indeed, the Democrats have also taken up the cry, and the idea seems to have considerable public support, as the deficit has thoroughly frightened the voting public with the prospect of a strapped and mortgaged economic future for the country, for generations to come. (*See also* Reaganomics; David Stockman; Stock Market Crash of 1987; Tax Reform; Trade Policies.)

DEMOCRATS

All in all, the Democrats, as the opposition party, had a rough time of it during the Reagan years, even though they managed to win back the Senate from the Republicans in 1986 and maintained their majority in the House of Representatives throughout Reagan's two terms.

In presidential politics, the elections of 1980 and 1984 kept with a trend that had been developing since the end of World War II. Since Franklin D. Roosevelt died in 1945, no Democratic president has served two full terms in office, and no Democratic president, as we approach the election of 1996, has managed to get elected to two terms.

Of the Democratic presidents since Roosevelt, only one elected incumbent ran for reelection; Jimmy Carter lost his bid for a second term in 1980. Harry Truman and Lyndon Johnson both won elections, but they became president on the deaths of their predecessors; Truman succeeded Roosevelt and Johnson succeeded John F. Kennedy. Kennedy, elected in 1960, did not live to seek reelection in 1964. The Republicans, on the other hand, have managed to reelect three incumbents in the postwar era: Dwight Eisenhower, Richard Nixon, and Ronald Reagan.

In the twentieth century as a whole, only two Democratic elected incumbents have been reelected: Woodrow Wilson was elected in 1912 and 1916, and Franklin D. Roosevelt won the elections of 1932, 1936, 1940, and 1944. Altogether, this century has been dismal for Democratic presidential candidates and for incumbent Democratic presidents. As this book goes to press, the 1996 election has not occurred, and so Bill Clinton's fate lies months into the future.

On the other hand, the Democrats have dominated Congress for a good portion of the century. They held the House during Reagan's term, although they lost the Senate to the Republicans in 1980 and remained the minority party in the Senate for six years of the Reagan era, regaining the upper house in 1986. The new Democratic Senate majority proceeded to make life difficult for the administration during its final two years.

During Reagan's first term, the administration managed to form a working relationship with moderate and conservative Democrats in both houses of Congress; those Democrats who supported Reagan's economic policies came to be called the Boll Weevils and were rewarded with the Republican president's support in their reelection campaigns—at least Reagan did not campaign for their Republican opponents.

That sort of arrangement is not at all unusual in American history, since any president, in order to be effective, must form working relationships with elements of the opposition party, and the most effective presidents always managed to do just that. Many of Franklin Roosevelt's New Deal programs were passed by bipartisan coalitions in Congress, with considerable support from Republican liberals; Eisenhower, during the 1950s, often worked with Democrats and had a good rapport with Senate Democratic leader Lyndon Johnson; and Presidents Johnson and Nixon relied to varying degrees on bipartisan support in Congress. Reagan, in his first term, did so very effectively.

In Reagan's second term, the combination of a resurgent Democratic Senate majority and the weakening effects of the Iran-Contra affair lessened the president's dominance over Congress. Additionally, the lame-duck status imposed by the Twenty-second Amendment on every second-term president served to diminish Reagan's power; a president who cannot be reelected need not be feared by his opponents or, for that matter, his congressional allies.

Nevertheless, the failures of the 1970s, the unpopularity of President Jimmy Carter, and the rise of the Christian Right and New Right all undermined the Democratic party. Conservative campaigns succeeded in portraying the Democrats as the party of criminal-coddling, tax-and-spend liberals who could not be trusted to conduct the nation's business. Even in the middle 1990s, with a Democratic president in the White House, the Democrats have not fully shaken that image, and the party lost both houses of Congress to the Republicans in 1994. (*See also* Boll Weevils; Congress; Elections—Congressional; Gypsy Moths; Thomas "Tip" O'Neill.)

DEREGULATION

The federal government took on a regulatory role during the early 1900s, under the administrations of Theodore Roosevelt, William Howard Taft, and Woodrow Wilson. Roosevelt was the first president to involve himself in mediating labor disputes, and his administration saw the creation of such regulatory agencies as the Food and Drug Administration. Under Wilson, workman's compensation came into being, as did the Federal Reserve Board. Child-labor laws, antitrust laws, and other reform measures all were enacted during that era, and all contributed to a growing and increasingly active federal government.

During the 1930s, Franklin Roosevelt's New Deal ushered in a long period of even more stringent and pervasive federal regulation of business and utilities in the United States, and for decades government's regulatory role went without meeting any serious challenges. Federal programs and agencies promulgated regulations governing crucial aspects of workplace safety, saw to public-health regulations, mediated labor disputes, supervised workplace unionization elections, restricted various business practices, and set utility rates. To conservatives, the catalog of government involvement seemed endless.

Although conservatives such as Barry Goldwater (who wanted the government to privatize the Tennessee Valley Authority) and other rightists decried regulation, only in the 1970s did pinched financial conditions begin a mainstream trend of deregulation of American business and commerce.

Although fairly gradual deregulation began during the Nixon and Ford administrations and then picked up some steam during the Carter years, the Reagan administration took up the cause in an extensive cutback of federal regulations in any number of areas. The Reagan White House drastically deregulated banking and savings-and-loan practices. Anti-air-pollution measures and car-and-truck safety regulations were reversed, and the Interior Department opened federal forests, wilderness, and offshore waters for development. (See also Cabinet.) Even the Federal Communications Commission reduced its regulatory function for the broadcast industry.

As President Franklin Roosevelt ushered in a period of extensive use of the government's "instrumentalities" to regulate business and promote the public welfare, now President Ronald Reagan believed it was time to reduce government involvement and allow business and commerce freer reign. (See also Reaganomics; Reagan Revolution; Franklin Delano Roosevelt.)

Ronald Reagan believed that "government is not the solution to our problems; government is the problem." In this, he certainly had the business community's solid support, and deregulation held a high priority in the administration. Reagan's belief in deregulation as a governing principle dated back many years to his early days as a newly converted conservative. In the 1950s and early 1960s,

Reagan, on his speaking tours for General Electric, heard numerous complaints from his corporate audiences about the federal regulations that were expanding even during Dwight Eisenhower's Republican presidency. (*See also* Ronald Wilson Reagan.)

Like many conservatives, Reagan came to believe that federal regulation actually threatened basic American freedoms, and that the framers of the Constitution never dreamed the government they created would in turn create a vast and powerful bureaucracy whose regulatory powers, in the conservative view, threatened to displace legislative functions and people's basic rights.

In the 1970s, both during and after his time as governor of California, Reagan made deregulation a major theme in the public appearances and writings that served to build support for his 1980 White House run. President Lyndon Johnson's Great Society programs were still a recent memory, and Reagan correctly sensed that resentment over big government pervaded much of the nation's heartland. He therefore pitched a good portion of his precampaign to this widespread sentiment.

During his first year in the White House, President Reagan put Vice President George Bush in charge of a program to reduce what the administration considered unnecessary federal economic regulation. Vice President Bush's committee recommended eliminating waste by cutting pages from the actual books of federal bureaucracy's rules and regulations. The program ran into stiff opposition from House Speaker Tip O'Neill and many of the House Democrats, whom Reagan called the "tax-and-spenders." The administration announced a plan to cut federal expenditures by eliminating various "boards, agencies, and programs" in an effort to begin reducing the federal deficit, which in 1981 had hit $80 billion—nowhere near what it would be by the time Reagan left office in 1989. At the end of 1981, Reagan continued to preach the gospel of getting government regulators out of business's way, and the administration managed to cut approximately $40 billion of spending from the 1981 federal budget. But the deficit went up anyway. (*See also* Congress; Deficit; Democrats; Thomas P. "Tip" O'Neill.)

In 1982 the Grace Commission made further recommendations for cutting government waste. The crusade had mixed results, as the country experienced the worst recession since the Great Depression of the 1930s, but administration spending cutbacks and economic policies may ultimately have helped the economy to recover by 1984. (*See also* Grace Commission; Reagan Recession/Reagan Recovery.)

Reagan and his supporters continued to claim deregulation a triumph long after Reagan left office, but of course, there are differing views. Critics blame deregulation for a variety of serious problems such as the following:

During the late 1980s, many of America's nuclear power plants were aging and deteriorating. But as a result of cutbacks in nuclear safety regulations, many plants were simply allowed to fall into very hazardous conditions. The nation would have to spend perhaps $200 billion over the next decade to rectify the situation.

Across the country in the late 1980s, during the last years of Reagan's presidency and into the tenure of the Bush administration, the federal government agreed to bail out thousands of savings-and-loan institutions that failed over the past few years or were about to fail. Some critics maintained that deregulation played a major part in the savings-and-loan disaster; in any case, the bailout cost American taxpayers untold hundreds of billions of dollars.

Reagan's airline-industry deregulation raised serious questions about airline safety, as the federal government had weakened or abolished rules that guided airline safety and airplane construction for the previous six decades.

Consumer advocate Ralph Nader, for one, denounced the administration's claims of deregulation's economic benefits as "ideological arithmetic" that disregarded the human cost in terms of injuries, illnesses, and deaths. (*See also* David Stockman.)

E

During the administration of President Gerald Ford, the heads of government of the leading industrial democracies began holding annual meetings. They called these meetings economic summits, even though they were not dedicated solely to economic issues; the presidents and prime ministers discussed whatever vital issues confronted them, including international politics, security, and anything else they considered pressing.

The leaders have continued to hold these economic summits, sometimes called the G7 (for "group of seven") meetings, from year to year, in various locations, and they try, with varying degrees of success, to keep the pomp and circumstance to a minimum. The conditions can be described as semiformal to informal; the participants hold roundtable discussions and consult each other privately or in smaller groups. As international conferences go, the economic summits are comparatively freewheeling and flexible in the relations between the national leaders who attend.

When President Reagan attended his first economic summit in Ottawa, Canada, in the summer of 1981, he was, in his own phrase, the "new boy in school." One of his main contributions at Ottawa, according to his own account and others, was to convince the participants to address each other by their first names, and he began by introducing himself as Ron. When, some years later, Japanese prime minister Yasuhiro Nakasane attended his first economic summit,

Reagan asked him what his wife called him. When the prime minister answered, "Yasu," Reagan said, "Well, Yasu, my name's Ron."

Despite differences in philosophies—Mitterand, for instance, was a socialist, while British prime minister Margaret Thatcher and President Reagan were fiscal conservatives—the group tended to help whoever was up for reelection or a confidence vote that year. According to former Treasury Secretary and White House Chief of Staff Donald T. Regan, the leaders would make sure the candidate's name figured prominently in their published communications. They would place the candidate at the center of nearly every photograph taken during the summit. Ideological agendas had no bearing on the matter, Regan reported. They liked to help and support one of their own in that exclusive and curious fellowship.

The fellowship and relative informality did not displace the seriousness of the occasions. The idea was for the leaders to meet and discuss mutual concerns in relative isolation, away from inquiring reporters and cheering crowds, so that the yearly sessions would not bog down in observing protocol, conducting press briefings, or attending public functions.

The following is a short summary of the major points of each economic summit that Reagan attended.

1981, Ottawa. As Reagan prepared to attend his first economic summit, his advisers warned him that he might encounter some bad feeling, as some other nations blamed America's high interest rates for their economic troubles. In fact, others present did criticize the United States for high interest rates; Reagan told his assembled peers that he had inherited the rates from the Carter administration and that he wanted them lower, too. He told the group that he wanted to control America's deficit, which concerned the others.

Reagan and British prime minister Margaret Thatcher stood for free trade. Japanese prime minister Zenko Suzuki agreed in principle but was unwilling to open Japanese markets to less restricted imports. French president François Mitterand was particularly critical of American interest rates. West German chancellor Helmut Schmidt muted his own criticism, even though everyone present knew him to be highly adverse to Reagan's economic policies.

Reagan and Thatcher talked privately during the summit and began forming a friendship that has endured since both left office. They found common cause in their general economic thinking and free-trade advocacy, but Thatcher worried that Reagan would have trouble reducing his deficit. Events proved her correct.

Reagan got the feeling that his fellow leaders at Ottawa thought his domestic economic-recovery plan would not work. They wished him good luck, but he suspected they did not agree with his "radical" notions of tax cuts and reducing the government's role in the national economy.

1982, Versailles. The 1982 summit took place in June, during the war between Britain and Argentina over the Falkland Islands. The war was very much on the assembled leaders' minds, and the proceedings became somewhat awkward when Thatcher found out from her foreign office back in London that the Japanese were going to vote in favor of a proposed United Nations resolution calling for a cease-fire. As the British insisted that there could be no cease-fire without an unconditional Argentine withdrawal, a vote for the resolution was in effect a vote against Britain. (*See also* Falklands War.)

President Reagan and the American delegation caused more awkwardness when, through a series of botched instructions, American ambassador to the United Nations Jeanne Kirkpatrick withdrew her vote against the resolution and changed it to an abstention. Then, when journalists were allowed to question the leaders at a lunch in the palace at Versailles, one asked Reagan about the confusion at the United Nations in New York. Reagan had heard nothing about it and could not answer the question.

Otherwise, the 1982 summit stuck to economic issues, and there was quite a bit of talk about the impact of new technologies on employment in the industrial nations. President Mitterand of France, the summit's host, presented a paper on the subject. The rather academic atmosphere of the conference oddly contrasted with the opulent surroundings of the palace in which it took place.

1983, Williamsburg, Virginia. This may have been Ronald Reagan's favorite economic summit, since the "Reagan recovery" from the worst recession since the 1930s was in full swing, and the summit seven appeared suitably impressed. Reagan later compared their opinions on his economic recovery programs to those they expressed two years earlier at Ottawa. West German chancellor Helmut Kohl, who had replaced Helmut Schmidt and was attending for the first time, asked the president to explain the "American miracle."

Prior to the summit, Reagan's White House advisers and Secretary of State George Shultz had decided to prepare the president for the event just as they prepared him for news conferences and debates. They staged a mock conference, with staffers impersonating the participating leaders.

Shultz and White House deputy chief of staff Michael Deaver hatched the plan after the embarrassment at Versailles, when Reagan could not answer questions about the United Nations vote on the Falklands resolution and other issues. To Reagan it probably seemed pretty normal, as his aides often prepared him for various functions in similar fashion.

Arms-control negotiations dominated the agenda at Williamsburg. The United States was negotiating with the Soviets to produce the Intermediate Nuclear Force and Strategic Arms Reduction treaties, but nothing much was happening at that point, as Mikhail Gorbachev had not yet come to power, and American-Soviet relations were icy. The summit seven agreed in principle that they should issue a "security statement" about the negotiations to solidify support for NATO's position on arms control. (See also Arms Control/Arms Race; Leonid Brezhnev; Cold War.)

Western Europe was covered with tactical and strategic missiles aimed at the Soviet Union, and the Soviet Union had thousands of strategic and tactical missiles aimed right back at Western Europe. Even so, it took some work to arrive at a consensus among the summit seven.

Canadian prime minister Pierre Trudeau at first wanted to "speak more softly" about deterrence and to try not to antagonize the Soviets. Japan's Nakasone wanted to extend the arms-reduction goal worldwide, rather than allow reductions only in Europe and thus leave the rest of the world, particularly Japan, still vulnerable to nuclear targeting. West Germany's Kohl, whose centrally located country had long been in the Soviet Union's nuclear crosshairs because of NATO's heavy deployment in the West German countryside, wanted a serious statement of support.

Ultimately, the summit seven issued a statement calling for arms reduction based on equality and verifiability. They called for an INF agreement as soon as possible. The statement called the collective security of the seven nations "indivisible" and noted that, should an INF agreement not be reached, the United States would go ahead with its planned deployment of new intermediate missile systems in Western Europe.

Once the statement was prepared, Mitterand and Trudeau refused to support it, calling it warlike. According to Reagan's account, the discussion grew heated, and when the conference broke for lunch, Mitterand and Trudeau walked together apart from the group as they all made their way to the place of repast.

After lunch the participants assigned their foreign ministers to revise the statement so the two dissenters could support it, but without watering down the essential message. There was more argument among the leaders during the afternoon, but somehow the issue got resolved, and the statement went out essentially intact. Even so, at one moment Trudeau objected to a phrase that called for freedom for people everywhere in the world. Trudeau thought that the statement seemed a slap at the Soviet Union. According to Donald T. Regan's account, President Reagan rapped his glasses on the table and snapped, "Damn it, Pierre! How can you object to that?"

Another notable development at the London summit concerned terrorism. Secretary of State Shultz wrote a strongly worded antiterrorism statement, and the seven leaders all signed it. The statement called for "closer cooperation and coordination between police and security organizations and other relevant authorities, especially in the exchange of information, intelligence, and technical knowledge" in combating terrorism. The leaders further agreed to cooperate in expelling or barring known terrorists from their respective nations, including terrorists and abettors of terrorism who held diplomatic status.

The summit seven assembled for a formal dinner the final night, and Queen Elizabeth, Prince Philip, and Queen Mother Elizabeth attended. At Trudeau's request (or prodding), President Reagan entertained the party by reciting "The Shooting of Dan McGrew," by Canadian poet Robert W. Service. Reagan had memorized it years earlier and entertained his children with it. The Queen Mother chimed in whenever the president reached the repeating line, "the lady named Lou."

1985, Bonn. President Reagan's participation in the Bonn summit was marred by the controversy over his accepting Chancellor Kohl's invitation to speak at the Bitburg cemetery, where SS members were buried. In the American media, and possibly in other nations' press coverage as well, the Bitburg controversy overshadowed the economic summit. (*See also* Bitburg.)

At the summit itself, French president Mitterand caused a stir by expressing doubts that the annual summits were particularly relevant anymore and wondering aloud if he would continue to attend. Japanese prime minister Nakasone defended the summits and chided Mitterand for taking neighboring democracies for granted. Nakasone felt decidedly isolated in Asia surrounded by pseudodemocracies and dictatorships.

In Bonn, Mitterand hammered away at a favorite theme; he favored a monetary conference of the seven nations to discuss exchange rates and other monetary issues. Reagan noted that at Williamsburg, two years earlier, the group had set its finance ministers to preparing a report on world financial matters, and the report was due in June. Reagan told Mitterand that it was best to wait and see what the report said.

Reagan encountered some skepticism on his plans for the Strategic Defense Initiative, but nothing strikingly significant emerged from the summit that for years has dwelt in the shadows of Bitburg in the world's memory.

1986, Tokyo. According to Margaret Thatcher, the main issues at the Tokyo summit were political rather than economic. The Americans had recently bombed Tripoli, Libya, and the Americans wanted a strong communiqué on terrorism. But the persistent issue of Japanese market restrictions still played heavily in the proceedings.

The West had spent several years trying to get Japan to open its markets, with frustrating results. Japan had a large trade surplus in 1986, and the Japanese allowed the yen's value to go up. The first development pleased Japanese businessmen and industrialists; the second did not. Japan still levied some stiff import taxes on many Western products, so all was not smooth between Prime Minister Nakasone and his fellow club members. (*See also* Japan.)

There was more harmony on the subject of terrorism. Shultz again drafted a statement that Reagan and Thatcher endorsed, and the summit seven signed on to "strongly reaffirm" their condemnation of "international terrorism in all its forms." (*See also* Hostages and Terrorists.)

1987, Venice. Arms control figured prominently at the Venice summit. Chancellor Kohl wanted short-range tactical nuclear weapons removed from Germany, but Prime Minister Thatcher disagreed, as British forces were stationed in Germany, and she did not want their protection removed.

Reagan favored Kohl's position on the ground that if they made headway in accepting the Soviet proposal for removing the short-range INF missiles, then that might lead to a later agreement to remove the long-range INF missiles. Thatcher, facing declining polls at home and a bitter controversy over health-care issues that threatened her Conservative party's lead in Parliament, stood firm on postponing any removals. She needed to show her electorate that she put Britain's interests first.

Reagan faced problems at home, too. The Iran-Contra scandal was at the top of the news, and many political commentators asserted that the president seemed out of touch and less of a presence than he had been, both at home and abroad. The next presidential election was a year and a half away, and pundits spoke of Reagan's lame-duck status.

The nation, and probably the president as well, was preoccupied with Iran-Contra, and Iran-Contra would continue to dominate the coming summer's headlines.

1988, Toronto. Ronald Reagan's final economic summit involved a good deal of talk about the General Agreement on Tariffs and Trade (GATT). America's huge trade deficit gave rise to a protectionist sentiment in Congress and among the public, and Reagan's own approaches to the subject were ambiguous. He called himself a free trader, but gave in to certain protectionist impulses, although he remained generally committed to free-trade principles. (*See also* Trade Policies.)

Agriculture figured as the thorny issue at Toronto. The Japanese, in particular, were stiffly protectionist in subsidizing and protecting their nation's agricultural industry. Many Third World nations wanted to export their agricultural products more freely, but the agricultural protectionism that Japan, France, and others among the summit seven practiced frustrated that ambition. Margaret Thatcher, for one, wanted her summit partners to open their agriculture markets. In her memoirs, she referred to this strain of protectionist policy as a "wealthy western protection racket."

The summit took no action on GATT, leaving that issue to the GATT negotiators. Reagan put forth an objective of achieving zero agricultural subsidies by the year 2000, but the other summit leaders thought it unrealistic and omitted it from the summit's communiqué.

Thus ended Ronald Reagan's participation in the yearly economic summits. At the next one, in Paris in 1989, George Bush attended as President of the United States.

ELECTIONS—CONGRESSIONAL (1980, 1982, 1984, 1986)

The Democrats were the majority party in Congress for a good deal of the twentieth century. After winning a majority in the House of Representatives in 1930, they held it, except for a brief interlude during the late 1940s and early 1950s, until the Republican sweep of 1994. Likewise, the Democrats dominated the Senate for many years before the 1994 elections, except for a period during the late 1940s and for six years during the 1980s.

President Reagan faced a Democratic House for all his eight years in office, but had a Republican Senate until the 1986 elections. One of the hallmarks of his first term was his administration's ability to outmaneuver the congressional Democrats, despite their House majority; in the Senate, too, where the Republican majority was not overwhelming, the administration had to call upon many skilled operators to work around the Democrats. Even so, during his first term, Reagan mostly got his way in Congress. Many conservative Democrats (the Boll Weevils) supported his economic policies, while some Republicans (the Gypsy Moths) often opposed the administration.

During his second term, Reagan faced more gridlock in Congress, as the Democrats became more contrary and resistant in the House and the Republicans lost the Senate in the 1986 midterm elections. Iran-Contra, too, eroded a good deal of the administration's power and influence on Capitol Hill.

Going into the 1980 election, the Democrats held 58 Senate seats to the Republicans' 41. The election gave the GOP a majority of 54 to 46. In the House of Representatives, the Democrats held their majority, but the margin went from 273 to 159, to 243 to 192.

In 1982 the nonpresidential party made gains in Congress. This is a normal pattern in American politics, but it was accentuated because the election took place at the height of the Reagan recession, when the president and the Republican party both were in trouble in the public-opinion polls. The Democrats closed the gap in the Senate by one seat. Going into the 1982 election, the Republicans held 54 Senate seats to the Democrats' 45 (there was one independent). After the election, the Republicans lost the one independent, and the Democrats now held 46 seats to the Republicans' 54.

In the House, the Democrats, still the majority party, made major gains. Going in, the House score stood at 241 Democrats versus 192 Republicans, and two seats were vacant. The 1982 election changed the score to 269 Democrats versus 166 Republicans. The House vote was widely regarded as a serious setback for the Reagan administration.

Reagan won a landslide reelection in 1984, but his coattails did not extend to Congress. The Republicans did manage to pick up 14 new House seats (which made for a balance of 253 Democrats versus 182 Republicans) but lost two Senate seats, weakening the GOP's command of the upper house with a tally of 53 Republicans versus 47 Democrats.

The greater shock to the administration came in the midterm

election of 1986, when the Democrats regained control of the Senate while maintaining a large majority in the House, thus making themselves once again the majority party in Congress. The new Senate had 55 Democrats and 45 Republicans. There was again economic trouble during that year, and unemployment reached its highest level since 1982. However, President Reagan himself stood well in the polls, even though the Democrats won the Senate back.

In the House of Representatives, 259 Democrats lorded it over 176 Republicans in the 100th Congress. The renewed Democratic domination of Capitol Hill caused severe problems for the Reagan administration during its remaining two years. (*See also* Congress; Democrats; Iran-Contra; Reagan Recession/Reagan Recovery; Thomas "Tip" O'Neill; Unemployment.)

ELECTIONS—PRESIDENTIAL (1980 AND 1984)

In 1980 President Jimmy Carter became the fourth twentieth-century incumbent to be voted out of office, joining William Howard Taft (1912), Herbert Hoover (1932), and Gerald Ford (whom he had defeated in 1976) in this dubious fraternity. Former California governor Ronald Wilson Reagan won the presidency in 1980 with 43,899,248 votes; President Carter won 35,481,435 votes, and independent candidate John B. Anderson won 5,719,435. The electoral vote was Reagan 489, Carter 49, and Anderson none.

The 1984 election was even more of a blowout, as President Reagan polled 52,609,797 votes (525 electoral votes) to Walter Mondale's 36,450,613 votes (13 electoral votes). In 1980 Carter carried only five states; in 1984 Mondale carried only Minnesota (his home state) and the District of Columbia. Reagan inflicted on the Democrats two of the most overwhelming elective landslides in American history.

Ronald Reagan was a very skilled campaigner, and his long years of performing stood him in good stead for the battles of the political arena. In 1980 he often came across as warm and gently self-mocking, whereas Carter often seemed distant, self-righteous, and humorless (none of which the former president actually is).

Carter also had the bad luck to suffer the indignities of the Iran hostage crisis (still unresolved on election day), as well as the political fallout from a troubled economy, fraught with drastic inflation and high unemployment.

In 1984 Reagan, now the incumbent, had had nearly four very visible years in the public eye, putting his actor's charisma to work in very effective ways. Few administrations have so well manipulated the media to such advantage. Reagan's public appearances were very carefully staged; he often dodged reporters with great acumen, and nearly always appeared hale, hearty, smiling, waving to bystanders— every inch a president pleased to be out among, and seen by, his people, even though he in fact was kept at a great distance from them.

Under Reagan, the presidential photo opportunity reached its zenith, as his handlers raised it to high art. The superstar president was photographed, filmed, and videotaped talking to common folks, helping teenagers load sandbags in a disaster area, and holding a weeping girl in his arms at the funeral services for the *Challenger* astronauts. Few presidents have managed their public relations so masterfully; perhaps only Franklin Roosevelt was Reagan's equal in this respect. Even Dwight Eisenhower was not quite the performer that Ronald Reagan was.

In his two presidential election campaigns, Reagan brought the full force of these talents to bear. His opponents' lack of performing expertise only served to accentuate Reagan's skill. Reagan also was fortunate in that, by 1984, the economy had noticeably recovered from the serious recession of the early 1980s.

The recession, the worst economic downturn since the Great Depression, may well have made Reagan yet another one-term president had it continued. But the economy rebounded, and the "Reagan recession" was forgotten in the wake of the "Reagan recovery." Reagan sailed to a second term in 1984. (*See also* Jimmy Carter; Debates; Ronald Wilson Reagan; Reagan Recession/ Reagan Recovery.)

F

FALKLANDS WAR

The United States did not become directly involved in the war between Great Britain and Argentina over the Falkland Islands, but the administration clearly backed the British, once diplomacy had failed and war was imminent.

Argentina had for some years insisted that the British Falklands, which the Argentines called Las Malvinas, rightly belonged to Argentina. In April 1982, Argentina invaded the Falklands, subduing the very small British force that was there. In the resulting diplomatic crisis, President Reagan had Secretary of State Alexander Haig shuttling between Buenos Aires and London, trying to find a diplomatic solution to avoid war.

According to some historians, Haig may have inadvertently given the Argentines the impression that the United States would not side with Britain if war broke out, leading the Argentines to believe that the Reagan administration did not necessarily disapprove of Argentina's invasion. The Argentines also may have believed that Reagan's Central American policy would dictate siding with Argentina, as Reagan seemed to value any possibility that South American nations would be able to help America's anticommunist stance in Central America.

On the other hand, others have noted that Haig and Jeanne Kirkpatrick, the U.S. ambassador to the United Nations, seemed to be the only ones in the administration who grasped the situation's seriousness. The two officials were at odds; Kirkpatrick wanted the United States to back the Argentines, since they were assisting in training Nicaraguan Contras. Haig, on the other hand, saw the invasion as violating international law and reminded his colleagues, and the president, that America's relationship with Great Britain was paramount. Defense Secretary Weinberger supported the secretary of state in this view.

Haig's announcement that the United States would afford all possible material help to Britain short of actual American intervention came as a bitter shock to Argentina and caused considerable ill feeling in many Latin American capitals. That Argentina had launched a war of aggression cut no particular ice with many Latin Americans, who resented the British presence in the Falklands.

The British made relatively short work of the Argentines, and American standing in South America may have been damaged, although it is difficult to assess the long-range impact of American policy regarding the Falklands War. At the same time, the relative brevity of the war may have helped halt a rapidly growing antagonism between Latin American nations and Western Europe; a prolonged war between Britain and Argentina, with the British at least diplomatically supported by their NATO allies and the United States, could have destabilized relations with Latin America.

GERALD FORD

Thirty-eighth president of the United States, Gerald Rudolph Ford took office upon Richard Nixon's resignation in August 1974. After losing the 1976 election to Jimmy Carter, he left the White House in January 1977. Ford served as a congressman from Michigan for twenty-five years and was the Republican minority leader in the House when Richard Nixon nominated him for vice president. He was the first vice president appointed under the provisions of the Twenty-fifth Amendment, following Spiro Agnew's resignation. (*See also* Twenty-fifth Amendment.)

Former governor Reagan challenged President Ford for the Republican presidential nomination in 1976. Ford had not been elected either vice president or president, and so Reagan felt politically secure enough to challenge this unusual opponent, who was far more moderate in his politics than Reagan was and who did not command the conservative right's support.

The primary battle between Ford and Reagan was fierce, and going into the convention, Ford's nomination was not a sure thing, even though he held a slim lead over the challenger. But the few remaining uncommitted Republican delegates ended up supporting Ford, and the president was nominated on the first ballot. Almost immediately, the assumption arose that Ronald Reagan would be the top contender for the party's 1980 nomination, as Ford was constitutionally prohibited from seeking another term if he won in 1976, since he had filled more than two years of Richard Nixon's second term.

Reagan's and Ford's political paths crossed for the second time in 1980, after Reagan had secured the nomination. Ford remained very popular among Republicans, and early in the primary season, polls showed that the former president could deny Reagan the nomination were he to enter the race. Ford was the one Republican who would be a stronger candidate than Reagan, but Ford was not interested in running for president again. However, once nominated, Reagan suddenly, and publicly, considered asking Ford to be his running mate.

The idea of a former president running for vice president was unusual, to say the least, but for a brief time, speculation was rife that Ford was interested. The Reagan camp floated trial-balloon reports that Reagan and Ford might put together a plan for a sort of copresidency—as an ex-chief executive could not realistically return to the executive branch in a subordinate position—even though there is no constitutional provision for such an arrangement. Reagan, in his memoirs, claimed that Ford indeed was interested in the proposal.

According to Reagan, the deal fell apart when Ford demanded concessions. In Reagan's later descriptions, however, these alleged concessions seemed to be the very deal that the Reagan camp appeared to offer in the first place—a sort of coequal relationship between president and vice president.

Whatever the state of affairs may have been, Gerald Ford did not sign on as Ronald Reagan's running mate, and the nomination was offered to George Bush. Gerald Ford continued to live in retirement, as a former president of the United States.

FOREIGN POLICY/FOREIGN RELATIONS

The Reagan administration conducted a general foreign policy that was decidedly bipolar and interventionist during the first term and a good part of the second. Early on, the administration set out to reverse what it saw as a decline in American power. Reagan's foreign policy relied largely on military solutions involving overt intervention along with covert operations. In the process, Reagan revived the old Cold War rhetoric of a world divided between two rival superpowers, and added his own gloss by calling the Soviet Union the "evil empire."

Besides determining to reestablish American military superiority over the USSR, the Reagan administration actively sought to minimize Western Europe's and Japan's pursuit of independent policies with regard to the Communist bloc or the so-called Third World. Domestic critics were frequently branded unpatriotic for their opposition. The administration sought to rule the roost, and insisted to both foreign allies and domestic political critics that support for Reagan's foreign policies was mandatory.

America's 1983 invasion of Grenada served as an exemplar of Reagan's "preventive intervention" policy. Similarly, the 1985 bombing of Tripoli was an example of limited but devastating payback for terrorism. The administration's commitment of naval and marine forces to Lebanon (which ended in the disastrous and tragic 1983 car-bombing of the Beirut marine barracks that killed over two hundred marines) also was part of a highly militarized approach to foreign relations. Reagan's interventionist principles were also manifested in overt and covert operations particularly in Central America and the Middle East.

Reagan was quite blunt and candid in his intentions: The United States would use its great military power as an active tool of diplomacy, and any crisis involving American interests might involve American military action. This stance largely defined the administration's foreign policy during the first term.

Events during the second term had a moderating effect on Reagan's policies. At home, financial imperatives forced cuts in the defense budget and halted America's massive arms buildup. Overseas, Soviet leader Mikhail Gorbachev's interest in easing Cold War tensions—indeed, in ending the Cold War itself, provided the United States and the Soviet Union could come to some crucial agreements—induced a curb on Reagan's rhetoric and adventurism. The superpowers now wanted to talk, and a new generation of Soviet leadership understood the economic problems facing the Soviet Union far better than did its elderly predecessors; the Soviets now needed to cooperate with the West.

China also remained problematic. Alienated from its former Soviet ally (despite Gorbachev's attempts to normalize relations), it played a sort of approach-avoidance game with the United States. The Reagan administration toyed with the idea of restoring normal relations with, and weapons sales to, Taiwan, both of which had been discontinued by President Carter in 1978. Beijing was angry, and when Reagan first took office, there was a chill in Sino-American relations that began to thaw only after it became clear, yet again, that the United States and the People's Republic of China needed each other for economic and strategic reasons.

Reagan's initial stance toward China had the effect of under-mining the rapproachment that Nixon and Carter had worked for. Under Carter, the United States formally recognized China, established an embassy in Beijing, opened trade relations, and negotiated a possible alliance. This was "playing the China card" against the Soviet Union, as relations between the two Communist giants were hostile, and there had even been military clashes along their common border. (*See also* Yuri Andropov; Anticommunism; Arms Control/Arms Race; Beirut Marine Bombing; Brezhnev Doctrine; Central America; China and Taiwan; Cold War; Mikhail Gorbachev; Grenada; Hostages and Terrorists; Middle East; Persian Gulf; Muammar Qaddafi; Reagan Doctrine; Strategic Defense Initiative.)

G

GENDER GAP

In the presidential election of 1980, only 47 percent of female voters voted for Ronald Reagan, as opposed to 55 percent of male voters. Historian Paul Boyer has noted that this was the widest discrepancy between female and male voters ever recorded in an election for president. For all of Reagan's presidency, his support was consistently stronger among men than women, thus the "gender gap."

Reagan appointed several women to high government posts. He picked neoconservative Democrat Jeanne Kirkpatrick as ambassador to the United Nations, Margaret Heckler as secretary of health and human services, and Elizabeth Dole as secretary of transportation. Anne Gorsuch Burford was a high official in the Environmental Protection Agency. Finally, President Reagan made the historic appointment of Sandra Day O'Connor as the first female associate justice of the Supreme Court. But Presidents Nixon, Ford, and Carter had each appointed more women to federal offices, albeit none as visible as the women Reagan appointed.

In 1983 Reagan got himself into trouble on the gender front when he quipped that, were it not for women's civilizing qualities, men would still be dressing in skins and "carrying clubs." Although some found the comment well-meaning but clumsy, many feminists called the comment patronizing, in the sense that it advocated a subservient role for women.

At the 1983 National Women's Political Caucus convention in San Antonio, Texas, the president came under extended and severe criticism. Various speakers described Reagan as hopelessly unresponsive to women's issues and utterly failing to understand the lives of contemporary American women. The *St. Louis Post-Dispatch* pointed out that while those words were harsh, they nonetheless accorded with public-opinion-poll figures, which showed that 68 percent of women Republicans favored reelecting Reagan, as opposed to a solid base of support among Republican men of 82 percent. Among the general public, most polls in 1983 showed only 33 percent of women voters favored reelecting President Reagan.

At the time of the 1983 polling—during the summer—Reagan's approval ratings were not at their highest; however, the gender gap plagued him throughout his presidency, even in the good times of public approval. One *U.S. News and World Report* article identified him as the first modern president to be notably less popular with women than men, and pointed out that even women in the administration were becoming alienated. For example, Justice Department official Barbara Honegger quit her job working on a project to identify laws that discriminated by gender. Honegger charged that the project itself was false, and told the press that the president had "betrayed" women. Reagan, in turn, stated that he would match his administration's record on women's issues against that of any other presidential administration.

According to feminist critics, the administration's welfare and social-spending cutbacks affected women more adversely than men, since women outnumbered men as beneficiaries of such programs as Aid to Families with Dependent Children, food stamps, medical programs, federally subsidized day-care programs, and legal aid.

U.S. News and World Report also reported feminist dissatisfaction with the administration's record of enforcing antigender bias laws.

The Reagan administration claimed that its policies benefited women by eliminating most federal estate taxes that hurt widows, reducing marriage penalties in federal taxes, and increasing women's buying power by reducing inflation. This defense left many feminist critics unmoved.

The gender gap never was resolved during the Reagan years. Eventually, it faded as a topic of media coverage, and public interest moved on. But Reagan continued to have less support among women than among men, although the president's support overall kept his poll ratings high for most of his presidency.

BARRY GOLDWATER

Longtime senator from Arizona Barry Morris Goldwater, as the 1964 Republican presidential candidate, gave his supporter Ronald Reagan his first national political spotlight by assigning the actor and aspiring politician a prominent role in the campaign.

Although Goldwater lost badly to President Lyndon Johnson in November, he was instrumental in advancing Reagan's new career. Reagan's campaigning for the senator, which culminated in Reagan's famous nationally televised speech for Goldwater on October 27, 1964, had much to do with his election as governor of California two years later, in 1966.

Until the 1964 campaign, Reagan was a registered Democrat, even though he had become increasingly active in conservative Republican politics. In 1960 he campaigned for Richard Nixon for president; at Nixon's request, Reagan kept his party affiliation, claiming to be a Democrat for Nixon, and tried to influence conservative Democrats to bolt their party in favor of the GOP candidate.

In 1964 Reagan was appalled at the massive federal spending that President Johnson poured into Great Society programs, like the War on Poverty, and became convinced that Barry Goldwater was the man to reverse this liberal trend and lead the nation back to sound conservative principles. Reagan's help at first met distrust from many of Goldwater's operatives, but the candidate himself accepted Reagan's support and praised the speech that Reagan was delivering around the country on the campaign's behalf.

"The Speech," as it was known, was the same one Reagan gave on national television to such great effect—that effect being mostly, of course, on his own political prospects. One immediate result of Reagan's televised speech, however, was that $1 million in campaign contributions poured into Republican national headquarters virtually overnight.

The speech for Goldwater really was quite similar to Reagan's standard banquet speech that he gave when he traveled the country for General Electric. He assailed big government and called upon the current generation to keep its "rendezvous with destiny," by voting for a new conservative agenda. Reagan quite openly borrowed "rendezvous with destiny" from Franklin Roosevelt, a president many of Reagan's audiences resented. But whatever the original source, Reagan's rhetoric struck responsive chords, and now, in 1966, he put his years of performing experience at Barry Goldwater's disposal. In the process Reagan established himself as a national political presence.

Almost from the day after the 1964 election, California Republicans regarded Ronald Reagan as a prospect for the 1966 gubernatorial election, and Reagan spent the next two years traveling around California for speaking engagements, banquets, and political meetings. Overall, he conducted himself as a candidate while maintaining that he had not yet decided to run but was traveling around to survey conditions and prospects in the state.

During the 1960s, Barry Goldwater was the leader of the same conservative movement that Reagan would lead during the 1970s. Goldwater's presidential candidacy signaled the trend away from big government and heavy social spending and toward conservative economic policies and social values. It was this resurgent conservative trend that led to Reagan's election as president in 1980. Goldwater, however, launched his campaign in an era that was still generally liberal, and he faced an incumbent who had enormous support simply for having succeeded the assassinated John F. Kennedy. No Republican could have defeated Lyndon Johnson in 1964. The GOP also fared poorly in Congress. Riding Johnson's coattails, the Democrats massively increased their majorities in both Houses. But 1964 was a personal triumph for Ronald Reagan.

For years afterward, many Republicans fondly recalled Reagan's famous speech for Goldwater. Republicans often thought of Goldwater as a sort of mentor, or at least a forerunner, to Ronald Reagan as the conservatives' national standard-bearer. It came as a shock to many Reagan supporters, therefore, and perhaps to Reagan himself, when Goldwater endorsed President Gerald Ford for the 1976 Republican nomination. Many Reagan supporters believed that an endorsement from Goldwater would help shore up support for Reagan in the Republican party's right wing.

Barry Goldwater remained a prominent conservative spokesman until he retired from the Senate in 1987, although he left his mark on American politics. He lacked Reagan's easygoing charisma, but served as a trailblazer for the future conservative leadership. (*See also* Christian Right/New Right; Sandra Day O'Connor; Ronald Wilson Reagan.)

MIKHAIL GORBACHEV

The final leader of the Soviet Union, Mikhail Gorbachev presided over both the end of the Cold War and the end of the Soviet Union itself, though not intentionally. Gorbachev sought to reform the Soviet system rather than abolish it, and he sought to improve relations with the West. He realized that his predecessors' hidebound policies, both foreign and domestic, were outdated, inappropriate, and no longer tenable. He failed to realize that those adjectives applied to the entire Soviet system itself, and the Soviet Union survived the Reagan presidency only by about two and a half years.

Gorbachev, who held the posts of first party secretary and Soviet president, came to power in 1985, upon the death of Konstantin Chernenko. He quickly set about liberalizing domestic legal and social policies by introducing freedom of speech (up to a point) and loosening emigration laws. This glasnost (openness) and perestroika (new thinking) delighted civil libertarians and dismayed hard-line Communists.

Eventually, in the later 1980s and early 1990s, the civil libertarians themselves were dismayed when Gorbachev to some extent retreated from his liberalism; he sought to stay in power by appeasing some of his conservative opponents, who still exerted considerable power in the Supreme Soviet. He also had to tread a careful path in regard to Soviet-U.S. relations for the same reason—he could not afford to appear to make wholesale concessions to the Americans.

Ronald Reagan and Mikhail Gorbachev developed an important working relationship under initially adverse conditions. Gorbachev first came to power during a chilly and dangerous period in super-power relations; the Soviet downing of KAL Flight 007 was quite recent, and Gorbachev's immediate predecessors ended up taking hard lines against the United States, even though Yuri Andropov, at least, had expressed interest in reviving the détente of the 1970s.

Also, Gorbachev had to reckon with the Reagan administration's hard-line policies. The days of Reagan's "evil empire" rhetoric were only a year or so in the past, and little significant progress had been made in any dealings between the superpowers.

Gorbachev's task was further complicated by Reagan's policy of American military superiority (the arms race had all but bankrupted the Soviet economy) and Reagan's determination to develop the Strategic Defense Initiative (SDI, often known as Star Wars). Gorbachev sought to ease the competition while continuing to rigidly oppose SDI. Reagan's antimissile program therefore loomed as the major stumbling block in arms-reduction negotiations, and a considerable obstacle to normalizing relations.

Gorbachev's task, therefore, was twofold: to achieve reform in both domestic and foreign policies. The young leader knew that the old ways would no longer work. The Soviet Union faced devastating economic problems, and superpower relations had deteriorated to their lowest and most dangerous state since the Cuban Missile Crisis of 1962.

Gorbachev and Reagan met to discuss arms control in Geneva, Switzerland, and Reykjavik, Iceland. At Geneva, in 1985, the two presidents at one point took a break from the formal negotiations and strolled to a nearby boathouse on the Lake Geneva shore, where the Americans had set up a comfortable sitting room. Settled in easy chairs by the fireplace, the two leaders had a more or less private session to get acquainted. The chat did not advance the negotiations, but it began a personalized working relationship between Gorbachev and Reagan. They discussed East-West mistrust, reviewed some Cold War history, and then, on the walk back to the main hall to rejoin their delegations, each invited the other to visit his country. The two leaders got along distinctly better than their wives did. (*See also* Nancy Davis Reagan.)

The Geneva summit was not entirely successful, and the next meeting, in Rekyavik, also had only limited success. But the personal diplomacy between the two opened a new era of contact between the Soviet Union and the United States. Gorbachev became very popular in America (although his status in his own country began to slip as the Soviet economy declined and the Soviet Union's international position steadily weakened), and Reagan's visit to Moscow was a popular success.

Gorbachev remained in many ways a solidly traditional Soviet ruler, in that he threatened or even resorted to using military force against secession-prone Soviet republics, and he wanted to maintain Soviet hegemony in the Eastern bloc. Gorbachev also seriously feared SDI and did not view it merely as some sort of bargaining chip. He was loath to expose his regime to free elections and attempted to retreat from his own reforms in his last years as Soviet president in order to placate the hard-liners in his politburo.

Still, Gorbachev formed a productive relationship first with President Reagan and then with President Bush, whom he had gotten to know during the Reagan administration. (*See also* George Bush.) Gorbachev's role in the notable arms-control treaties of the 1980s must not be underestimated; both Reagan and Bush needed a working partner on the other side, and Mikhail Gorbachev was that man.

Gorbachev survived a highly public coup attempt by antireform hard-liners during the summer of 1991. At year's end, he lost his power and his post and presided over the end of the Soviet Union.

Early in 1996, Mikhail Gorbachev announced that he would run for the presidency of Russia. In the June balloting, he won less than 1 percent of the vote. (*See also* Arms Control/Arms Race;

Brezhnev Doctrine; Cold War; Foreign Policy/Foreign Relations; Reagan Doctrine; Strategic Defense Initiative.)

GRACE COMMISSION

Officially known as the Private Sector Survey on Cost Control, the Grace Commission was formed in 1982, when President Reagan asked J. Peter Grace, of W. R. Grace & Company, to head a panel of business leaders who would study the federal government's operations and make recommendations to reduce waste and promote efficiency.

The Grace Commission's reports covered a wide variety of government enterprises and functions and made over two thousand recommendations that covered everything from privatizing many federal functions to eliminating paperwork costs. The commission, in short, concerned itself with the nuts and bolts of running the government.

Among the Grace Commission's findings were that it cost the United States Army over four times as much in administrative expenses simply to issue a paycheck as it cost a private business to do the same thing; half of the federal government's computers were obsolete to the point of uselessness; the Veterans Administration paid between $100 and $140 in administrative costs to process, but not actually pay, a single medical claim. Perhaps the most startling finding was that the government had no centralized management for its financial and accounting activities.

Reagan claimed to have implemented over half of the Grace Commission's recommendations and to have eliminated a good deal of waste. The president's claim has been disputed by critics and by former members of the administration. (*See also* George Bush; Deregulation.)

GRENADA

The 1983 American invasion of Grenada alerted the world to the Reagan administration's willingness to use military force. Neighboring governments had been consulted in advance, and many supported the invasion, but the Reagan administration did not consult British prime minister Margaret Thatcher, even though Grenada was a member of the British Commonwealth. This did not sit well with the British, but the United States decided to risk some amount of English disfavor.

The October invasion forcibly removed a Marxist regime that had overthrown the previous prime minister, and, according to the administration, seemed to be forging ties with Moscow. The administration also claimed that American medical students on the island were in imminent danger from the Grenadan government; there also were Cubans in Grenada—some were aid workers, and some apparently were military personnel.

Army and marine elements went ashore, and the navy successfully interposed itself between the island and any possible military action from Cuba. The invasion was brief, relatively inexpensive, and incurred few casualties—although many mental patients died when their hospital was mistakenly bombed.

In the United States, the invasion was by and large a public-relations success, although it did occasion some protest. On the world scene, Reagan's action did little if anything to moderate Cold War tensions; quite the opposite, as it seemed to support Soviet perceptions of American militancy in international affairs.

GYPSY MOTHS

The Reagan administration gave the moderate and liberal Republican members of Congress the nickname "Gypsy Moths" for their uncertain allegiance to the administration and their unreliable support for Reagan's programs. While the Boll Weevil Democrats supported key elements of Reagan's economic policies, the Gypsy Moth Republicans opposed many of these same policies. They often attacked the administration's proposed budgets, sometimes demanding restoration of liberal funding programs and opposing Reagan's intended cutbacks.

During Reagan's first term, the Gypsy Moths wanted, among other things, to continue funding Amtrak, energy for low-income households, education, youth job-training programs, and guaranteed student loans. Many of these senators and representatives had worked quite well with the Carter administration and supported many of the former president's moderate social programs.

The Gypsy Moths caused headaches for the Reagan administration and served to restrain some of its more militantly conservative intentions. Among the more prominent Gypsy Moths were Margaret Heckler of Massachusetts (who, perhaps ironically, later became Reagan's secretary of Health and Human Services), Larry DeNardis of Connecticut, William Green of New York's silk-stocking district, House minority whip Robert Michel of Illinois, Claudine Schneider of Rhode Island, Carl Pursell of Michigan, Gary Lee of New York, Norman Lent of New York, and Edward Bell Madigan of Illinois. (*See also* Boll Weevils; Congress; Democrats.)

H

HOSTAGES AND TERRORISTS

International terrorism has developed as a phenomenon mainly since the end of World War II. It has figured in liberation movements in Israel, Algeria, and Vietnam, and even to some extent in Canada. During the 1960s, Arab groups began employing terror as a major tool in their campaigns against Israel; the Palestinians resorted to terror in their quest for a Palestinian state.

During the 1970s, hostage taking increased as a terrorist weapon. There were many instances of hostage taking, but probably the most notorious occurred at the 1972 Olympics in Munich, West Germany, when Palestinian terrorists seized eleven Israeli athletes in the Olympic village. After several days of negotiating for safe passage out, all the hostages and terrorists died when West German security forces and the Palestinians shot it out at Munich's airport.

There were numerous other highly publicized hostage crises during that decade. The 1976 crisis that ended with the famous Israeli raid on Entebbe, Uganda, put a new cast on the matter. Israel freed all but four of the hostages held by the Palestinians with a daring nighttime raid deep into Ugandan territory in which all or most of the terrorists were killed, along with at least twenty Ugandan soldiers. The Israeli raid served notice on the world of a new and aggressive willingness to react violently to terrorism, even at the risk of hostages' lives.

The Israeli example may have influenced President Carter to approve the ill-fated raid into Iran to rescue the Teheran hostages.

(*See also* Jimmy Carter; Persian Gulf.) Ronald Reagan took office in 1981 after severely criticizing Carter for the way he handled the Iran crisis. Reagan insisted that he would never have entered into negotiations with the Iranians or with any terrorists, and he hinted from time to time that any raid he authorized would have succeeded.

But President Reagan found himself confronted with the different shades of terrorism nearly from the start, as state-sponsored, liberationist, even lunatic-fringe terrorists took hostages and attempted to black-mail the administration and the United States.

Early on, the administration took the position that the Soviet Union supported most of the world's terrorist groups as part of its Cold War against American interests. Secretary of State Alexander Haig and CIA Director William Casey were the most outspoken proponents of that view, although a State Department intelligence report cast doubt on their position. In the first two years of his first term, the president tended to support Haig's and Casey's contention. The evil empire, in administration rhetoric, had strong ties with all international terrorists.

While the Reagan administration likely overstated the Soviet connection to world terrorism, it is still true that the Teheran hostage crisis belonged to a disturbing new variety of international terrorism. State-sponsored terrorism—that is, terrorism sponsored and sometimes even carried out by governments, as opposed to insurgent groups or liberation organizations—became more and more evident after the mid-1970s. While the Iranian government did not initiate the taking of the American hostages in 1979, it quickly endorsed the action and then used the hostages as bargaining chips in its attempts to extort concessions from the United States and other Western nations. Libya and Syria also engaged in state-sponsored terrorism, as did other Third World nations.

State-sponsored terrorism became, in George Shultz's phrase, part of an undeclared war against the West. Nations encouraged terrorism by funding terrorists, giving them weapons and training, issuing them passports, and even providing asylum in safe areas to protect them from their target countries' prosecution or vengeance.

Perhaps because the Teheran hostage crisis was so recent, administration members spoke frequently about terrorism and often reiterated the policy that the United States would not negotiate with terrorists and that terrorism against Americans anywhere in the world would provoke a strong response. But the administration faced no tests of its resolve during most of the first term. Despite its rhetoric, the Reagan administration exerted something of a moderating influence when Israel invaded Lebanon in 1982 in retaliation against terrorist acts by the Palestine Liberation Organization.

The administration convinced the Israelis to refrain from trying to exterminate the PLO and to agree to an expulsion. The United States then assisted the PLO in its exit from Beirut. Later, Reagan stationed marines in Lebanon to preserve the peace and to help keep the feuding Lebanese factions apart, and perhaps also to avert another Israeli invasion.

The plan backfired when a terrorist bomb killed 241 marines in their Beirut barracks in 1983. It was the single largest loss of life of American military personnel since the Vietnam War.

Throughout the world, terrorists remained active. Arab terrorists most frequently attacked Israelis; the Irish Republican Army carried out terrorists acts in England; and terrorists were believed to be sponsored by Iran, Syria, Libya, North Korea, and a few other states. Attacks on Americans were too infrequent and scattered to claim consistent media attention, even after the 1983 Beirut marine bombing. All that changed during Reagan's second term. (*See also* Beirut Marine Bombing; Middle East; Persian Gulf.)

On June 14, 1985, TWA Flight 847, en route from Athens to Rome, was hijacked by two terrorists. Of the 153 passengers, 135 were Americans, and the Reagan administration now contended with the worst American hostage crisis since Teheran. The terrorists forced the pilot to fly the plane back and forth between Beirut and Algiers; on the ground in Beirut, the hijackers beat and then murdered Robert Dean Stethem, a diver in the United States Navy. They dumped his body on the tarmac, then flew back and forth between Algiers and Beirut yet again.

On the ground in each of the two capitals, the terrorists released most of the passengers, but on June 16, the plane landed in Beirut a final time, and thirty-nine hostages, all of them Americans or crew members, were held captive in Lebanon by the terrorist group Amal.

The terrorists had taken the hostages in order to force Israel to release about seven hundred Shi'ites from an Israeli prison. The prisoners had been arrested in Lebanon by Israeli forces for "security offenses." The terrorists found it easier to hijack an American plane than to strike at Israel because Americans were more vulnerable at international airports. That the United States had stationed marines in Beirut and had launched a naval bombardment of Moslem positions in Lebanon in 1983 helped fan resentment; for all these reasons, these terrorists chose to take Americans hostage.

The crisis was complicated by the high public profile of the captors and the hostages themselves. In Beirut the hostages were shown in public, not bound and blindfolded as the Teheran hostages had been, but instead being taken to a restaurant, walking about in escorted groups, and to some extent speaking to the press. One hostage was designated spokesperson and talked to the media about the terrorists and their aims.

The hostages were kept clean and fed and telegenic as the Amal leader, Nabih Berri, conducted a media campaign for the Shiite prisoners' release and to show the world what a good time his hostages were having in his charge. In a particularly bizarre episode in the generally bizarre situation, Berri ordered one hostage released when he was found to have a heart condition. At a packed press conference, Berri embraced the man and gave him a handgun as a gift, joking that he might need it to defend himself. The man was placed aboard a plane bound for the United States amid much commotion and the loud farewells of Nabih Berri.

Meanwhile, President Reagan received a letter at the White House that read, "We implore you not to take any direct military action on our behalf. Please negotiate our immediate release by convincing the Israelis to release the 700 Lebanese prisoners as requested. Now." The letter bore the signatures of thirty-two of the thirty-nine hostages.

The Israelis showed surprising flexibility and let the United States know that they would free their prisoners if requested to do so.

It is questionable, though, if the generous Israeli offer did the trick, or if some adroit and somewhat threatening signals from the White House may have effectuated the end of the crisis. Reagan had persuaded Syrian president Hafez Assad to intercede. Perhaps more to the point, the administration also conveyed to Berri in no uncertain terms that the United States would hold him personally responsible if anything untoward happened to the hostages.

Unexpectedly, even Iran had a hand in resolving the crisis. Apparently, Hashemi Rafsanjani, then speaker of the Iranian parliament, helped President Assad negotiate with the terrorist leaders in Lebanon who were, after all, sponsored by Iran. Rafsanjani may have wanted to defuse the crisis to avoid any immediate problems with the United States. In any case, his participation encouraged CIA Director William Casey and National Security Adviser Robert McFarlane to press on with the initiative that culminated in the Iran-Contra scandal. (See also Iran-Contra.)

However it all came together, Berri released all the hostages at the end of June, and President Reagan's public-opinion ratings shot skyward, in striking contrast to Jimmy Carter's fate of having a hostage crisis help destroy his presidency.

While the TWA hostage crisis held center stage, during that June there was another terrorist attack on Americans in Central America. On June 19 in San Salvador, guerrillas attacked a café and killed thirteen people, four of whom were United States marines and probably the intended targets. The president chose not to retaliate. Besides contending with the hostage crisis in Lebanon, Reagan also had publicly opposed counterattacking terrorists if doing so would involve large-scale civilian deaths, and the Salvadoran guerrillas were too well insulated amid the general population to allow for a "safe" retaliation.

The next high-profile hostage incident, like the TWA crisis, featured one particular act of singular brutality—in this case, the murder of an elderly, wheelchair-bound man. In early October 1985, the Italian cruise ship *Achille Lauro* was hijacked by Palestinian terrorists. There were about four hundred people aboard, many of whom were crew members, since most of the passengers were ashore in Alexandria, Egypt. The terrorists held the remaining crew and passengers hostage against a demand that Israel release fifty Palestinian prisoners.

Many of the passengers were elderly Americans, and the terrorists murdered one in a hideous way. Leon Klinghoffer, nearly seventy years old and confined to a wheelchair, was aboard with his cancer-stricken wife. The terrorists shot him, then threw his body and the wheelchair overboard. On October 9, the hijackers landed in Egypt and "surrendered" to a representative of the Palestinian Liberation Organization. Egypt allowed the PLO to put the hijackers on a plane bound for Tunisia, but the plane was intercepted by American F-14 attack jets and forced to land at a U.S. air base in Sicily. There, the Italians demanded that the United States surrender the terrorists. The Italians refused to extradite the Palestinians to the United States, but tried and imprisoned them in Italian courts.

The entire situation outraged much of the world, particularly some of America's allies. Italy, for one, did not appreciate being involved in a possible confrontation with the PLO, as the Italians feared terrorist retaliation. Further, President Reagan may have unwittingly sent the PLO a message that, counter to usual American policy, the United States was ready to deal with the PLO as a sovereign state.

This latter misunderstanding came about when the terrorists first surrendered in Egypt; Reagan told the press that he hoped the PLO would subject the hijackers to some form of justice. This could possibly have been taken to imply that the United States recognized the PLO as having jurisdiction, which would be tantamount to affording unofficial recognition. That would contravene Reagan's own policy of treating terrorist organizations as outlaws—Reagan previously had steadfastly refused to negotiate with terrorists, and here he was, in effect asking the PLO to try the hijackers under their own justice system (assuming that such a system existed).

However, Reagan's order to intercept the hijackers' plane countermanded any implication that the United States was willing to deal with the Palestine Liberation Organization.

As for the murder of Leon Klinghoffer, no one ever stood trial for killing the elderly man. Klinghoffer's wife, already ill at the time of the hijacking, died several months later.

The most enduring and strenuous of the hostage crises, which lasted into George Bush's presidency, concerned hostages in Lebanon. The terrorist group Hezbollah during the 1980s seized a number of Westerners, both American and European. Various deals were made over the years, and some hostages were released, though most of the Americans remained in captivity for years at a time. At least one, CIA agent William Buckley, was brutally murdered by his captors. Another hostage was photographed being hanged, but American intelligence agencies could not verify the pictures' authenticity. During Reagan's second term, the administration resorted to secret arms sales to Iran to persuade Iranian moderates to intercede with Hezbollah. (*See also* Iran-Contra.)

Several hostages were released, to great publicity and considerable rejoicing, but the public and the released hostages themselves at first knew nothing of the Reagan administration's secret diplomacy. Publicly, the president maintained that the United States would not negotiate with terrorists, while in secret the president's men were doing just that.

During the next two years, several more hostages were released. When the Iran-Contra scandal broke in 1987, the first of the freed former hostages, Father Lawrence Martin Jenco, told reporters that he would rather have remained in captivity than have his release secured by an arms-for-hostages deal.

The scandalous revelations took the luster off the administration's achievement. To many people, it appeared that the administration had caved in and lost its will to be tough with terrorists. Some hostages had been freed, but through secret bribery rather than through strength and resolve. It grew even worse when the Iranians themselves boasted publicly of having bilked the United States of money and arms.

Another source of frustration and anger for the United States was Libyan leader Muammar Qaddafi, who was widely considered a key sponsor of terrorists. He was rumored to have sent Libyan hit men into the United States to kill President Reagan, and he supported a terrorist attack on a discotheque in West Germany. In response, President Reagan ordered a bombing raid on the Libyan capital of Tripoli in 1986. (*See also* Muammar Qaddafi.)

After a long series of international terrorist incidents, many of which involved other nations' citizens, Secretary of State George Shultz decided in May 1986 to introduce terrorism onto the agenda at the yearly meeting of the leaders of the seven leading industrial democracies. Reagan agreed that Shultz (himself the target of several assassination attempts by terrorists; in 1988 a bomb exploded just behind his car in La Paz, Bolivia) should press the point when the leaders met in Tokyo.

Shultz circulated a statement to the summiteers urging a coordinated antiterrorist strategy, and the seven leaders issued a joint declaration that their nations would take action against individual terrorist acts and would sanction states that sponsored terrorism.

The declaration's effect is debatable as is Reagan's entire record on dealing with terrorism. The president consistently enunciated a tough antiterrorist stand, and on at least one occasion (the bombing of Tripoli) reacted strongly and decisively to terrorist acts. On the other hand, the TWA hostage crisis forced the United States to ask other parties to intercede. Even though Robert McFarlane conveyed an undisguised threat to Nahib Berri, the administration still did not manage to free the TWA hostages by mere force, nor even by unilateral American action.

Finally, the administration sought to resolve the most enduring and aggravating hostage situation of all, the Hezbollah hostages in Lebanon, by resorting to secret bribery. None of the foregoing is wrong in and of itself, but one must notice a striking contrast between the rhetoric and the reality. The man who won the presidency at least partly by condemning his predecessor for dealing with terrorists, had to deal with them himself, all the while insisting that he was doing no such thing.

In a rare and frightening situation during his first term, the president had a highly unusual personal encounter with a terrorist act. In October 1983, coincidentally on the same day that he decided to take military action in Grenada, Reagan and Secretary of State George Shultz went out to play some golf at the Augusta National Golf Course in Georgia. At the sixteenth hole, several Secret Service agents stopped the game and shepherded the golf party into White

House limousines. A gunman had driven a truck through one of the course's gates and now held seven hostages in the pro shop, among them two White House assistants. The gunman threatened to kill the hostages unless he had a meeting with the president.

By 1983, Reagan had frequently publicized his policy against responding to any terrorist's demands, but the situation's immediacy no doubt had its effect on him. For one thing, the Secret Service agents told Reagan that the gunman was obviously deranged and might very well start killing hostages. Reagan telephoned the pro shop, but the gunman hung up on him, as he had demanded a direct meeting.

Reagan refused the Secret Service's request that he leave for Washington immediately; he was in no danger himself and reasoned that such a sudden move would alert the press that something was up, and he feared that curious reporters might inadvertently find out about the decision to invade Grenada. In any case, the gunman surrendered a few hours later, the hostages unharmed. (*See also* Middle East; Persian Gulf.)

HUD Scandal

One of the major scandals of the Reagan administration occurred in the Department of Housing and Urban Development. A creation of Lyndon Johnson's Great Society, HUD had been targeted by conservatives for extinction, but events took another course.

Samuel Pierce, the HUD secretary, was the only member of Reagan's cabinet to serve the full eight years, although Pierce himself had little contact with the president or the White House. Known around the administration as "Silent Sam," Pierce was a Wall Street lawyer who owed his appointment to the fact that the Reagan people wanted an African-American at HUD. Pierce would be visible, but also reliably conservative.

During Reagan's first term, budget director David Stockman made deep cuts in HUD's budget, costing the department personnel and forcing it to trim its programs. In the wake of the cuts, many career civil servants left HUD, and the administration replaced some of them with political appointees, many of whom either knew little about the department and its programs (like Pierce himself) or were conservative opponents of the department and sought to undermine it from within.

Several of the former HUD officials became consultants in the construction business and had as clients construction companies seeking federal funding. Later investigation suggested that Secretary Pierce and some of his aides may have used several billion dollars of HUD's money at least partly in private transactions that awarded contracts to friends and associates. Apparently, many of these contracts went into constructing luxury apartment houses, golf courses, country clubs, and other such projects. But the money did not serve the purpose for which HUD was created, funding the construction of low-income housing.

Haynes Johnson, in his study of the Reagan years, *Sleepwalking Through History*, compared the HUD scandal to the Teapot Dome scandal of the Warren G. Harding administration of 1921 to 1923, as both scandals involved making profits from political connections and government contracts. Johnson termed the scandal an "utter betrayal of public trust."

The scandal broke publicly after the Reagan administration left office. In 1989, during President George Bush's term, the HUD abuses were revealed through congressional investigation. Many public figures were implicated in the HUD scandal; one was former Interior Secretary James Watt, who had allegedly collected sizeable fees merely for contacting HUD operatives on behalf of his clients. Even John Mitchell, who had been both attorney general and campaign manager for President Richard Nixon and who served prison time for his role in the Watergate scandal, was involved in the HUD misdeeds. Pierce himself came under criminal investigation; Mitchell, however, died soon after the scandal became public.

I

Iran-Contra

The Iran-Contra affair (also known as Contragate, Iranscam, and Iranamock, among other sobriquets) was the biggest single scandal of the scandal-ridden Reagan administration, involving as it did an arms-for-hostages deal, possible embezzlement, several criminal indictments, trials, and considerable bad press for the Reagan administration, which had previously stood so high in the public's esteem.

No evidence has ever shown that President Reagan himself violated any laws, but many of his underlings did, and there was conflicting testimony as to whether the president understood that illegal actions were being taken, and as to whether he authorized them. That Oliver North and Fawn Hall destroyed a good many written records pertaining to the Iran-Contra affair has made it difficult to get at the truth of the matter. The full truth probably never will be known.

One of the most striking aspects of the Iran-Contra affair is the number of White House officials who sought to deceive Congress, thwart its will, and then lied to congressional investigating committees. Individuals such as William Casey, John Poindexter, and Oliver North seemed to function in a world in which Congress mattered little if at all, except as an obstacle to circumvent or a nuisance to placate, so that they could get on with their work of enforcing the Reagan administration's Central American policies. They showed a blatant disregard for legality, apparently believing

135

that the White House stood above the law without accountability to Congress.

According to the independent counsel's report on the Iran-Contra scandal, completed and released in 1994, long after the Reagan administration left office, even though there never was any reliable evidence that President Reagan himself violated any criminal laws, Reagan "set the stage" for criminal activities by encouraging and ordering continued support of the Contras after Congress passed the Boland Amendments to cut off the Contras' funding.

Reagan violated the spirit if not the letter of the law, for he determined to circumvent the will of Congress, and Congress has the constitutional authority to allocate or curtail funding for presidential actions. Reagan specifically created a climate in the White House that precipitated alternative actions of questionable legality and outright illegality, and the president's own actions may have violated civil laws while stopping short of criminality.

The president's underlings, however, committed specific criminal acts. The Iran-Contra affair involved high administration officials secretly selling arms to Iran in return for Iranian promises to get the terrorist group Hezbollah to free its American hostages.

These same officials used the profits from the arms sales to give financial support to the Contras in Nicaragua, without the knowledge or consent of Congress, in violation of federal law. National security adviser John Poindexter and his aide, Marine Lieutenant Colonel Oliver North, alledgedly covered up the deal by falsifying or destroying documents and lied to Congress about their activities.

As with the Nixon administration's Watergate scandal, the question on everybody's mind seemed to be, *What did the president know, and when did he know it?* To this day, Ronald Reagan claims that the skullduggery of Iran-Contra occurred behind his back, and that he had no knowledge of any wrongdoing until after the fact; he also claims to have gone public almost as soon as he knew and never to have consented to or participated in any cover-up.

Some administration officials, such as White House press spokesman Larry Speakes, support Reagan's claims of ignorance, but others, such as former National Security Adviser Robert McFarlane, later said that the president knew about the arms-for-hostages deal from the beginning, had verbally approved the plan, and later may have known about the diversion of funds to the Contras. McFarlane has written that President Reagan told him to do whatever was necessary to keep the Contras going, and the former national security adviser apparently interpreted this as an authorization of extraordinary methods, including the illegal.

President Reagan recorded his own version of the arms-for-hostages deal in his post–White House memoir, *An American Life*. By his account, McFarlane first explained the preliminary proposals to him as Reagan recovered from cancer surgery in Bethesda Naval Hospital in July 1985. McFarlane told him of contacts with Israeli officials who said that a group of "moderate, politically influential Iranians" wanted to reestablish a relationship with the United States, since the Ayatollah Khomeini would soon die. Reagan gave McFarlane permission to meet the Iranians and see how the situation might develop.

Reagan saw McFarlane's news as a possible opening to potential good relations with Iran, since Khomeini was rumored to be very ill, the Iranian economy was faltering, and the Iran-Iraq war remained bogged down in a bloody and expensive stalemate. (*See also* Persian Gulf.) Restoring friendly terms with Iran would make good strategic sense, since Iran bordered the Soviet Union, and such a move might undercut Soviet overtures to Iran.

Something else in McFarlane's report caught the president's attention; according to the Israelis, the moderate Iranians indicated that in order to show their sincerity, they might try to persuade the Hezbollah to release the seven American hostages in Lebanon. Reagan wrote that he was very eager to explore yet another possible way to secure the hostages' release; he told McFarlane that the United States would send a team to Israel to meet the officials who offered to act as go-betweens for the Iranian moderates. Thus began the Iran-Contra affair, by President Reagan's account.

The Iranians' initiative via Israel to the United States was likely prompted by the fact that, in the mid-1980s, the stalemated Iran-Iraq war was costing both nations heavy casualties and material damage.

Iraq, more or less on friendly terms with the United States, had ready access to American arms and spare parts. Iran, on the other hand, had been hostile to the United States since the Ayatollah Khomeini's Islamic revolution overthrew the Shah, and especially since the hostage crisis of 1979 to 1981 that undid Jimmy Carter's presidency. Although the United States played both sides of the war at different times, for the most part American policy favored the Iraqis and opposed the Iranians.

Hezbollah, a terrorist group in Lebanon, had held seven Americans hostage for some years, and the group was more or less supported by Iran. This was one of the great sore points between the United States and Iran, and the Reagan administration had long made a priority of securing the hostages' release. Altogether, the Israeli contacts offered a number of attractive possibilities to the president: undermining the Ayatollah, contact with potentially friendly Iranian elements, and release of the American hostages.

Consequently, secret diplomacy commenced as agents of the Reagan administration set out to offer the Iranians arms and spare parts in exchange for helping to free Americans held hostage by the various terrorist groups in Lebanon. This was a potential public-relations bomb, as American voters would probably react adversely to such doings. Iran, after all, was widely seen as an outlaw state, and there was still a good deal of hostility toward the Iranians left over from the hostage crisis. The administration feared that any aboveboard dealings with Iran would be seen by the public as breaking bread with the very outlaws who had imprisoned and abused Americans in Teheran.

There was sure to be considerable public outrage at the idea of giving the Iranians weapons, even if the object was to free Americans.

The administration conducted the arms-for-hostages negotiations in secret; an Israeli official introduced McFarlane to an Iranian businessman named Manucher Ghorbanifar. The unlikely Mr. Ghorbanifar claimed to represent moderate elements in the Iranian government who wanted to undermine the Islamic revolution. Ghorbanifar told McFarlane that his contacts wanted the United States to sell them arms so that Iran could win the war against Iraq, regain America's friendship, and, in return, prevail upon Hezbollah to free the hostages in Lebanon.

The arms-for-hostages deals were partly successful, and several American hostages were released, although the public did not know at first about the arms sales. The Reagan administration went to great lengths to keep them secret and, whether the president knew about it or not, a cover-up was in fact conducted by high officials. Prominent in this cover-up was the terminally ill CIA director, William Casey, as well as McFarlane; McFarlane's deputy, John Poindexter (who later succeeded McFarlane); and their assistant, Oliver North. (*See also* William Casey and the CIA.)

The plot thickened considerably when somebody had the bright idea of using the profits from the arms sales to fund the Contras. North called this a "neat idea" and claimed it as his own inspiration, though others—including, of all people, Ghorbanifar—also claimed to have come up with it. Both men later denied having had the idea at all.

The main problem with the neat idea was that it was illegal. The Boland Amendments clearly forbade aiding the Contras in their guerrilla war against the Sandanista government in Nicaragua, but in the memorable words of North's secretary, Fawn Hall, the participants had to find a way "above the written law." The Boland Amendments had to be circumvented, and, of course, Congress kept in the dark. There had to be an apparatus for getting money to the Contras, and this apparatus would be by necessity secret, and by definition against the law.

North and Casey (the latter was dying of a brain tumor, unbeknownst to all, except, possibly, Casey himself) decided to get around the Boland Amendments by "privatizing" the Contra aid; that is, by fund-raising among private citizens and foreign governments. Further, they began disguising some of the aid they did get to the Contras, by giving the guerrillas weapons and materials for free, diverting funds for humanitarian aid into military equipment, and, of course, using the funds gained by the secret arms sales to the Iranians.

While aiding the Contras was illegal, selling arms to the Iranians inhabited a gray area. Some authorities hold that the sales were not in and of themselves illegal, since the ban on dealing with the Iranians was a matter of the administration's own policy; there was no law against such actions. The independent counsel, however, believed that the sales violated federal statutes that regulated the export of arms and armaments. In any event, the administration kept the contacts secret for political reasons, and so that there would be no questions about the disposition of the profits from the arms sales—which were, after all, illegally going to the Contras.

Among the many legal questions raised by the administration's actions is whether the CIA's involvement was legal, since the CIA must specifically answer to designated congressional committees about its operations. But, under Casey, the CIA became simply the tool of White House policy. According to the independent counsel, many senior CIA officers were wary of this state of affairs, and some of them resented it, but being career officers who did not want to offend their superiors, they went along with Casey's orders.

The decision to sell arms to Iran triggered a series of incidental illegalities, many of which may have been committed out of simple, though inexcusable, ignorance of the laws governing transactions of this sort. For one thing, North conducted the arms sales so that they made profits, and by law any such profits from selling federal properties were to go to the United States Treasury and not into secret accounts set up by North.

North also later claimed to believe that channeling funds from the sales to the Contras did not violate the Boland Amendments, since the administration was not using money that had been appropriated by Congress. Actually, the same federal laws that govern the profits from sales of federal properties also mandate that the executive branch may not spend funds on its own that Congress has not appropriated. The Oval Office, after all, is not a business concern that may conduct its own profitable transactions, nor is it allowed to fund its own activities; such autonomy would remove the presidency from any sort of accountability. On every point, the redoubtable Lieutenant Colonel North was out of line.

North and his secretary, Fawn Hall, went into a frenzy of shredding documents once the investigations into the Iran-Contra affair got underway. This was purposeful destruction of evidence, and the very act suggested conscious wrongdoing; after all, North, Poindexter, and others, including Richard Secord, a retired air force general who participated in the Iran-Contra transactions, knew what the Boland Amendments were, even if North was unclear on other aspects of the law. They may have been destroying evidence for political purposes, but destroying evidence is illegal, and North and Hall surely must have known that.

A colorful detail of the shredding anecdote also indicates that the shredders understood that they were committing illegal acts. North and Hall smuggled evidence out of their office once federal investigators showed up. The colonel and the secretary hid the offending documents under their clothing and sneaked by the agents, thus engaging in some felonious cloak-and-dagger tomfoolery. When an observer sets aside the incident's comical aspects, there remains the cold fact that Oliver North and Fawn Hall actually concealed evidence on their persons and removed it from a scene being searched and investigated by federal officers with a search warrant.

The scandal became public in the fall of 1986, through an odd chain of events. On October 5, the Sandanistas shot down a cargo plane over Nicaragua; the plane carried weapons meant for the Contras that General Secord had purchased. The pilot, Eugene Hassenfus, survived the crash and came clean to his Sandanista captors, telling them that he was part of a secret plan to get American aid to the Contras. Hassenfus gave further details at a press conference in Managua on October 9; his account was sketchy but accurate enough to send the CIA and other high-level participants into a flurry of evasive activity.

Then, on November 3, a Lebanese magazine called *Al Shiraa* broke the story of the arms-for-hostages deal. It printed a sketchy and only partly accurate account, but that same day, Iranian government officials confirmed that the deals had indeed been made and proudly smirked that the alleged "moderates" were loyal Iranians who took the Americans to the cleaners for the greater glory and profit of the Khomeini government. A political cartoon that appeared sometime later in American newspapers showed the Ayatollah handing out clown costumes to various members of the Reagan administration.

Within days, Reagan administration officials were denying knowledge of the *Al Shiraa* revelations. At the same time, Oliver North continued his efforts to carry on the dealings with the Iranians, although an Iranian representative told North on November 8 that Iran would make no more deals until several Shiite terrorists held in Kuwait were released. North returned to Washington and assisted in the developing cover-up.

Casey, North, and Poindexter proceeded to release misleading and outright false information to Congress and the press. The evasive trio tried to shift most of the blame onto Secretary of State George Shultz, who actually opposed the whole plan from the beginning. The secretary later ran into some trouble with investigators, since it was clear that he knew about the affair as it unfolded, even though he thought it foolish and advised against it. He was never charged with any crimes.

President Reagan, on November 13, portrayed the arms-for-hostages deals as an attempt to make an opening to Iran, in the spirit of Richard Nixon's opening to China, and criticized the media for blowing the story out of proportion. The president also claimed that the United States only sent a few defensive weapons and spare parts to the Iranians in order to strengthen the moderates in the Iranian government. Finally, Reagan denied that what had occurred was an arms-for-hostages deal.

Attorney General Edwin Meese began an investigation of the affair but went about his task in a slow and slipshod manner, thus allowing Oliver North, Fawn Hall, and other members of North's staff several days to hold the shredding parties referred to above. Still, Meese and the president revealed to the media on November 25 that there was evidence of a diversion of funds from the Iran deals to the Contras, and Reagan announced that he had accepted Poindexter's resignation and fired Oliver North.

As the president's approval ratings sank in the national polls (in early December, Reagan had a Gallup Poll approval rating of only

46 percent; it had dropped twenty-one points in only one month, which was a Gallup Poll record), he appointed a special board to review the affair. When the Tower Board, composed of Texas senator John Tower, former Secretary of State Edmund Muskie, and former National Security Adviser Brent Scowcroft, issued its report late in February 1987, it hurled several bombshells.

Harshly critical of White House chief of staff Donald T. Regan, the report accused him of trying to exert undue control over the White House staff in general and over the national security adviser in particular. Regan, said the report, was present during the planning of the arms-for-hostages "initiatives," and he should have seen to it that things were done in an orderly and legal way.

Regan was the report's most famous target; he had enemies in the administration, and many of them, including the first lady, now believed he should resign as soon as possible. He hung on for what many thought an unseemly period of time, however, not wanting to appear to quit because of the Tower report. In the end, that impression proved impossible for Regan to avoid. (*See also* National Security Advisers.)

The administration was further assailed during the summer of 1987, when Congress convened a special committee, made up of members of both houses, to investigate the affair. The hearings, usually presided over by Hawaii Democratic senator Daniel Inouye, of Watergate fame, had the ironic, unlikely, and unintended effect of making a popular hero out of Oliver North. Even so, it was the administration's darkest hour, as intricate tales of cover-ups, secret deals, and other misdeeds filled the nation's television and radio airwaves. Reagan's reputation with the public suffered, and a good deal of the administration's effectiveness was diluted.

The joint committee concluded, among other things, that the White House operatives engaged in deception and in violations of the law, and that the president had lost control of these officials. The Tower report implied, and the congressional report now specified, that Ronald Reagan should have known what his men were up to.

North, Poindexter, Defense Secretary Caspar Weinberger, and others were indicted on federal criminal charges. North and

Poindexter stood trial and were convicted but won appeals to overturn the convictions. In 1992 President Bush pardoned Weinberger before the former secretary could stand trial.

Former President Ronald Reagan appeared as a defense witness at Poindexter's trial; the testimony was videotaped and released to the public. The independent counsel's report commented on that testimony; portions of the report are summarized below.

Five years after President Reagan left office, independent counsel Lawrence E. Walsh and his staff in the Office of the Independent Counsel (OIC) issued their report and published their conclusions. According to the report, Reagan proceeded with the Iran initiative without notifying Congress, though such notification was required under the National Security Act and the Arms Export Control Act. The White House functioned in "extreme secrecy" and "without accountability," and Poindexter, North, and others "invited" criminal activities, such as profiteering from the arms sales, diverting funds, and destroying evidence.

Reagan allowed the National Security Council personnel to create false accounts of their activities; part of the false account, according to the OIC, held that the president had no knowledge and did not authorize the initial sales of arms to the Iranians during the fall of 1985. At the time, Attorney General Meese expressed concern that the arms sales may have been illegal; part of the cover-up was meant to conceal the fact that the president had authorized the arms sales.

Walsh's office found no evidence that Reagan knew anything about the diversions of funds to the Contras, despite McFarlane's testimony. Walsh had some questions on this point, but North's destruction of evidence effectively blocked Walsh's line of inquiry.

Walsh concluded that Reagan was not really concerned about how his subordinates carried out his policy to pursue the Iran initiative and get around the Boland Amendments to fund the Contras. This stance effectively freed McFarlane, Poindexter, and North to operate without oversight or accountability.

In 1990 Reagan gave videotaped testimony at Poindexter's trial, and winked and smiled at the defendant during questioning. The public saw the tape a little over a month later. The former president claimed memory lapses about conversations with Poindexter, and the defense counsel tried to show that Reagan knew about and approved Poindexter's activities. Reagan did call the Iran-Contra affair "a covert action that was taken at my behest," but showed no detailed knowledge of the matter.

Walsh wanted to question President George Bush about the Weinberger pardon, but Bush refused to be deposed. Walsh considered seeking a grand jury subpoena for Bush's testimony but in the end decided that he would not resort to such a measure unless he meant to seek a criminal indictment, and that was unlikely. Walsh also did not want to appear to be retaliating for the Weinberger pardon and therefore dropped his quest to depose the incumbent president.

The independent counsel concluded that Reagan, Shultz, Weinberger, Casey, and their respective assistants all carried out two programs that went against congressional policy and against "national policy" as well. These men "skirted the law," some actually broke laws, and all of them participated in a cover-up.

Walsh's report called the Iran-Contra affair an abuse of power and charged that President Reagan set the tone for the actions taken by his underlings. But Walsh did not hold those underlings blameless, for, according to the report's concluding section, when any president, for whatever motive, skirts the law, then his subordinates have an obligation to resist; their loyalty to the Constitution of the United States and to the rule of law must come before their loyalty to the president.

Congress, the report reminded the nation, has the duty and authority to make sure that a president, his cabinet, and the entire administration remain faithful to that constitutional loyalty. The system of checks and balances is inherent in the constitutional system, which all federal officers, including presidents, take an oath to preserve and protect.

The scandal left Ronald Reagan's presidency in a shambles. Much of the American public now mistrusted him, the media compared the scandal's immensity to Watergate, and there was talk of impeachment. The president, on advice of some older associates, called in former senator Howard Baker to take the job of White House chief of staff, to help clean up the mess the scandal had left, and to rebuild the Reagan presidency.

During 1988 the scandal lost its central place in public attention, although the media continued to cover its various developments. But Ronald Reagan won back the American public. In one of the most amazing political resurrections in American history, if not the most amazing, Reagan finished his term as one of the most popular of all presidents, ranking with Dwight Eisenhower and Franklin Roosevelt in that regard.

It would be difficult to imagine nearly any other president recovering from a scandal of such proportions. (*See also* Boland Amendments; Hostages and Terrorists; National Security Advisers; October Surprise; Donald T. Regan.)

Ronald Reagan presidential portrait (Archive Photos)

PEORIA, ILL., NOV. 3 1980. Thousands turned out to cheer their candidate on the final day of campaigning in Peoria. Former President Gerald Ford lends his support to Ronald Reagan and running mate George Bush. (AP/Wide World Photos)

WASHINGTON D.C., SEPT. 25, 1981. The nine justices of the Supreme Court, including the newly sworn-in Sandra Day O'Connor, pose with President Reagan in the conference room of the Supreme Court. From left: Harry A. Blackmun, Thurgood Marshall, William H. Brennan, Warren Burger, President Reagan, Sandra Day O'Connor, Byron White, Lewis Powell, William Renquist, and John Paul Stevens. (White House photo by Bill Fitz-Patrick, AP/Wide World Photos)

WASHINGTON D.C., SEPT. 17, 1982. President Reagan and Philippine President Ferdinand Marcos stand at attention during the official White House reception for the visiting leader. (AP/Wide World Photos)

WASHINGTON D.C., MAY 12, 1983. President Reagan talks with Secretary of State George Shultz in the Oval Office after Shultz returned from a 17-day trip to the Middle East to help in negotiations in foreign troop withdrawals in Lebanon. (Photo by Ron Edmonds, AP/Wide World Photos)

WASHINGTON D.C., JAN. 21, 1985. President Ronald Reagan repeats the oath of office of the president as his wife Nancy holds the Bible during the ceremony under the Rotunda of the Capitol in Washington. (Photo by Bob Daugherty, AP/Wide World Photos)

BITBURG, WEST GERMANY, MAY 5, 1985. West German Chancellor Helmut Kohl, West German General Johannes Steinhoff, President Ronald Reagan, and General Matthew B. Ridgway walk over the Bitburg military cemetery behind crosses on their way to lay wreaths together on the graves. Among those graves here are 49 of former SS members of Nazi Germany. (AP/Wide World Photos)

ARLINGTON, VA., JULY 2, 1985. President Reagan hugs Sherry Sierralta, sister of Robert Stethem, as first lady Nancy Reagan looks on at Arlington National Cemetery after the President and Mrs. Reagan laid a wreath at the grave. Stethem was killed by terrorists aboard a hijacked plane in Beirut, Lebanon. (AP/Wide World Photos)

BURBANK, CALIF., DEC. 1, 1985. President and Mrs. Reagan are surrounded by Hollywood friends in Burbank, Calif., after the taping of a CBS-TV special honoring The President entitled "All Star Party for Dutch Reagan." Seated from left: Maureen Reagan, President and Mrs. Reagan, and Michael Reagan. Standing from left: Frank Sinatra, Burt Reynolds, Dean Martin, Eydie Gorme, Vin Scully, Steve Lawrence, and Paul Keys. (Photo by Scott Stewart, AP/Wide World Photos)

NEW YORK, DEC. 6, 1985. President Reagan gives Mrs. Reagan a puppy in their New York hotel suite. The dog, a King Charles spaniel named Rex, is an early Christmas present. (Archive Photos)

BETHESDA, MD., JAN. 6, 1987. President Ronald Reagan receives a traditional phone call from congressional leaders informing him the 100th Congress has convened and is ready to conduct business. The president took the call in his Bethesda Naval Hospital room. (Photo by Terry Arthur, Archive Photos)

WASHINGTON, D.C., JULY 7, 1988. President Reagan and Vice President Bush confer on the Colonnade just before attending a lunch with political advisers on campaign strategy. (Archive Photos)

WASHINGTON, D.C., OCT. 9, 1987. President Reagan talks with Supreme Court nominee Robert Bork who said that he would not withdraw his nomination to the Supreme Court. (AP/Wide World Photos)

WASHINGTON, D.C., DEC. 10, 1987. President Reagan speaks with Soviet leader Mikhail Gorbachev as they walk towards the entrance of the White House.(Photo by Dennis Cook, AP/Wide World Photos)

YORBA LINDA, CALIF., JULY 19, 1990. Presidents (L-R) Ronald Reagan, Richard Nixon, George Bush, and Gerald Ford share a light moment in The Richard Nixon Library and Birthplace in Yorba Linda, Calif. (Photo by Barry Thumma, AP/Wide World Photos)

Ronald Reagan with his family. (Archive Photos)

J

JAPAN

During the Reagan presidency, two areas dominated American-Japanese relations: defense and trade. Japan emerged as a major player in the world economy in the 1970s; with its impressive productivity and technological inventiveness, Japan rose as an economic power, highly competitive in international markets but protectionist and restrictive in regard to opening its own home markets to imports.

Concerning security, Japan's location east of the Soviet Union and China was highly strategic, and in theory a strong Japanese navy could impede the Soviet navy's passage through the many Japanese straits if the necessity arose. But Japan proved resistant to strengthening both its defense budget and its armed forces (known in Japan as the Defense Forces), as militarism was in severe disrepute in postwar Japan. Japan's Western allies, particularly the United States, wanted the Japanese to upgrade their military forces and take a more active defensive role in East Asia, to counterbalance potential Soviet or Chinese threats.

In 1982 Yashuhiro Nakasone became Japan's prime minister, and he made relations with the United States a high priority. Nakasone clearly understood that Japan faced new imperatives as an economic power and a leader in the world community. Early on, the prime minister made a bold and politically risky move by visiting South Korea to try to improve still shaky postwar relations with that nation and ameliorate some of the anti-Japanese feeling that still gripped

East Asia. The Asian fear of Japan was becoming sharper with Japan's new power and prominence.

With its restrictive import policies and aggressive entry into foreign markets, Japan was often blamed (though not entirely accurately) for trade imbalances; the American public in particular tended to resent the Japanese for the United States' trade deficit. A growing sentiment for protectionist trade policies, at least regarding Japan, took root in American public opinion, and various political figures took up the cause as well.

Japanese investments in the United States also caused much ill feeling, even though a case could be made that such investment was beneficial and, in any case, Japan was not the foreign nation whose investors owned the most in the United States. During the entire Reagan era, the British, the Dutch, and possibly the Canadians each held more investments in the United States than did the Japanese.

The Reagan administration's Japan strategy aimed at getting the Japanese to ease or lift restrictions on trade. It was a long and drawn-out process of negotiation and wrangling, and at times it led to virtual economic war between the two nations, particularly during Reagan's first term. Finally, in 1986, after some difficult negotiations, the Japanese agreed to expand American access to the Japanese market in telecommunications, medical equipment, and pharmaceutical products. But problems remained, owing chiefly to difficulties inherent in the Japanese economy itself.

Secretary of State George Shultz, an economist by training and formerly one of Richard Nixon's Treasury secretaries, tried to explain to the administration and to the American public that Japan was not responsible for America's economic problems during the 1980s, nor was Japan necessarily just being stubborn about lifting its import restrictions. Contrary to public perception, Shultz explained, during the Reagan years Japanese markets actually were more open to imports than they had been a decade earlier, and American companies were doing more business and selling more products in Japan than ten years before. Consequently, the American trade deficit could not solely be attributed to Japan's trade policies.

Second, according to Shultz, the Japanese had savings well in excess of their own domestic investment. This meant that Japan had to maintain a high employment rate, and it needed to export considerably more than it imported. This internal imbalance could not easily be fixed, just as the Americans had no magic wand to wave over their own domestic economic problems.

The imbalanced economic relationship between the two countries encompassed certain defense issues. Since the Cold War began, Japan had afforded the United States a strategic base for operations and for impeding the movements of a strong Soviet fleet into the Pacific. Japan provided bases during both the Korean War and the Vietnam War. In order to keep the harmonious relationship with Japan going over the years, the United States accepted Japanese trade and import restrictions and allowed Japanese access to American consumer markets. At the end of the Reagan years, scholars George Friedman and Meredith LeBard point out, the United States had a trade deficit with Japan of about $52 billion.

While President Reagan tried to persuade Prime Minister Nakasone to open Japan's market in the spirit of free trade, American trade policy with Japan still veered into protectionism to a considerable extent, and the trade imbalances, as well as other problems between the two nations, remained unresolved when Reagan left office.

The second broad category of issues, defense, entailed its own complex problems, all concerning the desire of the United States and other Western powers to convince Japan to play a more significant role in military matters, juxtaposed against many East Asian nations' underlying mistrust and fear of a remilitarized Japan. That inherent conflict produced a highly ambiguous situation in the world's potential balance of military power.

Still, the Reagan administration and its successors have tried to persuade Japan to increase its military strength and contribute to the overall Western alliance, rather than continue to be protected by American forces against possible aggression by the Soviets or, now that the Soviet Union has collapsed, China. The problem has become more complicated since the Cold War's end; many members of the United Nations have even criticized the Japanese for insufficient participation in the Desert Shield and Desert Storm coalitions during 1990 and 1991.

But the Japanese stubbornly resisted expanding their military during the Reagan years. The Japanese have come to find militarism distasteful, and when American military strategists visit Tokyo to confer with their counterparts in the Defense Forces, the sessions are held with little or no public notice, often in hotel rooms rather than in government conference facilities. A postwar antimilitarism, combined with some degree of traditional xenophobia, keeps the military in check in Japanese society.

The Japanese constitution, which was actually written by the American occupiers during the late 1940s, specifically forbids Japan to rely on war as a tool of policy. Succeeding Japanese governments have refrained from projecting Japanese power overseas at all, and have resisted most American and United Nations requests to contribute troops for various overseas functions.

Many observers predict that Japan may become less averse to military expansion now that the Cold War is over and the country is a major economic power in a new world order. That remains to be seen.

The military issues, as well as the trade issues, remained unresolved when the Reagan administration left office. In more recent years, the Japanese economy has run into some trouble, and Japan seems not quite the invincible economic power it appeared to be several years ago. But in a changing world order, Japan figures to be a major factor for the United States for years to come. (*See also* Economic Summits; Foreign Affairs/Foreign Policy; Trade Policies.)

K

KOREAN AIRLINES FLIGHT 007

One of the most serious single incidents during the chilly Cold War period of Ronald Reagan's first term was the Soviet downing of Korean Airlines Flight 007. The incident was a human disaster and a setback to any fragile progress in superpower relations.

On August 31, 1983, the airliner, carrying 269 persons (including Congressman Larry McDonald), strayed into Soviet airspace, undoubtedly by accident. Soviet planes, thinking the intruder a military aircraft, shot it down, and all aboard were killed.

International outrage put the Soviets on the defensive; instead of apologizing, the Soviets called the airliner's intrusion a provocation by the West and, for reasons difficult to understand, the Soviets would not admit that the incident was a simple case of mistaken identity. Had they done so, they would still have been criticized but probably would not have provoked such widespread anger in the international community.

Soviet leader Yuri Andropov and President Ronald Reagan exchanged angry words in a series of speeches and public comments. The KAL Flight 007 incident became the focus of an acrimonious public debate between the two superpowers, as U.S.-Soviet relations, already in a hostile and dangerous state, suffered further, owing largely to Andropov's stubbornness. Reagan, while angry, commented that he could only act within limits, for the United States was not about to go to war over the incident.

On the other side, the Soviets at first would not budge from their inexplicable stance of blaming the West, and Andropov continued to call the incident a Soviet reaction to Western provocation. But after about a week, the Soviets claimed that the mistake had been made because of poor visibility in that sector of Soviet airspace. However, CIA intelligence reports alleged that visibility was fairly clear that night and that the Soviet jets took plenty of time studying the Korean plane before firing on it. Still, Andropov, when he finally spoke publicly about the incident, continuted to blame the United States for using the airliner as a spy plane.

While not actually a central issue in the ongoing Cold War of the 1980s, the downing of KAL 007 nevertheless hurt the Soviet Union's international standing, helped to make the Reagan administration appear more reasonable, and added fuel to the hostile fires on both sides. Had Andropov not died shortly afterward and Chernenko shortly after that, there is no telling where U.S.—Soviet problems might have led, without the more progressive leadership of Mikhail Gorbachev. (*See also* Yuri Andropov; Cold War; Foreign Policy/Foreign Relations.)

L

LAFFER CURVE

A supply-side economic principle delineated by economist Arthur Laffer in 1974, the Laffer curve was later adopted by Ronald Reagan to explain and justify his devotion to supply-side economics.

According to legend, Laffer drew his famous curve on a cocktail napkin in a bar, in order to explain supply-side economics to President Gerald Ford's White House chief of staff, Richard Cheney, who would later serve President Bush as secretary of defense. Laffer drew a line of tax rates between zero and 100 percent and explained that, at either end of the line, taxation would not produce any revenues for the government. At zero, no taxes were collected, and at 100 percent, no one would work if everything he or she earned would be taken by taxation.

Laffer's principle held that actual tax revenue would increase as taxation decreased from 100 percent, as people would have incentive to earn more income and therefore would pay more taxes, rather than searching for loopholes to avoid excessive taxation.

The Laffer curve was a teaching device, at least in its napkin form, but Ronald Reagan was entirely taken with it. Reagan first heard about it early in 1980, as he was preparing his campaign for the Republican presidential nomination. According to David Stockman, the candidate related his personal experience to Laffer's principle, recalling that during his Hollywood days, a movie star would graduate into a higher tax bracket after making four pictures during the course of a year. Consequently, movie stars would quit work for the year after making their fourth film. The high tax rates of the time—during World War II—therefore produced less work and less tax revenue.

According to Stockman, the flaw in attempting to translate Laffer's teaching device into practical economic policy was that it would require an economy with no inflation; as production increased, so would the gross national product and so would tax revenues. When Reagan took office, the economy had for several years been suffering rapid inflation. Inflation pushes wage earners into higher tax brackets, so, according to Stockman, when you stop inflation, you also stop tax-bracket elevation, which is an inherent tax cut.

Upon taking office, Reagan attempted to end inflation and simultaneously cut taxes by 30 percent. The Laffer curve, said Stockman, could not entail both actions, deflation and cutting taxes.

Other critics, such as historian Michael Schaller, have pointed out that, while the Laffer curve seems sound in principle, neither Laffer nor anyone else could figure out what would be an ideal tax rate. This defect meant that the Laffer curve had no real practical value and could only describe abstract economic principle. However, the curve became popular with supply-siders, such as Republican congressman Jack Kemp of New York and Republican senator William Roth of Delaware, who put together the famous Kemp-Roth bill, which proposed cutting federal income taxes by 30 percent.

In 1980 candidate Reagan was under the economic tutelage of Arthur Laffer and others who believed in the Laffer curve and supply-side theory. Reagan's support for massive tax cuts and his belief in the Laffer curve gave George Bush, Reagan's chief rival for the Republican nomination, the opportunity to utter one of the most memorable phrases of the campaign. Bush called the Laffer curve and the tax-cut proposal "voodoo economics." That phrase came back later to haunt both President Reagan and Vice President Bush. (*See also* George Bush; Deficit; Reagonomics; Reagan Recession/ Reagan Recovery; David Stockman; Tax Reform.)

M

MEDICAL CONDITIONS

Many American presidents suffered illnesses during their terms of office, and eight died (four by assassination). Lincoln suffered several ailments, including a mild form of smallpox; George Washington spent some time bedridden; Andrew Jackson's health was frail when he lived in the White House; Lyndon Johnson proudly showed America his scar from gallbladder surgery; John F. Kennedy spent a few weeks on crutches because of his back problems and suffered a highly publicized virus attack after that.

Grover Cleveland had cancer surgery in secret, aboard a private yacht on Long Island Sound, and served the remainder of his second term with a rubber plug in his palate. Woodrow Wilson suffered a devastating stroke, spent the remainder of his presidency seriously disabled, and remained debilitated for the rest of his life. Franklin Roosevelt, a paralytic since age thirty-nine, suffered from congestive heart failure during World War II and died of a stroke. Jimmy Carter, like Napoleon, had severe hemorrhoids. Dwight Eisenhower suffered a near-fatal heart attack toward the end of his first term, but won a second term all the same. Richard Nixon had phlebitis and pneumonia.

The list could go on. In the twentieth century, presidents have been particularly prone to incapacitating illness, and rare was the modern chief executive, like Harry Truman and Herbert Hoover, who managed to get through a term unhindered by rebellious physiology.

Ronald Reagan, the oldest president of all, had his share of health concerns, ranging from a gunshot wound to cancer. The first lady, too, underwent cancer surgery during her husband's presidency.

Reagan's first presidential health crisis came, of course, as a result of the 1981 shooting. As Reagan stood by his limousine, John Hinckley's bullet hit the car and ricocheted into the president's body, entering his chest under the left arm; the bullet, flattened by hitting the car, made a narrow slit like a knife wound, hit Reagan's seventh rib, then literally tumbled into the left lung and stopped less than an inch from Ronald Reagan's heart. The bullet was a "devastator," designed to explode on impact, but this one did not.

Doctors discovered the bullet hole as they examined the president in the emergency room of George Washington University Hospital. He was gravely wounded, over seventy years old, albeit in excellent physical condition, and his chest cavity was filling with blood. He was showing signs of incipient shock as he was placed in the hospital's trauma unit and his blood pressure was dangerously low.

Doctors determined that the president's left lung had collapsed, and it took them some time to locate the bullet in the president's chest. Meanwhile, a thoracic tube was inserted into the chest to ease the president's breathing and promote the lung's reinflation. He breathed through an oxygen mask. Finally, the doctors decided that Reagan was losing too much blood and surgery was necessary. They feared that the president's stomach might be filling with blood.

There was no blood in the president's stomach, and the surgeons managed to remove the bullet from the lung, after first considering that they might have to leave it in. Reagan also received five units of blood before surgery; the blood loss combined with the signs of incipient shock presented a major worry, but the surgical team averted both problems.

Reagan awoke some hours later, at first thinking he could not breathe. He was on a respirator, which did his breathing for him, but patients often feel unable to breathe with a tube down their throats.

On his fifth day in the hospital, after steadily improving, Reagan ran a fever of 103. The doctors put him on antibiotics and Tylenol. Soon after, Reagan developed anorexia and was able to eat only very small amounts of food, and sometimes none at all, over the next few days.

Within another few days, the doctors had Mrs. Reagan take the president on short walks up and down the halls. He was again on the mend, improving rapidly, but still hardly able to eat. But after not too long, his appetite returned.

Reagan returned to the White House on April 11. Although more seriously ill than the public realized, he still was making a remarkable recovery, especially considering his age. One of his doctors told Mrs. Reagan that the president had the body of a man nearly twenty years younger. Still, on doctors' orders, he spent the first three weeks out of the hospital working a very short schedule, taking plenty of bed rest, and altogether pacing himself carefully. Within a fairly short time, he was no longer incapacitated at all. (*See also* Assassination Attempt.)

In 1985 President Reagan checked into the Bethesda Naval Hospital in Maryland for his annual physical examination, and doctors discovered a small polyp in his colon. They decided to remove it as a precautionary measure; it is routine in such instances to test for malignancy.

The president spent the morning before surgery drinking Go Lightly, a liquid that thoroughly cleans out the bowels with, Reagan later wrote, "a vengeance." When the surgeons removed the polyp, they found another larger and flatter polyp in the colon, which looked like it could be precancerous or already malignant. The doctors considered whether to let the president go to Camp David and return for surgery the following week or perform the surgery during the weekend, since Reagan was already in the hospital and already thoroughly purged by the Go Lightly. For Reagan it was no contest; rather than endure another round of going lightly, he decided to stay in the hospital.

The doctors told Reagan that the second polyp looked "suspicious," and they were checking the surrounding lymph nodes for malignancy. They expected to see biopsy results on the coming Monday. Oddly, Reagan's older brother, Neil, had undergone an identical operation two weeks earlier.

The biopsy showed cancerous cells in the tissue sample, but

the doctors told the president that they thought they had got the cancer out. They added that Reagan would need annual checkups for five years.

It became evident, as time went on, that the surgery had in fact removed the cancer. A section of Reagan's colon was removed as a further precaution. The surgery was successful but also revealed that Reagan had diverticulosis, a common inflammation of the intestine which is not serious, although it can be irritated by small bits of food such as nuts and seeds. Diverticulosis can become diverticulitis, which is more serious and often involves significant pain and fairly lengthy hospitalization.

Only ten days after Reagan left the hospital, he went back in. A biopsy showed a small bump on his nose to be a carcinoma. The cancer was the sort that sometimes develops from sun exposure, but it was not yet dangerous.

Early in 1988, Reagan underwent a transurethral resection to alleviate an enlarged prostate. This condition commonly affects men of Reagan's age (and younger, for that matter), and the surgical technique is routine and involves no intrusive penetration of the skin. Possibly owing to his age, Reagan remained in the hospital for several days longer than had been expected, although the procedure was entirely successful.

Reagan's health problems during his presidency were fairly common for people his age, and he possibly owed his rapid recuperations from the gunshot and cancer surgeries to his excellent physical condition. Even in his seventies, he followed a consistent regimen of diet and exercise, and spent time working on his ranch in California, chopping wood, fixing fences, and performing other outdoor tasks that provided good physical workouts.

Reagan had been physically fit all his life; he was a lifeguard as a young man and then, as a movie actor for years, he had to keep in shape. The years of conditioning stood him in good stead in his old age.

In his seventies, Reagan was noticeably hard of hearing, and toward the end of his first term, he sometimes appeared in public wearing a hearing aid.

In 1994, over five years after leaving the White House, Reagan revealed he had Alzheimer's disease, for which there is no treatment. He has stopped making formal public appearances, although he continues to attend church in Bel Air, California. He has not become reclusive, but he no longer makes speeches or attends public functions.

Nancy Reagan had her share of health problems, too, during the White House years. In October 1987, a mammogram showed what appeared to be a tumor in Mrs. Reagan's left breast. Before undergoing a radical mastectomy, she said to her husband, "I guess it's my turn."

The tumor was malignant, but the laboratory analysis of the lymph nodes and tissue samples revealed no further malignancy. Consequently, Mrs. Reagan's doctors ordered no further treatment other than periodic examinations.

Nancy Reagan had no other serious illnesses during her White House residency, but she did injure herself in a fall during the 1984 presidential campaign. The president and first lady spent the final night of the campaign in a hotel in Sacramento, California, and their bed stood on a platform. During the night, Mrs. Reagan got up to find an extra blanket and, having forgotten about the platform, fell, slid across the floor, and hit her head on a chair.

The next day, Mrs. Reagan's speech was slurred and she had difficulty maintaining her balance. She experienced memory lapses and years later could not recall much of the day, nor even that a doctor had examined her. The doctor found that she had suffered a concussion.

Considering their ages, both Reagans were healthy for most of the eight years they spent in the White House. Their respective bouts with cancer were serious but not unusual for people their age. The assassination attempt, of course, was not a normal event either in Ronald Reagan's life nor in American presidencies in general. Reagan also beat the old American superstition that a president elected in a year that ends in zero will die in office. (*See also* Twenty-Year Curse.)

MIDDLE EAST

President Reagan inherited a diplomatic mess in the Middle East, as has every American president since Franklin Roosevelt. When he took office in early 1981, the Middle East was as unstable and as dangerous as ever. The Iran hostage crisis was just ending; the devastating and dangerous Iran-Iraq war raged in the Persian Gulf; and civil war continued in Lebanon. Israel and its Arab neighbors continued to coexist in a hostile and belligerent atmosphere, although Israel and Egypt had come to terms under the Camp David accords brokered by President Jimmy Carter.

American relations with Libya were deteriorating rapidly, and the Soviet Union had mired itself in a civil war in Afghanistan.

Early on, the administration continued the policy of preventing Soviet influence in the area. Secretary of State Alexander Haig wanted Israel, Saudi Arabia, Jordan, and Egypt to join in an alliance that would block Soviet diplomatic designs in the Middle East, but Middle Eastern nations were more interested in feuding with each other than in joining a concerted anti-Soviet front. Fundamental to Reagan's Middle East policy were the assumptions that Israel was still the strongest American ally in the region, and that Syria had become a Soviet client state.

Some situations quickly got out of hand. In 1982 Israel, with the Reagan administration's tacit approval, invaded Lebanon to destroy or at least expel the Palestine Liberation Organization, which based its headquarters in Lebanon and controlled portions of Lebanese territory. Israel proceeded to besiege and bombard the Lebanese capital city of Beirut, causing worldwide concern. The Lebanese situation deteriorated further. Christian Lebanese leader Bashir Gemayel was assassinated in September 1982, and the murder was followed by mass killings of Palestinian refugees by the Christian Lebanese Phalangist militia.

Lebanon slid further into chaos, and the United States, France, and Italy sent in peacekeeping forces to try to counterbalance the Christian forces, who in turn faced superior Shiite Muslim and Druse military forces supported by Syrian army units. Western support for the Christians alienated many Lebanese Muslims, and in

April 1983, a band of suicide terrorists killed sixty-three people at the American embassy in Beirut.

The venerable battleship USS *New Jersey* shelled Shiite and Druse positions near the Lebanese coast. In retaliation, on October 23, 1982, a truck bomb blew up the United States Marine barracks in Beirut, killing 241 marines. In January 1984, President Reagan withdrew American land forces from Lebanon, and the civil war flared up again, with considerable loss of life among the warring Lebanese factions.

Meanwhile, the ongoing problem of the Palestinians living under Israeli rule in areas that Israel seized during the Six Day War of 1967 aggravated the Middle East situation. At the end of 1987, the *intifada*, or uprising, began against the Israeli occupying authorities, and for the next three years there were continual clashes between Israeli soldiers, Palestinian residents, and Israeli settlers in the West Bank. The *intifada* resulted in many deaths, destruction of Palestinian homes by Israeli soldiers in retribution for bombings and other terrorist attacks, and even some clashes between Israeli authorities and Israeli settlers. Settlers also were sometimes killed by Palestinian attacks.

The PLO was not fully in control of the *intifada*, and in 1988 PLO leader Yassir Arafat finally agreed to declare that Israel had a right to exist. The pronouncement came under considerable American prodding, and it made possible the beginning of a dialogue between the PLO and Israel, who had previously refused to communicate directly with each other.

When Reagan left office, Israel and the PLO had not come to an agreement concerning the establishment of a Palestinian state in the occupied territory. (*See also* Beirut Marine Bombing; Foreign Affairs/Foreign Relations; Persian Gulf; Muammar Qaddafi.)

N

NATIONAL SECURITY ADVISERS

Also known as the national security director, this is a cabinet-level post; the national security adviser presides over the National Security Council, which, however, is not an executive department. The post of national security adviser and the council were created after World War II, and thus began an inherent rivalry with the secretary of state and the State Department, since two bodies now dealt with the same problems, and the State Department lost its imprimatur as the sole purveyor of the president's foreign policy. The national security adviser strikes some observers as a second secretary of state.

During President Nixon's first term, for instance, his reliance on Henry Kissinger isolated and devalued Secretary of State William Rogers. In Nixon's second term, Kissinger became secretary of state, and briefly held both posts simultaneously. His eventual successor as national security adviser went largely ignored. During President Carter's single term, the bad blood between Zbigniew Brzezinski and Carter's first secretary of state, Cyrus Vance, became legendary.

When Ronald Reagan ran for president in 1980, one of his campaign pledges was to downgrade the position of national security adviser in order to facilitate more cohesive conduct of foreign policy and to reduce the red tape and superfluous functions that he and his conservative constituency saw as plaguing the government. It is ironic, then, that President Reagan ended up relying heavily on his national security advisers, and that he ultimately went through six of them. Prior to his presidency, there had been a total of only ten.

Several of Reagan's national security advisers caused him and the administration, and the country, a great deal of trouble. Two of them, Robert McFarlane and John Poindexter, were instrumental in precipitating the Iran-Contra scandal. But the first embarrassmant came when Richard Allen got caught in some dubious practices.

Allen was a hard-line right-winger, and his appointment may have been meant to placate ultraconservative Republicans. Allen also probably reflected the administration's first-term Cold War stance. In any case, he helped a Japanese magazine arrange an interview with Nancy Reagan. The grateful and gracious Japanese editors gave Allen a cash gift of a thousand dollars. Additionally, Allen accepted a gift of several watches from another Japanese friend; and in an unrelated matter, investigation revealed that he had given some incorrect information on the financial disclosure forms he had to fill out when he got the job.

This may not have been a major scandal, but it was troubling that a national security adviser would accept gifts from foreigners and inaccurately report personal finances. Also, Allen did not address these issues until he was under investigation by the FBI. While it is true, for instance, that he might have insulted the Japanese editors by declining the cash gift, the proper procedure most likely would have been to disclose the gift immediately and turn the money over to the government.

Whatever the proprieties, Allen had to resign. He was replaced by William Clark, one of Ronald Reagan's old political associates. Clark was Governor Reagan's chief of staff in Sacramento and later served on the California Supreme Court. Clark first joined the administration as a foreign policy adviser in the State Department, and at his Senate confirmation hearings could not name several leaders of important nations nor answer questions about certain international controversies with American allies. Though he was confirmed, he had already embarrassed the administration.

The administration was not sufficiently embarrassed, however, to refrain from appointing Clark to fill the departing Allen's post.

Clark did not turn out to be a powerful national security adviser, but he was conscientious and kept President Reagan fully apprised of administration foreign-policy operations. Allen had been sadly deficient in this respect. Clark served from 1982 until he replaced James Watt as secretary of the interior in late 1983. (*See also* Cabinet.)

Clark's successor as national security adviser was his deputy, Robert McFarlane. McFarlane was a career Marine officer who had worked for presidents before, both as an assistant to Secretary of State Henry Kissinger and as a White House national security aide under Richard Nixon and Gerald Ford. McFarlane was unpopular with the press and soon developed a reputation for peremptory behavior. The Beirut bombing, the invasion of Grenada, and the events that triggered the Iran-Contra scandal all occurred on McFarlane's watch as national security adviser.

Some members of the administration have treated McFarlane very unfavorably in their respective memoirs, but it is difficult to discern if these reviews are accurate, or if they are essentially self-serving, or even attempts to blame McFarlane for the Iran-Contra scandal, thus protecting the authors themselves and shielding President Reagan from some of the more serious charges that the scandal entailed.

McFarlane served for two years and resigned for reasons not entirely clear. There were rumors that White House Chief of Staff Donald T. Regan forced McFarlane out, but Regan has denied that. Regan himself came under severe criticism by the Tower Board for some of his actions in regard to Iran-Contra. (*See also* Donald T. Regan.)

McFarlane's name became prominent in the news later on when, as a former adviser, he was publicly implicated in the Iran-Contra scandal. In February 1987, he sat for an hour-long interview with reporter Ted Koppel on the ABC news show *Nightline*, and then, a few days later, attempted suicide.

When McFarlane quit the post in December 1985 he was succeeded by Admiral John Poindexter, another career military man who, like his predecessor, moved up to the main job from the position of deputy. Poindexter lasted for just under a year, resigning in

November 1986, on the very day it was revealed that White House operatives had funneled profits from the Iran arms sales to the Contras. Poindexter was forced out, faced congressional investigations and, later, criminal charges.

Poindexter's successor, Frank Carlucci, had extensive foreign-policy and foreign-service experience. He had served as President Carter's ambassador to Portugal and held other government positions as well. However, he did not remain on the job long and in 1988 replaced Caspar Weinberger as secretary of Defense. Carlucci's successor was General Colin Powell, who later gained international fame as chairman of the joint chiefs of staff during Operation Desert Shield in 1990 and the Persian Gulf War in 1991. (*See also* Central America; Iran-Contra.)

NEW DEAL COALITION

The presidential election of 1980 ushered in a period of realignment in American national politics, and many voting groups that had been reliably Democratic since the Franklin Roosevelt era defected en masse to the Republicans. Some of these groups were key elements of the so-called New Deal coalition, the collection of political interests that had coalesced around President Franklin Roosevelt and his New Deal policies during the 1930s. Some elements of the New Deal coalition became bastions of Reaganism.

The New Deal coalition was composed of urban ethnics, urban and rural blacks, labor-union members, liberals from the middle classes and the professions, and the budding class of technocrats. After Roosevelt's death in 1945, these groups formed the Democrats' basic national consituency and contributed heavily to maintaining the Democratic majorities in Congress, even as Republicans won the White House in 1952, 1956, 1968, and 1972.

The upheavals of the 1960s and 1970s began the coalition's undoing, as the sexual revolution and social protest movements alienated many of these aging consituencies and helped drive them into the conservative Republican fold. Just as the New Deal coalition itself was born of realignment (blacks, for instance, had voted solidly Republican prior to the New Deal era), so it was undone by yet another realignment, as conservative white southerners, white ethnics, union members, professionals, and large portions of the middle classes began defecting to the GOP.

During the 1970s and even as early as 1968, some politicians competed for what they recognized as a newly conservative constituency. In 1968, for instance, Alabama governor George C. Wallace bolted the Democratic party and ran for president at the head of the new American Independent party, campaigning directly to the conservative white elements of the old coalition. He polled nearly ten million votes—one reason why Richard Nixon's victory over Vice President Hubert Humphrey was such a squeaker.

In 1972, Wallace campaigned for the Democratic presidential nomination, appealing directly to the same elements he had tried to reach in 1968. He left the campaign after being shot by a would-be assassin; his wounds left him partially paralyzed. Wallace supporters no doubt contributed to Nixon's reelection landslide, but Democratic nominee George McGovern proved a weak candidate, unable to appeal to conservative Democrats.

The ongoing realignment came to full fruition with the advent of Ronald Reagan. Besides carrying the traditionally reliable Republican constituencies in both 1980 and 1984, Reagan scored heavily with the white middle classes, professionals, and laborers who previously were reliably Democratic.

A conservative element also emerged within the black middle class, and it, too, favored Reagan. Nonetheless, African-Americans and other racial minorities did not swing into the Republican column in large numbers during the Reagan years. These groups stayed in the old liberal fold; some of the remaining New Deal constituencies figured significantly in electing Bill Clinton president in 1992.

On the other hand, some of the more traditionally conservative constituencies moved even farther to the right, particularly when they began to believe that President Reagan was not entirely committed to their agenda. Many of these disaffected Republicans today form the political base for such extremists as Pat Buchanan.

Buchanan claims to wear the Reagan mantle, but actually embodies an old-time populism considerably to the right of more conventional Republican conservatives, including Ronald Reagan.

The various realignments during the past political generation have not resulted in any sort of general moderation in American politics, and some of the movement among constituencies has contributed to a polarization every bit as severe as in Franklin Roosevelt's day. Then, as now, various elements of the electorate who felt disaffected, neglected, besieged, or disenfranchised sought new and even radical solutions to their ongoing sense of frustration and exclusion. There are always politicians around who promise to provide those solutions. (*See also* Reagan Revolution; Franklin Delano Roosevelt.)

SANDRA DAY O'CONNOR

Nominated to the Supreme Court by President Reagan in August 1981, after Justice Potter Stewart retired, Sandra Day O'Connor was the first woman ever nominated and confirmed as an associate justice. Previously, she had been a deputy county attorney in San Mateo, California, the assistant attorney general of Arizona, an Arizona state senator, majority leader of the Arizona state senate, a superior court judge, and an appeals court judge.

Justice O'Connor was the first of Reagan's Supreme Court nominees; since she was an active Republican, many greeted her appointment with foreboding. Many liberals feared she would be the first soldier in a conservative assault on a generation of liberal judicial rulings. This has not entirely proven true. O'Connor is conservative, but she is not any sort of ideologue, and the "Reagan Court" that began with her appointment has not proven to be the hornets' nest of reaction that many critics feared.

Actually, the announcement of her nomination dismayed and frightened many conservatives. While liberals feared her conservatism, many movement conservatives of the Christian Right considered her insufficiently conservative. That President Ronald Reagan nominated such a person to the Supreme Court gave an unwelcome jolt to the doctrinaire ultraconservatives who counted on Reagan to promulgate the Christian Right's judicial agenda, which was to overturn *Roe v. Wade* and throw out most, if not all, of the Warren Court's civil-rights rulings. Moral Majority leader Jerry Falwell went so far as to say that "all good Christians" should oppose O'Connor's nomination. Senator Barry Goldwater, O'Connor's fellow Arizonan and longtime associate, countered that "every good Christian ought to kick Jerry Falwell right in the ass."

Justice O'Connor has been conservative on matters of criminality and has authored Court opinions that limited a suspect's Miranda rights. She often concurs in rulings that favor state powers over federal powers, and has supported states' rights to criminalize homosexual practices. She has voted conservatively on other moral issues before the Court, and has caused considerable bad feeling in gay communities and among others who believe the government, state or federal, has no place in the nation's bedrooms. While many conservatives welcome such rulings, there are other conservatives who believe that government should stay out of people's private lives.

To the surprise of some and the relief of others, and to the chagrin of many conservatives, Justice O'Connor voted against overturning or limiting *Roe v. Wade*, the decision that liberalized abortion laws.

While more conservative than liberal, she has shown little tendency toward political orthodoxy and has proved more moderate than many of her critics feared, or some of her supporters hoped. (*See also* Gender Gap; Supreme Court and Federal Judiciary.)

OCTOBER SURPRISE

A persistent rumor, which was never substantiated, held that the Reagan campaign conspired with the Iranians to keep the Teheran hostages in Iran until after the presidential election of 1980. Even Ronald Reagan's daughter, Patti Davis, has publicly expressed suspicions that the Reagan team may have made some sort of deal to that effect.

Actually, the term *October surprise* originated in the Reagan camp. During the 1980 campaign, longtime Reagan aide Michael Deaver coined the phrase to express the possibility that if President Carter managed to get the Iran hostages freed just before the election—that is, if Carter pulled an "October surprise"—then he would gain heavily in the polls and win the November election. Deaver believed that Reagan's lead in the public-opinion polls was not all that secure, as he led Carter only by about ten points during early September, and so such a coup by the president was possible.

According to rumors that circulated during the Reagan presidency and afterward, Reagan's people came to terms with the Iranians and promised to sell them arms and other military necessities for their war against Iraq if they would agree not to release the hostages until after the election. If true, this attempt to parlay the hostages' plight into a political weapon may have fallen under the legal definition of treason. It would also have been a violation of federal law against private citizens conducting foreign policy.

Suspicions were fueled particularly by the Iran-Contra affair, which involved illegal arms sales to the Iranians. But the evidence put forth by proponents of the "October surprise" theory has proved flawed, even though some highly reputable journalists have come to believe the allegations.

The theory might be yet another in a long line of American political myths surrounding major events. These myths have a strong hold on popular imagination even in the face of overwhelming evidence to the contrary. No real evidence shows, for instance, that Franklin Roosevelt had prior knowledge of the Japanese attack on Pearl Harbor, nor that John F. Kennedy was assassinated by any sort of conspiracy, nor that Abraham Lincoln's secretary of war played any role in Lincoln's murder. Not only are these beliefs unsubstantiated, but there is considerable evidence to disprove them in each case.

Nonetheless, many people prefer to believe that Roosevelt allowed the Japanese to attack, that the CIA (or whoever) killed Kennedy, and that Secretary Edwin Stanton was in league with John Wilkes Booth. In the case of the October surprise, *Newsweek* magazine published an informative and convincing refutation of the rumors, yet they persist. And so, the October surprise takes its place with the other conspiracy myths in the dark playground of American imagination.

The *Newsweek* report poked holes in the conspiracy theories by showing that various key figures were unreliable in their testimony (one was indicted for perjury and had a long record of dishonesty). It also showed that others (including future CIA Director William Casey) who supposedly disappeared at just the right moments to attend secret meetings with Iranians were actually operating in full view at the very times they were allegedly missing. Casey, for one, had not even left the country, and his whereabouts were fully accounted for when, according to the October-surprise rumors, he was secretly in Spain, meeting with Iranian representatives.

Patti Davis wrote that she believed her father cut a deal with the Iranians during the campaign. She gathered from something she overheard that her father had knowledge of the impending release of the hostages on his inauguration day. He had not taken his oath of office and so was not yet president; it seemed odd to her that he would have knowledge of events in Teheran that day. Davis wrote in her memoir, *The Way I See It,* that she concluded a shady deal had been made.

In fact, President Carter called Reagan's people at seven o'clock that morning to bring them up to speed on the Iranian situation. Carter told Reagan's aides that the hostages were about to leave Iran. Reagan's aides did not want to awaken him to take the president's call, so they later informed the president-elect of Carter's news.

Newsweek pointed out that there were contacts between the United States and Iran during the crisis; the Carter administration sought diplomatic solutions after the failed rescue attempt, but such contacts broke off in September when the Iran-Iraq war erupted. That some sort of negotiations were going on while Carter was still president was not entirely secret, but times of crisis always provide climates for rumormongering, misconceptions, and mythmaking.

Additionally, individual Iranians sometimes got confused about their own contacts with the United States. Various public perceptions and a bit of misreporting by some individuals probably misidentified Carter's representatives as representatives of Reagan, and this likely helped give rise to the conspiracy rumors. One Iranian involved in the contacts mentioned Reagan in his diary, but, according to *Newsweek,* this reference probably was simple confusion, as the Iranian diarist seemed unsure who was president of the United States, Carter or Reagan. Many foreigners have trouble distinguishing between a president and a president-elect (so do some Americans), and some of the Iranians may have been unsure as to with whom they were dealing. If this was the case, then confusion may be one of the key elements that fueled the rumors.

In more recent years, the rumors have faded to the sidelines of public consciousness, but historical rumors have a way of resurfacing, and the October-surprise myth may yet take its place in America's political folklore. (*See also* Jimmy Carter; Hostages and Terrorists.)

THOMAS P. "TIP" O'NEILL

A Democrat from John F. Kennedy's old congressional district in Massachusetts, Tip O'Neill was the House majority leader during the Nixon presidency and Speaker of the House during the Carter years and most of Ronald Reagan's presidency.

In 1980 Reagan was elected president, and the Republicans won control of the Senate. The Democrats held on to their majority in the House, but lost a significant number of seats. With Jimmy Carter defeated, and Edward Kennedy submerged in a Republican Senate, O'Neill became the principal and most visible leader of the National Democratic Party, as well as President Reagan's main opponent in Washington. O'Neill, a self-described New Deal liberal, saw it as his task to stand for the old New Deal coalition's agenda, in opposition to the new conservative regime.

One administration official described the Speaker as a formidable opponent and an old-fashioned welfare-stater. O'Neill himself considered this description essentially correct. Reagan later wrote that he realized early on that O'Neill viewed him as "the enemy," and was not entirely unoffended when, upon first meeting O'Neill, the Speaker commented to the new president that he was "in the big leagues now." Reagan replied that he thought eight years as governor of California was "hardly the minor leagues."

In Congress the Reagan administration won victory after victory during the first years, and O'Neill led a very beleaguered and unpopular opposition. The Speaker often encountered hostility from members of the public for his stand against the genial and popular president, and he even received a few death threats. In Washington itself, during 1981 and 1982, Reagan's White House had O'Neill and the Democrats outgunned; the Speaker acknowledged that Reagan's political aids and advisers were a strong, capable, and savvy group, and he lamented their success in winning the support of the Boll Weevil Democrats away from the Democratic Party's agenda.

Speaker O'Neill and President Reagan often clashed in the public arena, exchanging political barbs and personal insults. O'Neill accused Reagan of being a "rich man's president" and compared Reagan's supply-side economic policies to Herbert Hoover's. The president attacked the Speaker as a tax-raising liberal and even ridiculed the portly congressman's weight by joking that he stayed in shape by jogging around O'Neill. O'Neill found this latter jibe quite offensive.

The two enemies did manage, eventually, to have a fairly civil relationship in private, and even swapped a few Irish jokes and baseball stories over drinks in the White House after business hours. Reagan described O'Neill as friendly and charming when off-duty but "as bloodthirsty as a piranha" when it came to politics.

Despite Democratic gains in the House in the 1982 midterm elections, Reagan remained powerful and won a landslide reelection in 1984. O'Neill never really got the better of the president, but he remained an effective counterbalance to the administration in the House. After 1982 Congress was less compliant with Reagan's wishes and policies, and the Iran-Contra affair considerably weakened the administration on Capitol Hill. O'Neill believed himself to have been more effective in opposing Reagan under these conditions in the second term.

In 1986 the Democrats strengthened their House majority and took back the Senate. Tip O'Neill retired from Congress and from politics, satisfied that he had helped to keep the Reagan Revolution somewhat in check. He wrote two books and appeared in several television commercials before his death in 1994. (*See also* Boland Amendments; Boll Weevils; Congress; Democrats; Elections—Congressional; Gypsy Moths.)

P

At least since the end of World War II, the United States has maintained a strong naval presence in the Persian Gulf. The area is of strategic and economic value; a large part of the world's oil supply comes from Saudi Arabia, Kuwait, and Iraq; and Iran, for years an American ally, flanks the southern Soviet Union. Since the late 1940s, the Soviet Union has competed for influence in the area; both superpowers identify the Persian Gulf as a region of critical interest.

Disruptive events in the Persian Gulf region during the 1970s and 1980s caused major headaches for the United States. Iran and Iraq, the area's two major powers, vied for local domination, and either nation's preeminence represented a threat to American interests and to the security of the other gulf states. Iran's growing instability further aggravated matters. The Soviets quickly tried to exploit America's problems; many analysts believe that the 1979 invasion of Aghanistan was a flanking movement in the wake of Iran's Islamic revolution, to counterbalance America's preponderant influence in the Persian Gulf region and in the Middle East overall.

In previous decades, the United States often propped up friendly regimes and undermined those that favored the Soviet Union. For instance, an American-backed coup d'état in the early 1950s restored Shah Reza Pahlevi to the Iranian throne after pro-Soviet elements overthrew him.

When the shah finally fell during the Carter years, Iran became an anti-American Islamic fundamentalist republic. In 1979 zealous Iranian students attacked the American embassy compound in Teheran, took Americans hostage, and launched the crisis that ultimately helped destroy Carter's presidency and contributed heavily to Ronald Reagan's election victory in 1980. (*See also* Elections—Presidential; October Surprise.) Presented with the students' fait accompli, the Ayatollah Khomeini's revolutionary government endorsed the hostage taking, and the crisis went beyond terrorism into a sustained crisis that threatened to undermine America's position in the gulf, the Middle East, and perhaps the world.

While the hostage crisis frustrated the United States, conditions in the region took an even more dangerous turn when war erupted between Iran and Iraq in 1980. For much of Reagan's presidency, the United States played both sides of the Iran-Iraq War, fearing that outright victory by either side would enable the winner to dominate the gulf.

As the troubles in the gulf worsened, events transpired in other parts of the Middle East that made America's gulf allies leery of American fortitude. Saudi Arabia, Kuwait, and some of the other gulf states began mistrusting American commitment in 1983 shortly after 241 marines died in the suicide bombing of their barracks near the Beirut airport. The United States pulled out of Lebanon. The withdrawal planted doubt in Saudi and Kuwaiti minds as to whether the Americans would honor commitments in the gulf if their forces also suffered casualties there. (*See also* Beirut Marine Bombing; Middle East.)

The war threatened the other gulf states' shipping in the Persian Gulf, and their desire for security gave an opening to the Soviet Union. This disturbed the Reagan administration, as it had the Carter administration. The Carter Doctrine of 1979, a response to the Soviet invasion of Aghanistan, asserted that "any attempt by any outside force to gain control of the Persian Gulf region will be regarded as an assault on the vital interests of the United States of America, and such an assault will be repelled by any means necessary, including military force." The Reagan administration had to judge if Soviet overtures to the Kuwaitis and Saudis might qualify as the sort of attempt that the Carter Doctrine identified as a provocation. (*See also* Reagan Doctrine.)

Such concerns became more immediate as the war between Iran and Iraq wore on. In time, after sustaining defeats and enduring barbarous chemical-weapons attacks, the Iranians gained the upper hand in the war. In the middle 1980s, Iran and Iraq fought a series of massive battles that involved terrible losses on both sides but put the Iranians in a position possibly to overrun the southern half of Iraq and, according to former Secretary of State George Shultz, then threaten Saudi Arabia, Kuwait, and other gulf states, such as the United Arab Emirates and Oman.

The war had already cost perhaps a million lives by 1987, and now Iran drove deep into Iraqi territory; in the north Iranians were near the Iraqi capital of Baghdad, and in the south they occupied Iraqi territory on the gulf coast. Now Iran, more than Iraq, posed a threat to gulf shipping, and indeed the Iranians mined the gulf. Worse, to American thinking, the Iranians were in a position to close the Straits of Hormuz, thus bottling up the Persian Gulf itself.

Were Iran to close the straits, besides playing havoc with oil shipping to and from the gulf, it would impair American naval movements in both the Persian Gulf and the Gulf of Oman. The United States found this prospect unacceptable.

But the United States was not happy with Iraq, either. If Saddam Hussein's Iraq became too strong, it, too, would probably threaten Kuwait and Saudi Arabia, and thus potentially control a major portion of the world's oil supply. Finally, either nation would pose a deadly threat to Israel, which was America's strongest ally in the Middle East. In anticipation of a possible threat, Israeli planes carried out an air raid on an Iraqi nuclear reactor amid combat between the Iraqis and the Iranians.

Despite periodic covert aid to the Iranians, after 1983 the United States in effect waged an undeclared war against Iran. The administration deployed a carrier battle group in the Persian Gulf, gave advice and supplies to the Iraqis, assisted Saudi Arabia in several aerial clashes with the Iranians, and, in 1984, reestablished formal diplomatic ties with Iraq.

By 1987 American ships periodically destroyed Iranian oil platforms in the gulf, usually in retaliation for various Iranian misdeeds. America's Iran policy became bolder as the Soviet Union declined. The competition for influence between the superpowers grew uneven as the Soviets had trouble at home and became mired in their frustrating Afghan war. For years the Soviets had a run of bad luck in the Middle East that their more recent moves did not rectify. They "lost" Egypt after the Six Day War of 1967, and in the 1970s and 1980s, the USSR had uncertain relations with Iran and Syria and lost ground with the Iraqis as the Americans aided Iraq's war effort.

The Iran-Iraq war dragged on for eight years, and both superpowers sustained international criticism for making no serious diplomatic efforts to stop it. The Soviets openly sold arms to both sides, as did France. Also, Reagan's claim that the United States stood ready to protect the Arab states around the gulf from Iranian aggression was undermined by the revelation that the administration had made arms-for-hostages deals with Iranians. Iran-Contra undermined Reagan's foreign policies, as well as damaging his standing at home. Nor was Reagan's position helped by the Iranians' effective use of their ill-gotten arms in several offensives against the Iraqis. (See also Iran-Contra.)

Reagan's Iran strategies proved no more effective than Carter's. Iran remained a "belligerent neutral" even after the war with Iraq ended, and it still threatens to close the Straits of Hormuz. During the early 1990s, the Iranians purchased a Soviet submarine, which increased their capability to bottle up the Persian Gulf. Reagan's policies did not eliminate Iran as an ongoing threat to American interests in the Middle East.

American relations with Iran were particularly confused and aggravated by the arms-for-hostages deals that led to the Iran-Contra scandal. The Reagan administration endeavored to undermine the extremist Islamic government by arming the more moderate Iranians who claimed to want to normalize relations with the United States, recognizing that the Ayatollah Khomeini would not live forever and postrevolutionary Iran would need to rejoin the world community. But the results of these dealings proved disastrous for the United States, and very nearly caused the ruin of the Reagan administration and the president himself.

Kuwait now sought outside help to guarantee its shipping's security. In December 1986, just prior to the Iranian assault on Iraq, the Kuwaitis and the Soviets negotiated a plan to reflag some Kuwaiti tankers as Soviet ships so that the Soviet navy could accompany and protect the tankers without violating any international law or provoking the Iranians or the Iraqis. Kuwait approached the United States with a similar plan, thus seeking both superpowers' protection.

Uncomfortable as the United States was with an increased Soviet naval presence in the Persian Gulf, Secretary Shultz advised the administration against objecting to the Kuwaiti plan. But he also advised that the United States allow Kuwaiti tankers to reflag as American ships and then afford the ships the proper American naval protection. Shultz worried that, were the administration to object to including the Soviets, this would in effect give the Kuwaitis more bargaining power when dealing with the United States.

In March 1987, the United States officially offered the reflagging option to Kuwait, and on April 6 several Kuwaiti oil tankers reflagged to American registry. Shultz intended the deal as a way to notify the Iranians, and anyone else concerned, that the United States had seriously committed itself to keep the Persian Gulf open to commercial shipping. Shultz believed that the commitment was essential, since American credibility had been undermined by the 1983 Beirut marine bombing. Many of the gulf Arab states, and possibly Iran, suspected that the United States would withdraw if American forces sustained any serious casualties and fatalities, as happened after Beirut. Shultz and others in the administration saw the Kuwaiti reflagging plan not only as a way to ensure open sea lanes in the gulf but also an opportunity to renew America's credibility in the entire Middle East.

Then, on May 17, events took another ugly turn when an Iraqi fighter plane attacked the American frigate USS *Stark*.

Thirty-seven sailors died when the plane's two Exocet missiles hit the ship.

Iraq later apologized for the attack, which no doubt was a mistake. The Reagan administration accepted the apology, and several years later the Iraqis paid monetary compensation for the crewmen who were killed, but the incident sent a jolt through official Washington and evinced public doubts about America's continuing role in the gulf.

The reflagging went on, but during the summer, the Saudis directly expressed their fears to American officials that the United States might pull out of the gulf, as they had pulled out of Beirut. Consequently, according to Shultz's memoirs, Saudi Arabia hesitated to join the Americans in protecting gulf shipping. The Saudis did not want to be left holding the bag.

Meanwhile, Shultz and the administration chose to react to Kuwait's overtures to the Soviet Union as a chance to promote Soviet-American cooperation, now that relations were so markedly improving between the two superpowers. Several Soviet ships soon joined the American naval forces in the Persian Gulf in the first such joint effort since World War II.

With all the foregoing, President Reagan escalated his anti-Iranian rhetoric and described Iran as an aggressor and the most likely enemy that American forces might have to fight in the gulf. The Iranians purchased Chinese Silkworm missiles; Secretary Shultz believed that Reagan may have been further motivated to villify the Iranians in order to counter the mounting Iran-Contra scandal at home. During the spring and summer of 1987, after all, Congress held its joint Iran-Contra hearings, and the administration suffered mightily in the public-opinion polls.

As the United States and the United Nations cast about for a way to end the Iran-Iraq War, on June 27 Iran attacked a Norwegian and a Liberian tanker in the gulf. Rumors circulated that the Iranians were about to put Hezbollah's American hostages on trial in Teheran. Other rumors held that an Iranian assault on Kuwait was imminent. A direct confrontation between American and Iranian forces was only weeks away.

On July 22, a reflagged Kuwaiti tanker hit an Iranian mine, and limped back to port with a large hole in its hull. Several days later, angry mobs in Teheran attacked the Kuwaiti and Saudi Arabian embassies. On August 1, Iranian government officials publicly called for the overthrow of the Saudi monarchy. Even amid its brutal and costly war against Iraq, Iran had decided to turn militantly hostile toward Saudi Arabia and Kuwait.

In the following weeks, the United States and the Soviet Union strengthened their naval forces in the Persian Gulf. Britain, France, Italy, the Netherlands, and even Belgium sent ships to support American and Soviet efforts. United Nations Resolution 598, which had hastily been passed only weeks earlier, now took actual effect. The resolution demanded a complete cease-fire between Iran and Iraq and the withdrawal of their forces back within their own borders.

The show of strength in the gulf waters moved the Iranians to invite the U.N. secretary-general to Teheran for a conference about the resolution. The Iranians, perhaps aware they had overreached, seemed willing at least to hear proposals for a negotiated end to the war. Even so, in late September of that year, there was a direct clash between American and Iranian forces in the southern part of the gulf, only forty miles off the island emirate of Bahrain.

The clash occurred when a United States navy helicopter attacked an Iranian amphibious landing craft that was laying mines. Only days later, the Iranian government agreed to begin implementing United Nations Resolution 598, providing that a U.N. commission investigate the war's origins. The Iranians were seeking, at least in part, validation of their charge that Iraq started hostilities.

Iraq *had* started the war. Saddam Hussein's forces invaded Iranian territory in 1980; both President Reagan and Secretary Shultz believed it would be just as well to permit the U.N. investigation, since it might give more incentive to Iran to end hostilities. Several other world leaders, among them Egyptian president Hosni Mubarak, credited both America's flexibility regarding Iran's request and the American attack on the Iranian craft with making both warring countries more amenable to negotiation. The United States needed to act directly to assuage any doubts other nations had about its fortitude and commitment. The naval attack, according to Shultz's analysis, supplied that assurance.

However, the Iranians still did not go quietly into the good night of negotiated peace, and there were further clashes between Iran and the United States in the gulf. American helicopters sank three Iranian gunboats in early October. A week later, the Iranians fired a Silkworm missile on a reflagged Kuwaiti tanker. In retaliation the United States blew up an Iranian oil rig and banned all Iranian imports into the United States.

Nearly another year went by before the Iran-Iraq War ended. The combatants agreed to a cease-fire in early August 1988. No doubt American and United Nations efforts brought about the war's end, and the shows of force convinced all concerned of America's seriousness. However, the United States took a distinctly harder line toward Iran than it did toward Iraq, probably because the Reagan administration still wanted to promote Iraq as a counterbalance to Iranian expansion in the gulf region.

Relations between the United States and Iran were further exacerbated in the summer of 1988 when the USS *Vincennes* shot down an Iranian passenger airbus over the gulf, after taking the plane for an attacker. Such terrible mistakes are not rare in war zones, but the United States sustained worldwide criticism, though subsequent investigation showed that no one aboard the *Vincennes* knew they were firing on a passenger plane. Over the years, before and after the airbus incident, there were dozens of near-misses of this sort, and it was virtually inevitable that sooner or later an incident would occur.

After the war ended, the United States continued to supply Iraq with technical assistance and other forms of aid, as did France and Germany. Iraq, though exhausted by the long war, continued to build its chemical arsenal and pursue its efforts to develop nuclear weapons.

Saddam Hussein maintained his expansionist ambitions and in 1990 Iraq invaded and occupied Kuwait. The invasion precipitated the year-long crisis that led to the Persian Gulf War in 1991. (*See also* Foreign Policy/Foreign Relations.)

PHILIPPINES

During the 1980s, events in the Philippines caused concern in the Reagan White House as the government of President Ferdinand Marcos and his influential wife, Imelda, became unstable and finally collapsed. American concern stemmed from several factors: The Philippine Islands are strategically located in the western Pacific; President Reagan worried that a rural guerrilla insurgency might lead to a communist takeover; the United States had two important military installations in the Philippines—Clark Air Force Base and the Subic Bay Naval Station.

President and Mrs. Marcos ruled the country with an iron hand and lived sumptuously in a sixteenth-century palace that the Spanish had built for their governor-general. Marcos imposed martial law in 1972 and canceled an upcoming presidential election, then stayed in power illegally. The state of affairs began to rapidly deteriorate on August 21, 1983, when Marcos's main opponent, the charismatic and popular Benigno Aquino, returned from exile only to be shot to death when he arrived at Manila Airport.

Immediately, speculation and rumors spread that Marcos ordered the assassination, and the government's position became less tenable. At the same time, the results of years of corrupt misgovernment became more and more apparent as the economy declined and unemployment climbed to 25 percent. In the United States, Reagan administration officials concluded that the Philippines would need alternatives to the Marcos regime.

In September 1984, Cardinal Jaime Sin, the Roman Catholic prelate of Manila, reported to President Reagan that Filipinos widely believed Marcos had had Aquino murdered. The people were turning against Marcos, Sin told Reagan—a situation that raised the chance of a communist takeover. Still, Reagan was inclined to continue supporting Marcos, since he believed the dictator to be the "best counterforce" to the communist insurgency in the countryside.

Reports from Manila became more disturbing. Ferdinand Marcos's health was failing, and Imelda was isolating him. Both Marcoses appeared out of touch with events in their country and did not understand the depth and extent of the popular resentment against them. Reagan sent Senator Paul Laxalt to talk to the Philippine president, and Laxalt strongly advised Marcos to hold a presidential election to show that the country was a democracy.

Marcos agreed to hold the election and announced that he would schedule it for 1987. Then, in November 1985, Marcos announced that he was moving up the date, to January 17, 1986.

If Marcos did this to throw the opposition off balance, he miscalculated. Eight different opposition parties united behind one presidential candidate: Corazon "Cory" Aquino, the slain opposition leader's widow. Marcos rescheduled the election again for February 7, but the race was on, and the dictator's days were numbered.

Marcos's stock fell further a few weeks after he announced the election when a court acquitted General Fabian Ver and twenty-five accused accomplices of murder in the death of Benigno Aquino. Three days later, Corazon Aquino's presidential candidacy became official. Aquino promised that, if elected, she would try to put Ferdinand Marcos on trial for murdering her husband.

During the campaign, the Marcos side portrayed Aquino as weak willed and easily fatigued because she was a woman. On election day, there was widespread voter fraud, and American news cameras photographed soldiers confiscating ballot boxes from polling places. The Reagan administration had sent a delegation to monitor the election, and the two delegation heads, Senator Richard Lugar and Congressman Jack Murtha, quickly concluded that President Marcos had stolen the election.

President Reagan, meanwhile, resisted suggestions that he call on Marcos to resign. Reagan remained inclined to support Marcos, but Shultz and others believed that Marcos's ouster was inevitable and might be accompanied by bloodshed if the United States did not somehow intervene. Marcos declared himself the winner, but events quickly went out of his control. Later in February, Defense Minister Juan Ponce Enrile and Lieutenant General Fidel Ramos resigned from the government, announced that they supported Corazon Aquino, and demanded Marcos's resignation. Marcos and General Ver meanwhile assembled a large force of army troops and tanks and prepared to attack Enrile and Ramos's army units. In Manila large crowds of civilians blocked Marcos and Ver's forces, and the soldiers turned back; this extraordinary popular intervention could easily have resulted in a massacre.

Cardinal Sin (who is famous for greatly enjoying and making jokes and puns about his name) now rejoined the fray and called for "peaceful change" that would entail Marcos's leaving office without bloodshed. Some of Marcos's opponents asked the American ambassador, Steven Bosworth, to press Marcos to leave, but Bosworth did not believe that an American request would have any effect.

The administration now came around to opposing the dictator. A White House press release supported Enrile and Ramos and expressed the opinion that the "ruling party" of the Philippines had committed fraud in the presidential election. The White House was receiving reports from its people in Manila that Marcos had lost virtually all his support and was isolated in his sixteenth-century palace.

On February 24, President Reagan sent private messsages to Marcos urging him to refrain from using force to stay in office. Reagan asserted that the crisis could be solved only by a "peaceful transition" to a new regime. Reagan's message served Marcos notice that the United States supported Aquino rather than Marcos.

Shortly afterward, Senator Laxalt personally called Marcos and assured him that President and Mrs. Reagan were concerned about Marcos's safety. Even so, on February 25, Marcos and Aquino both had themselves sworn in as president. This was a symbolic move on Marcos's part, for he was to leave the country that night on a United States Air Force plane. He had finally conceded the struggle, and Corazon Aquino became the president of the Philippines.

The new Filipino administration signaled to the Reagan administration that it "needed the legitimacy" that United States recognition would bestow. Secretary Shultz proposed a statement of recognition, but White House Chief of Staff Donald T. Regan objected that it was too strongly worded and gave the impression that the United States was in a hurry to dump Marcos. After arguing with Regan, Shultz secured President Reagan's agreement.

Shultz told the press that the president was "pleased" with developments in the Philippines, and the United States formally recognized Corazon Aquino as president.

The new president's gratitude to the United States was not boundless, and Aquino called for the immediate closing of Clark Air Force Base and the Subic Bay Naval Station; there was a distinct anti-American strain in Filipino politics, possibly because of America's support for Marcos over the years, and Aquino played to that during the campaign. Now she wanted the American military out of the Philippines.

At the same time, Aquino did not want to strike an outright anti-American pose. She eventually proved more reasonable on the subject of the American bases, which the United States closed out over the next few years. Aquino also made an official visit to the United States; she received a warm reception from both the president and Congress.

President Aquino served her full term, although she had to quell several military coup attempts. She had limited luck in combating the rampant government corruption that had taken hold throughout the Philippines, and her administration had to cope with a series of natural disasters, including a volcanic eruption. The American aircraft carrier USS *Abraham Lincoln* helped evacuate the volcano's victims.

Nevertheless, Aquino managed quite a few notable accomplishments as president. She and her supporters created a new democratic constitution, held local and national elections, reformed the economy and produced an economic upturn, and tamed and professionalized the army. The Aquino government managed to turn back the communist insurgency in some areas and at least held it in check during her term of office.

Finally, President Aquino stepped aside when her term ended, and one of her major supporters, Fidel Ramos, won the presidency in a free election.

Ferdinand and Imelda Marcos were flown to Hawaii, which they disliked. He insisted to his dying day that he was the rightful president of his country, and Imelda insisted that she wanted to return home to bury her husband. They also spent a good deal of their time in Hawaii trying to avoid lawsuits by Aquino supporters in American civil courts, as well as trying to fend off criminal indictments for alleged financial crimes in the United States.

According to President Reagan, during the Marcoses' time in Hawaii, they kept trying to contact the president and Mrs. Reagan and Senator Laxalt to seek support for their claims that they still were the legitimate president and first lady of the Philippines. They also continually tried to prevail upon the Reagans to intercede with President Aquino to permit them to retire to the Philippine island of Luzon.

The Reagans did in fact ask Aquino if she would agree to let the Marcoses return if they would give back money that they allegedly stole from the Philippine treasury. Aquino refused on the grounds that if Ferdinand and Imelda returned, they would attempt to rally support for overthrowing the new government. When Reagan found out that the Marcoses were, from their sanctuary in Hawaii, encouraging elements back home to raise a coup, he saw the wisdom of Aquino's decision.

After Ferdinand died in 1989, Imelda kept his body preserved, for eventual burial in the Philippines. During the 1990s, she and her late husband returned home, and she stood trial for her various misdeeds but won acquittal.

According to Secretary Shultz, an important aspect of American support for Aquino over Marcos was to break the precedent that the United States automatically supported brutal dictatorships simply because they opposed Communism. By Shultz's account, President Reagan never fully reconciled himself to this idea and always regretted having to "dump" Marcos, whom the president considered a reliable ally and anticommunist. But Shultz was highly pleased by the development, and later wrote that he hoped the Marcos case might set a new precedent once and for all.

PRESS RELATIONS

Every president since George Washington has had bumpy relations with the news media. The First Amendment to the Consitution guarantees a free press, and thereby ensures headaches for the president. In the twentieth century, radio and television have joined the print media in questioning presidents, making the conflict even more glaringly public. Even the administrations that have had the smoothest press relations have still found cause for complaint; Franklin Roosevelt and Dwight Eisenhower often complained about the sort of coverage their administrations received, and those two presidents were particularly well liked by many reporters.

Every president has felt mistreated by the press, and every president's supporters often feel that the press has it in for their president. Network television reporter Sam Donaldson has said that he believes he was every bit as tough on President Carter as he was on President Reagan, but Carter supporters excoriated him for being unfair to Carter, and Reagan supporters criticized him for his liberal bias in covering Reagan.

During the Reagan years, the press came under heavy criticism by Reagan supporters, and occasionally by the White House itself, for biased coverage. But veteran network correspondent David Brinkley notes that when a viewer writes in and accuses you of being biased, all that means is that he doesn't agree with you. Brinkley claims never to have received a letter that says, "You are biased. I agree with you." One can extend the argument to the White House press office; if the reporter's coverage is favorable, then he displays rare perceptiveness and objectivity, but if the coverage is unfavorable, then the reporter is biased.

Traditionally, the press in turn often feels mistreated by the White House, whoever may be president. In the case of the Reagan administration, reporters often smarted over being denied access to the president and being denied permission to cover certain major stories—for instance, during the invasion of Grenada, the military closed off the island to reporters, and so there was no news coverage on Grenada itself until days after the invasion. On the other hand, the press also got hold of details about the impending air raid on Tripoli, arms-for-hostages negotiations, and other data that may have compromised the administration.

The Reagan administration continued the time-honored practice of selective leaking, so as to plant seeds for favorable press coverage or simply to control the reporting of a news development. While reporters love leaks, many have an accompanying constitutional aversion to being used or managed by officials who seek to manipulate the news.

The Reagan White House was not the first administration to recognize that the press could serve as a de facto publicity service for the president's programs, policies, and image, but it mastered the art of press management to a degree unrivaled by any previous administration, including those of Franklin Roosevelt or Dwight Eisenhower. This entailed careful management of the president's public appearances, of photo opportunities, and of reporters' access to the president.

Indeed, the White House press staff saw to it that media access to the president was strictly limited; when the press got to question Reagan, it was usually under controlled conditions. White House news conferences took place with the dais set up before a doorway to a long, carpeted corridor, so television viewers saw the president answering questions as he stood before a passageway to the realm of the presidency itself. This made for a formal, nearly sanctified atmosphere, as opposed to the almost rowdy proceedings in recent administrations.

In accordance with the occasion's solemnity, reporters now had assigned seats and had to remain sitting until called upon when they raised their hands. They were unable to stand and shout and compete for the president's notice in the old-fashioned way. The new way enforced order and control.

Reagan's press people also made sure that the president did not fall into informal sessions with the press outside the context of a formal press conference, as previous presidents sometimes had. Reagan was always carefully briefed before meeting the press, and the White House staff did not like it when he was tempted to ad lib; as governor and as a presidential candidate, Reagan had already gotten into some trouble when he tossed off unrehearsed answers to inquiring journalists under informal, unmanaged conditions. During the first term, Reagan's press handlers developed the strategy of keeping the White House press corps at a signficant physical distance whenever President Reagan walked to and from a helicopter or Air Force One or a limousine or whatever.

Even these precautions were not foolproof, for Reagan had a tendency to try to answer some of the questions that the louder journalists managed to shout over the roar of helicopter engines or across the White House lawn or wherever the opportunity presented itself. Some of Reagan's press people have since written that such incidents were the White House staff's nightmare, for the president might misremember some detail or make some joke or remark that revealed too much or in any case say something that would make White House public relations more difficult.

No recent president held fewer press conferences than Reagan. During his first eight months in office, he held only three, rarely granted interviews, and at the conferences and interviews that did occur, he was prone to making pronouncements and answering single questions without follow-ups. Clearly, the Reagan White House was not press-friendly, although the president often tried to smooth things over by making favorable public statements about the press, lauding reporters as hardworking and honest people while chiding the American media for its allegedly liberal bias.

As Reagan's first year in office passed, and particularly after the assassination attempt, some of the more alert White House staffers detected Ronald Reagan's remarkable "Teflon" effect, which defied all logic. Democratic congresswoman Patricia Schroeder coined the term "Teflon President," and the term caught on. The president remained phenomenally popular regardless of how the press was treating him at a given moment. Sometimes criticism by the media seemed to enhance his popularity, as many voters perceived the press as mistreating him, and resented it.

James Brady was Reagan's original press officer but was gravely wounded when John Hinckley attempted to assassinate President Reagan only two months and ten days into Reagan's first term. Though Brady was left permanently disabled, he kept the official title of press secretary for Reagan's eight years in office, but the actual duties of chief press spokesman fell first to Larry Speakes (who, in his memoirs, wrote that he viewed the relationship between the White House and the press as "us" versus "them") and then to Marlin Fitzwater. (*See also* Assassination Attempt.)

As Reagan's chief press officer, Larry Speakes participated in the public relations and news management that characterized the White House press relations during the Reagan administration. In fact, Speakes went so far as to attribute other officials' words to Reagan and even made up fictitious quotes that he then told the press the president had said.

The first such instance that Speakes reported in his autobiography, *Speaking Out*, occurred during the crisis over the Soviets' shooting down of Korean Airlines Flight 007. During a meeting of the president, some White House personnel, and Congressional leaders, Secretary of State George Shultz commented that the crisis was not specifically a problem between the Soviet Union and the United States but a problem of the Soviets "versus the world." When Speakes briefed the press, he realized that Reagan had said very little during the meeting, so Speakes attributed Shultz's words to the president, telling the press, and by extension the world, that the president had said what in fact the secretary of state had said. (*See also* Korean Airlines Flight 007.)

Later at the Geneva summit between President Reagan and Soviet president Mikhail Gorbachev, Speakes grew concerned about the press coverage of Reagan's idea for the Strategic Defense Initiative and instructed one of his deputies to compose some false quotes for attribution to the president. Consequently, Speakes told the press that Reagan said to Gorbachev, "There is much that divides us, but I believe the world breathes easier because we are talking here together." Speakes thus gave the press a wholly fictional story of a conversation that never took place, and neither the president nor the White House staff ever disavowed Speakes's account.

Speakes saw nothing amiss in taking such liberties with the truth. The only regret he expressed about the Geneva quote was that the Soviets later could have claimed, quite truthfully, that they never heard such words as had been reported in the world media. But Speakes maintained that Reagan would not have disavowed Speakes' words and noted proudly that he had "been able to spruce up the president's image" by making use of his "P.R. man's license."

Marlin Fitzwater succeeded Larry Speakes as press spokesman

after Speakes left the White House to pursue a Wall Street career in January 1987. Fitzwater's own autobiography makes no mention of any Speakesian fabrication or misattribution of quotes, and overall, Fitzwater seems to have liked the press better than did Speakes. But when he left the White House with George Bush in 1993, the outgoing president refused to let the press ride along on the flight home to Houston, and Fitzwater's inward reaction was "I was glad. It was over. To hell with them."

The president's chief press officers were not the only ones who committed thoughts about the Reagan administration's press relations to paper. So did the president. The first lady, too, had her say in her memoirs. Unsurprisingly, both Ronald Reagan and Nancy Reagan expressed ambivalence about the press, and each gave the press mixed reviews, as journalists had given the two of them. Nancy Reagan's relations with the news media were bumpy throughout her husband's presidency.

The press made much—most of it critical—of her propensity for expensive formal clothes, her choice of White House china, her conflicts with Raisa Gorbachev, her conflicts with her children and stepchildren, and her relationship with, and alleged influence over, her husband. In 1981, the press reported, inaccurately, that Mrs. Reagan tried to get the Carters to vacate the White House early, so that the Reagans could have an easier transition. (*See also* Nancy Davis Reagan.)

The first lady's image suffered further damage when the press picked up negative reports leaked by White House officials who had their differences with her, most notably White House chief of staff Donald T. Regan, who also panned her after he left office, in his own White House memoir published while the Reagans still occupied the mansion. The news media gleefully publicized Regan's revelation that the first lady regularly consulted an astrologer. (*See also* Astrology; Nancy Davis Reagan; Donald T. Regan.)

Still and all, after a very rocky start during the administration's first year and a half, the first lady succeeded in making a favorable impression on the press with her performance at the annual Gridiron Dinner, in 1982. Traditionally, the after-dinner entertainment is supplied by the attendees—the president, other high government officials, and the Washington press corps. President Reagan enjoyed these dinners and performed in a few comedy skits; during the Bush administration, President Bush and Marlin Fitzwater staged a mentalist comedy act, very much like Johnny Carson's "Karnak the Magnificent" (during which President Bush wore a mystical-looking robe); other presidents have delivered comic speeches—John F. Kennedy was particularly adept at this.

In 1982 the first lady appeared on stage outlandishly dressed as a bag lady and sang a self-mocking parody of "Second Hand Rose." The performance was a hit, the first lady got a standing ovation, and the press let up on her, for a time at least.

President Reagan's own personal relations with the press ran the gamut that one might expect over the course of an eight-year presidency. While usually polite and publicly gracious, if evasive, in dealing with reporters, Reagan still had some unguarded, undiplomatic moments. There exists a videotape of the press stubbornly refusing to leave a conference room after being allowed in to take some photographs and ask a few questions before the president and some of his advisers began their meeting. The reporters and photographers did not respond to entreaties to finish up and get out, and the president, on tape, can be heard very distinctly to mutter, "The sons of bitches."

Generally, Reagan's comments on the press were more civil. When he began his presidency—in fact, when he first entered politics during the 1960s—Ronald Reagan already had been dealing with the press in one way or another for many years. He had been famous for a long time before becoming president, and thus belonged to a group that included such prepresidential celebrities as Washington, both Adamses, Jefferson, Madison, Jackson, and Eisenhower. All of those men were prominent in one way or another before entering politics, and all dealt with the press of their day. But Reagan was unique in having been a professional actor.

As an actor, Ronald Reagan was in the public eye as early as the late 1930s. His movies, career ups and downs, divorce, and remarriage all found their way into the press. When he took the oath as president in 1981, he already had been contending with a very nosy news establishment for over forty years.

Reagan wrote in his memoirs that he always believed that a free press was vital to America—a fairly standard thing for a politician to say. He also noted that, as a result of the Watergate scandal during the Nixon administration in the early 1970s, the press in general, and the White House press corps in particular, had become very skeptical and even cynical about politicians, the government, and especially the president.

It is difficult to assess Reagan's criticisms of the press on this score, especially since a number of major scandals took place in his administration , resulting in considerable bad press. It is understandable that Reagan would bristle at the media attention such scandals generated, but it is also understandable that the press would focus on those matters. (*See also* HUD Scandal; Iran-Contra; Wedtech Scandal.)

Interestingly, the public often shared the president's view of the press during the Reagan years. In 1986, a just-released American hostage blew up at the White House press corps. The president and first lady stood by impassively, giving what amounted to silent support as David Jacobsen shouted at reporters in the Rose Garden, "In the name of God, would you please just be responsible and back off?" Public reaction mostly favored Jacobsen.

Both the president and the former hostage were upset over the recent press revelations of the arms-for-hostages negotiations, and Jacobsen feared that the publicity might imperil further hostage releases.

Except for one early phase of Reagan's first term, a period characterized by the worst recession since the 1930s, and during the height of the Iran-Contra scandal, President Reagan's press relations never adversely affected his standing in the public-opinion polls. Even so, an overall assessment of the relationship between the Reagan White House and the press corps does not indicate that reporters treated Reagan any more brutally than Jimmy Carter, Richard Nixon, or Lyndon Johnson. In fact, Reagan received a good deal of favorable press and never suffered the nearly universal condemnation that afflicted President Nixon during the Watergate scandal. (*See also* Reagan Recession/Reagan Recovery.)

While many reporters were liberal during the Reagan years, as they are today, many—perhaps the majority—of the most prominent newspaper and magazine columnists were conservative. Also, whether the liberalism of many reporters actually affects their reporting is debatable and should really be examined as a case-by-case analysis. If one looks at the press coverage of the Reagan White House, can one honestly conclude that the press was consistently hard on Ronald Reagan?

Reagan's charisma and charming personality were not wasted on the Washington press corps, and many reporters are on record as saying they personally liked Ronald Reagan. By the same token, his more liberal predecessor, Democrat Jimmy Carter, had, by any analysis, a terrible relationship with the press once past the "honeymoon" that the press affords nearly any new president. The question may have more to do with perceptions and biases than with the reality of the balance, or lack thereof, in the give-and-take between any president and the American press.

Q

Muammar Qaddafi

Branded "the mad dog of the East" by President Reagan, Libyan leader Muammar al-Qaddafi was one of the nation's prime antagonists during the Reagan years. Libya is an oil-producing country, and Qaddafi used his national wealth to sponsor international terrorism and maneuver for power in the Arab world. Bitterly anti-Israeli and anti-American, his relations with his fellow Arab leaders were (and still are) mixed, as were his relations with European nations.

In the early 1980s, Qaddafi claimed most of the Gulf of Sidra as Libyan territory and objected strenuously to American naval patrols and maneuvers in what he regarded as his country's waters. There were infrequent and little-publicized clashes between Libyan and American airplanes over the Gulf of Sidra in 1981, and the Libyans always came out on the losing end of these encounters.

The clashes began after Reagan ordered the Navy Sixth Fleet to conduct maneuvers in the Gulf of Sidra during the summer of 1981. Qaddafi first made his territorial claims during the late 1970s, when the United States was distracted by the Iran hostage crisis and not likely to go out of its way to challenge him or engage his forces. In fact, President Carter canceled the Sixth Fleet's usual maneuvers in Sidra in 1980, although it is not clear that he did so in response to Qaddafi's claim.

In any case, Reagan determined to resume the maneuvers, as he wished to reinforce the international law that a nation can claim territorial waters only as far as twelve miles from its shores. For the United States to accept Qaddafi's claim that the entire gulf belonged to Libya would be to allow a precedent that could wreak havoc internationally if other small nations decided to emulate Qaddafi and expand their claims to territorial waters. Such a state of affairs could interfere with shipping and inhibit naval movement worldwide.

Late in August, Libyan planes fired at two American F-14s from the carrier USS *Nimitz*, sixty miles from the Libyan coast. The American planes shot the Libyans down. Reagan later wrote that within a few days of the clash, he received word that Qaddafi had been heard to say he wanted to have Reagan assassinated. Whatever the report's merit, it added to the growing conflict between the United States and Libya, which also had all the earmarks of a personal animus between Qaddafi and Reagan.

Qaddafi later reduced his claim on the Gulf of Sidra; instead of insisting that the entire gulf was Libyan, he drew an imaginary "line of death" in the water, though the location was uncertain, and dared anyone ("anyone" meaning the United States navy) to cross it. Despite the comic-opera aspects of Qaddafi's posturing, the situation was serious.

Qaddafi's enthusiastic support of terrorist activities endeared him to some Arab militants, though it alienated other Arab leaders.

One alienated Arab leader was Egyptian president Anwar Sadat. When Sadat was assassinated in 1981, Qaddafi went on Libyan television and celebrated his neighbor's death; many Islamic fundamentalists resented Sadat for making peace with Israel, and Qaddafi was not the only celebrant. Still, many more moderate Arabs in the Middle East regarded the Libyan leader as something of a loose cannon, and not the one to represent Arab interests to the world at large.

Qaddafi continued to find ways to make trouble in his own neighborhood. Libyan troops launched an invasion of Chad, Libya's southern neighbor, in December of 1982, and American intelligence agencies also suspected that Qaddafi was helping to plot a coupe d'état in Sudan.

France went so far as to send troops to Chad to help repel the invasion and to fight the Libyan-backed rebel guerrillas. The

United States contributed several AWACS planes and fighter escorts, and thus kept track of Libyan air and troop movements. Egypt, too, cooperated with the French and Americans in Chad, since its own interests very much concerned the rest of North Africa, particularly Sudan, which shared with Egypt the Nile River. Apparently, these movements sufficed to, in Secretary of State George Shultz's phrase, "scare off" Qaddafi and the Libyans from their adventurism in neighboring North African nations.

The next major clash between Libya and the United States came over four years later, during American naval maneuvers in Sidra, when Libyan planes again fired on American planes. The Libyans missed and the American planes did not respond, but later that day fighters from the carrier USS *Yorktown* sank a Libyan patrol boat. Then an American plane destroyed a radar installation at Sirte, Libya.

The next day, American naval forces sank two more Libyan patrol boats and attacked a Libyan missile launching site. That same day, the Libyans told the Italian ambassador in Tripoli that, if the United States escalated its attacks, the Libyans would attack military installations in Italy, and probably Italian islands in the Mediterranean. The Italians in turn told NATO of Qaddafi's threat, but the Americans in the Gulf of Sidra staged no further actions against Libyan forces, and Libya issued no further challenges at that point.

Still, Qaddafi postured, and within a day proclaimed a state of war between Libya and the United States. The Soviet Union, not in a friendly mood, issued condemnations of American actions in the Gulf of Sidra, but King Fahd of Saudi Arabia tried to persuade Qaddafi to calm down. Fahd later told Americans that, when he spoke to Qaddafi, the Libyan was barely coherent, enraged, and difficult to understand.

The situation drastically escalated on April 5, when a bomb destroyed a West German discotheque, killing two people and wounding 155, of whom between 50 and 60 were Americans. American intelligence reports indicated that the terrorists who planted the bomb had ties to the Libyans, and the Reagan administration decided to act.

On April 14, 1986, American planes attacked the Libyan capital of Tripoli in a bombing raid that caused serious damage and large loss of life. Among the dead was one of Qaddafi's children. At first, Qaddafi responded with a good deal of public anger. Then he abruptly quieted down, and Libya's involvement with international terrorism in time became less evident.

Qaddafi himself grew less assertive, and within a few years he no longer loomed so large over the Arab world. However, Libya has continued to stockpile chemical weapons, and the United States still considers Qaddafi a sponsor of international terrorists.

R

Nancy Davis Reagan

First lady from 1981 to 1989, Nancy Davis Reagan was a second-generation actress who married Ronald Reagan when he was an actor. She is his second wife, the mother of two children, and the stepmother of his two older children, from his first marriage to actress Jane Wyman.

Nancy Reagan's mother, Edith Luckett Davis, was a theatrical actress who spent a good deal of time on the road. She married Kenneth Robbins, a New Jersey car salesman, in 1917, and Nancy was their only child. Mrs. Reagan admits to July 6 as her birthday but does not like to reveal the year of her birth; she was probably born in 1921, according to most sources.

Christened Anne Frances Robbins, the baby was nicknamed Nancy, and she has gone by that name ever since. Her parents divorced soon after she was born, and Edith Luckett had to support her baby daughter. She resumed her acting career and went back on the road. She was penniless, without alimony; after a period of taking Nancy along on her travels, she left the toddler with her sister and brother-in-law in Bethesda, Maryland. Nancy's aunt and uncle gave her a stable home until her mother's remarriage.

When Nancy was about ten, Edith married Loyal Davis, a socially prominent Chicago neurosurgeon. Nancy now had a stepfather, a half-brother, and a stable life in Chicago, although Dr. Davis did not adopt Nancy until she was in her teens. According to Patti

Davis, Dr. Davis wanted his wife's daughter to "earn" the right to bear his name as his adopted daughter. But Nancy Reagan wrote lovingly of her adopted father and has never publicly expressed anger at his delay in adopting her.

Edith Davis acted on radio soap operas based in Chicago, including the old *Amos and Andy* radio show, in which white actors portrayed black characters. Apart from this, Edith Davis no longer pursued an acting career although the Davises kept up Edith's old show-business contacts. These associations later helped Nancy in her own acting career.

Nancy Davis attended the Girls' Latin School in Chicago and then Smith College. Her first serious boyfriend, a Princeton student, was struck and killed by a train in 1941. She later wrote of the incident that it was the first time she lost someone close to her; the couple had been considering marriage.

During summers off from college, Nancy Davis apprenticed at a New England summer stock theater; after the end of World War II, she made her professional debut with Zazu Pitts in Detroit, in a play called *Ramshackle Inn*. Pitts was an old friend of Edith Davis.

In New York, Nancy Davis renewed her ties with several of her mother's old friends, including such luminaries as Walter Huston, Lillian Gish, Spencer Tracy, and Katherine Hepburn. Her first (and only) major Broadway role was in the musical *Lute Song*, with Yul Brynner and Edith's old friend Mary Martin. It was Brynner's first major role also. The show ran six months (a respectable run in those days).

In time Nancy Davis went to Hollywood and was mentioned in the gossip columns as Clark Gable's frequent date. In the late 1940s and early 1950s, she appeared in several films. Her most famous role was as James Whitmore's wife in *The Next Voice You Hear*, a film about God speaking to the world through radio broadcasts. Mrs. Reagan believed her role was the first visibly pregnant character ever to appear in an American movie. She used a "pregnancy pad" to simulate the family condition.

By 1949 Nancy Davis had appeared in a number of films and was a moderately successful Hollywood actress—not a star but fairly well known and steadily employed. She played a series of featured parts in such films as *East Side, West Side*, with Barbara Stanwyck, James Mason, and Ava Gardner; *It's a Big Country*, with Ethel Barrymore, Gary Cooper, and Gene Kelly; and after her marriage to Ronald Reagan, they co-starred in *Hellcats of the Navy*.

This was the era of the Hollywood blacklist, when the House Committee on Un-American Activities held sensational and highly publicized inquiries into alleged communist influence in the motion-picture industry, and anyone in the business even remotely suspected of having communist connections usually was unofficially but effectively barred from movie or television work.

As it happened, a Hollywood newspaper listed Nancy Davis as a communist sympathizer. Probably, the report confused her with another actress named Nancy Davis, as had happened on occasion back in New York. Her friend, producer Mervyn LeRoy, informed the Hollywood press that the Nancy Davis under contract at Metro-Goldwyn-Mayer was not the same one suspected of communist sympathies. Davis was upset, and to reassure her further, LeRoy called the president of the Screen Actors Guild, Ronald Reagan.

Thus did meet the future first lady and president of the United States. They began dating, got engaged, and married on March 4, 1952, shortly after Ronald Reagan's divorce from Jane Wyman became final. Reagan had two children from his first marriage—a daughter, Maureen, and an adopted son, Michael. Ronald and Nancy Reagan had two more children, Patricia Ann and Ronald Prescott. (*See also* Reagan Family.)

As Ronald Reagan phased out of show business and into politics, Nancy Reagan quickly adapted to her role as a political wife, although she continued to take occasional roles until the early 1960s, and in 1962 appeared in several network television plays.

She was California's first lady for eight years, from 1967 to 1975, and campaigned with her husband when he unsuccessfully sought the 1976 Republican presidential nomination, and in his successful presidential campaigns of 1980 and 1984. Like many political wives, Nancy Reagan became as much a public figure as her husband, and soon gained a reputation as one of his most influential advisers. But, like Edith Wilson and Eleanor Roosevelt, Nancy Reagan denied having any particular influence.

Nancy Reagan was controversial throughout her husband's political career. Outspoken in her support of his conservative policies, she delighted conservatives and infuriated liberals. She was also frowned upon by those who disapprove of active political wives, regardless of their politics. It became clear early on that the Reagans were a team, and Ronald Reagan's prominence would entail prominence for Nancy Reagan.

As first lady, Nancy Reagan was determined to restore formality and sumptuousness to the White House. During the Carter presidency, a more or less egalitarian tone prevailed. State dinners were reputedly less stately, and various formal events seemed less formal than in previous administrations. The Reagans served notice on inaugural night that the new regime would return to more traditional and formal mores; the various inaugural balls were glittering gatherings of the Republican upper crust, who, for their part, were only too happy to turn out dressed to the nines to welcome the dawning of the new conservative era in Washington.

Criticism of Nancy Reagan began immediately. Her taste for expensive clothing and fine china provoked an explosion of protest and ridicule, and some of her critics thought it scandalous that she sometimes borrowed clothes and jewelry for state occasions. It is difficult to see what constitutes scandal in such instances, since those who supplied the items were retailers and designers, rather than Washington influence peddlers.

The new first lady also became the subject of unflattering and largely unfounded rumors, such as the erroneous report that she tried to get the Carters to vacate the White House even before the inauguration, so that the president-elect's family could move in early. Even more absurd, the writer Kitty Kelley, author of "unauthorized" biographies of such celebrities as Elizabeth Taylor and Frank Sinatra, wrote that the first lady had an affair with Sinatra in the White House.

But perhaps the two most persistent rumors that plagued Mrs. Reagan during her husband's presidency concerned her alleged influence on the president and her rivalry with Raisa Gorbachev, wife of the Soviet leader. The first lady was also plagued by highly public family conflicts, particularly with her daughter, Patti.

Patti Davis made a point of staying away from her family during most of the Reagan era, and published novels that thinly fictionalized her dysfuntional family relations. The president's older daughter, Maureen, wrote and spoke more kindly about her stepmother, as did Michael, the older son. The younger son, Ronald Prescott Reagan, maintained a public appearance of relative harmony with his parents, as he pursued careers first as a ballet dancer, then as a journalist.

Nancy Reagan's role and possible influence in the White House also came under fire from Donald T. Regan, who served both as secretary of the treasury and White House chief of staff. Regan and Mrs. Reagan had very unkind things to say about one another in public statements and their respective autobiographies; it was Regan who first broke the story that Nancy Reagan consulted an astrologer about scheduling some of the president's appointments, and alleged that the first lady scheduled some of her husband's surgeries and travel plans according to astrological forecasts.

Nancy Reagan's bumpy relations with Raisa Gorbachev occasioned considerable controversy and rumormongering. While Mrs. Reagan made no secret of her uneasy and difficult encounters with her Soviet counterpart, she maintained that she had no actual enmity or rivalry with Mrs. Gorbachev. According to Mrs. Reagan, the two were not entirely compatible, but they were not opponents either, and got on well enough once they became used to each other.

Even so, the antagonism between the two caused headlines when they first met at the Geneva summit in December 1985. Raisa Gorbachev displayed an often overbearing, even arrogant personality. The Soviet first lady dominated a photo session with Mrs. Reagan, during which she barked orders at all and sundry, held forth at length on various topics, and altogether put on a show of one-upping her American counterpart. Nancy Reagan was heard to ask an aide, "Who does this dame think she is?"

On another occasion, Raisa Gorbachev subjected both Mrs. Reagan and nearby reporters to a long lecture on world affairs. When the Soviet first lady finished, Mrs. Reagan tried to speak and Mrs. Gorbachev interrupted her. Obviously agitated, Nancy Reagan raised a hand and said, "Now I want to say something. Okay?"

In 1987, Mrs. Reagan underwent a radical mastectomy and, as she was recovering, President Reagan delivered the news that her mother, Edith Davis, had died. Mother and daughter were extremely close, and the loss was devastating. Her adopted father, Loyal Davis, had died in 1982.

The first lady involved herself in a highly publicized public-relations campaign against drug abuse, the famous "Just Say No" crusade. The campaign involved speaking appearances, visits to public schools around the country, and convocation of the first lady's Conference on Drug Abuse. She was also active in the Foster Grandparents' Program, which encouraged senior citizens to spend time with institutionalized children.

Nancy Reagan's role in history will probably be debated for many years to come. To what extent she influenced her husband may ultimately lie in the eye of the beholder. As to whether her alleged power and influence were proper or improper, it is well to remember that, for better or worse, a president has the right to turn for advice or information to anyone he chooses. How one may feel about the advice that he receives usually depends upon how one feels about the adviser, just as with other first ladies; those who agreed with what they stood for appreciated their influential role, and those who opposed them considered their activism inappropriate.

Nancy Reagan claims to have had no special influence on the president. That may or may not be true, and Mrs. Reagan herself may or may not be aware of the actual extent of her influence. Whatever the case, there are no clear rules or laws governing such matters, nor should there be. No one can fully separate personal from professional life, and that simple rule of reality applies as much to presidents and their spouses as to anyone else.

Nancy Reagan was, indisputably, vitally important to Ronald Reagan, and remains so in the former president's illness-ridden retirement. (*See also* Astrology; Reagan Family; Ronald Wilson Reagan; Donald T. Regan.)

RONALD WILSON REAGAN

Fortieth president of the United States, from 1981 to 1989, Ronald Reagan was the first president since Dwight Eisenhower (1953–1961) to serve two full terms. Elected at age sixty-nine (he turned seventy during his first year in office), Reagan was both the oldest man elected president, and the oldest president to serve. Previously, William Henry Harrison, who died after only one month in office, was the oldest elected president at sixty-eight, and Eisenhower, who turned seventy shortly before leaving the White House, was the oldest serving president. Reagan broke both records.

Ronald Wilson Reagan was born on February 6, 1911, in Tampico, Illinois, but spent most of his childhood in Dixon, Illinois. At birth he was described by his father as a "fat little Dutchman," and so "Dutch" stuck as his boyhood nickname. He was the younger of two sons; his brother, Neil, nicknamed "Moon," was two years older.

His father, John Edward Reagan, known to everyone, including his sons, as Jack, an alcoholic who held a series of sales jobs, wanted to establish his own business but never managed to make a go of it. An Irish-American Catholic, Jack Reagan was a lifelong Democrat who would be very conservative by today's standards, with his deep mistrust of government authority and passionate belief in individual rights.

Reagan's mother, Nelle Wilson, was a Protestant of Scottish-English extraction; she married Jack Reagan in Fulton, Illinois, in 1904. All four of Reagan's grandparents died before Neil and Ronald were born. The two boys, though taken to Catholic mass from time to time, were mostly raised in their mother's church, the Disciples of Christ.

As Jack Reagan changed jobs, the family lived in various parts of Illinois, including Chicago. Jack settled them in Dixon when Ronald Reagan was nine years old, in 1920. After that, for the most part, the family stayed put as Jack traveled to different areas for jobs. Reagan spent his teenage years as normally as possible under the family's rather straitened circumstances. He attended high school, played football, worked odd jobs (according to Reagan, he rescued over seventy victims during the several summers he worked as a lifeguard at the local lake), and grew into a popular and active young man. Under the tutelage of an English teacher, he became interested in theater and performed in school plays.

In 1932 Reagan graduated from Eureka College with a degree in economics, although, he wrote later, his secret ambition was to be an actor. As a preliminary step to pursuing an acting career, Reagan went into radio, still a fairly new medium and more accessible in the Midwest, hundreds of miles from New York and a couple of thousand miles from Hollywood. His first broadcasting job was as an all-purpose announcer for a station in Des Moines, Iowa.

At the end of his first season in Des Moines, during which he became the station's sports announcer, Reagan returned to Dixon, and he was there when Franklin D. Roosevelt was elected president in November 1932. Jack Reagan, one of the only Democrats in town, became a minor official in the local federal relief programs, and this was Ronald Reagan's first exposure to government service. His father, unemployed for quite some time (the Depression had hit in 1929, and Jack always had trouble holding jobs in any case), now was a government bureaucrat. Eventually, he took charge of the Works Progress Administration office in Dixon; the WPA was Roosevelt's landmark jobs-creation program and a crucial element of the New Deal.

Ronald Reagan eventually found another radio job, this time for a larger station in Davenport, Iowa, where he again was a sports announcer. After four years, he went to Hollywood, where he quickly found an agent, and the agent quickly found him work. Reagan signed as a contract player with Warner Brothers, thus beginning a Hollywood career that made him famous and led directly to his political career.

Reagan did well in Hollywood for many years. While never a top star, he was a star nevertheless, and racked up some famous roles, such as the Gipper in *Knute Rockne, All American*, and the young George Armstrong Custer in *The Santa Fe Trail*. As the rakish young swain in *King's Row*, Reagan spoke his single most famous line. Upon awakening from surgery, Reagan discovers that his girlfriend's hostile father, a surgeon, has amputated his legs. The horrified youth screams, "Where's the rest of me?" That question later served as the title of the first of Reagan's two published autobiographies.

During World War II, Ronald Reagan, now married to Jane Wyman and the father of a small daughter, Maureen, went into the Army Air Corps (despite an aversion to flying) and spent the war years making war movies, training films, and morale films, mostly in Southern California. At war's end, he was discharged, left the service, and resumed his civilian career as a movie star.

In 1946, Reagan and Wyman adopted a baby boy, Michael, but their marriage headed for the rocks as Reagan's career began to decline while Wyman's was on the ascent. They separated, then divorced a few years later so that Reagan could marry Nancy Davis.

Reagan was politically active during his Hollywood years. An ardent New Deal Democrat, he was an early member of the Screen Actors Guild and eventually became its president; Reagan is the only president of the United States to have been a union president and a member of the AFL-CIO. Reagan grew more conservative during the late 1940s, by his own account. At the end of World War II, he was still, he has written, very much a New Dealer, and believed that government was the solution to any number of social problems. However, as his postwar movie career waned and he worked as a corporate spokesman for General Electric, Reagan developed into a conservative. It was not a rapid process; during the senatorial campaign of 1950, for instance, he defended his friend Helen Gahagan Douglas against Richard Nixon's charges that she was a communist sympathizer.

But by the middle of the 1950s, Reagan, while still a registered Democrat, had become a conservative Republican in his thinking. He supported Dwight Eisenhower for president in 1952 and 1956 (Richard Nixon was Eisenhower's running mate both times), and when, in 1960, Reagan worked for Nixon's presidential campaign, he did not change his registration, because the Nixon camp told him he would be more effective as a very visible Democrat for Nixon.

Although he did not officially change his party registration from Democrat to Republican until 1964, Reagan established himself as a conservative spokesman; this may have cost him his job with General Electric, for the company fired him in 1962. There are two different stories behind Reagan and GE's parting of the ways. By one account, GE executives were disgruntled with the fact that Reagan, in his banquet speeches on the rubber-chicken circuit, spent more time campaigning against big government and elucidating conservative ideologies than pitching the company's products.

The other story is that GE fired Reagan because the company got nervous about a Justice Department probe into allegations that Reagan, when president of the Screen Actors Guild ten years earlier, was involved with a deal that allowed MCA, a large production company, also to act as agent for actors under contract to MCA itself. If true, this represented a conflict of interest, and Reagan stood vulnerable to accusations of abetting the deal for profit. Called to testify at a grand jury hearing in 1962, he claimed not to remember anything about the MCA deal. He was never charged, but it was rumored that GE feared continuing to employ Reagan might cause scandal.

Whichever story was true, after 1962 Reagan no longer was General Electric's spokesman, and he returned to acting to make a living. He hosted the *Death Valley Days* television program and made one more film, *The Killers*, in 1964. In an unusual bit of casting, Reagan portrayed a villainous businessman who, in one scene, physically strikes Angie Dickinson.

In 1964 Reagan essentially came out of the closet as a conservative Republican, campaigned nationally for Barry Goldwater and delivered a major campaign speech for the Republican presidential nominee in October. Two years later, in 1966, Reagan ran for governor of California as a Republican. (*See also* Barry Goldwater.)

Foreshadowing his later presidential campaign, as a gubernatorial candidate Reagan portrayed himself as an outsider, a nonpolitician seeking to bring government back in touch with ordinary citizens. He denounced high taxes, advocated reducing government's regulatory role, and recommended that spending be cut back. The candidate spent nearly as much time attacking the federal government as he did addressing state issues, and pundits speculated that he had national ambitions.

Reagan opponent Governor Edmund "Pat" Brown had in his two terms presided over a good deal of growth and expansion in California, as the state's landscape filled up with new freeways, business, and industry. Brown took a decidedly liberal approach to social spending, expanded the state's welfare system, and greatly expanded the state's water system. He also expanded the University of California; in that era of student unrest, this did not endear him to the conservative voters of Southern California. Reagan called Brown a liberal, "tax-and-spend" governor.

Brown inadvertently helped Reagan by waging an inept campaign. The governor had been popular, and he had won wide respect among national Democrats by trouncing former vice president Richard Nixon in the 1962 gubernatorial election. But in 1966, rather than run on his record, Brown waged a campaign of character assassination that included such absurdities as a series of ads reminding voters that Reagan was an actor, and an actor, after all, murdered Abraham Lincoln.

Reagan won the election, and at his midnight inauguration he already sounded like a candidate for national office. He told his audience that "freedom is a fragile thing and is never more than one generation away from extinction. It is not ours by inheritance; it must be fought for and defended constantly by each generation." (*See also* Astrology)

Reagan showed more flexibility and moderation than his campaign rhetoric and many of the statements he made as governor would indicate. It may be fair to characterize Reagan's governing style as an interesting blend of conservative rhetoric with moderate policies. While he mobilized the national guard against rioting students several times, and while he denounced rebellious youth in harsh, and often hyperbolic terms, he still did not cut education funds (as he had promised to do), and actually doubled overall state spending. He signed one of the nation's most liberal abortion bills into law and left the state's vast and complex welfare system solidly in place. Governor Reagan also approved the largest tax increase in California's history.

But Reagan remained a hero to conservatives and, as governor of the nation's then second-largest state, became a major figure on the national scene. Many Republicans considered him a contender for the 1968 presidential nomination. President Lyndon Johnson was widely expected to run (although a minority of commentators predicted he would not seek another term), and a number of Republicans vied for the privilege of opposing him. The front-runners were Richard Nixon and Nelson Rockefeller; Goldwater had no plans to seek the nomination a second time, and Reagan, though prominent, was definitely a second-rank contender.

In fact, the governor did make a fairly serious bid for the 1968 nomination. But in the end, he supported Nixon, who went on to defeat Vice President Hubert Humphrey in the general election. Reagan remained in Sacramento, where his conservative star continued to rise in the highly polarized political climate of the late 1960s and early 1970s.

Reagan remained a major political figure during Nixon's presidency. The Republican party's right wing supported him consistently and regarded him still as a future presidential prospect. When the Nixon administration foundered during the Watergate scandal, Reagan expressed support for the president but also made a few Watergate jokes in public. When Nixon resigned and Gerald Ford became president, in August 1974, the Republican party effectively split between Ford's moderate supporters and the conservatives who regarded Reagan as their standard-bearer.

Reagan left the governorship in 1975 after two full terms (he won a landslide reelection in 1970 against Democratic candidate Jesse Unruh, the "Big Daddy" of the California legislature) and remained in the public eye by hitting the lecture circuit, hosting a radio show, and writing occasional newspaper columns. The former governor now took solid command of the Republican conservative wing, and there was widespread speculation that he would challenge President Ford for the party's nomination in 1976.

Ford was vulnerable to challenge. In the midst of the Watergate scandal, President Nixon had named him vice president to replace Spiro Agnew, who had resigned in disgrace over his own scandal. It was the first time that a vice president had been chosen under the terms of the Twenty-fifth Amendment. When Nixon resigned,

Ford then became the only American ever to serve as president without having been elected either to that office or to the office of vice president. That alone made Ford vulnerable, but he aggravated the situation with his controversial pardon of Richard Nixon.

The foregoing, combined with a troubled economy, denied Gerald Ford the traditional sanctity that a party grants its own incumbent in election years. Normally, a president would not have to worry about getting nominated, but things were different in 1976. Adding to Ford's other difficulties, the resurgent conservative wing primed itself to claim the soul of the Republican party.

Reagan's challenge led to a bitter and rancorous primary fight. Right up to convention time, the press considered the contest too close to call. The fratricidal war between Ford and Reagan stood in stark contrast to the Democrats, who in effect anointed Georgia Governor Jimmy Carter as their nominee. At the Republican convention, the two camps competed for uncommitted delegates down to the wire, and President Ford won the nomination but lost the closely contested election to Carter.

During Carter's presidency, Reagan was generally regarded as the front-runner for the 1980 Republican nomination. After 1976, Reagan busied himself with public appearances, his newspaper opinion column, and his radio show (a fairly tame forerunner of Rush Limbaugh's). Reagan stayed visible and built political alliances within the National Republican Party. He used his leftover 1976 campaign funds to found an organization he called Citizens for the Republic, a conservative group that helped keep his political support intact for the coming 1980 campaign.

When Carter began his famous plummet in the opinion polls during the late 1970s, there was immediate media speculation that he would be a single-term president and that the front-runner for the Republican nomination, and therefore the presidency itself, was Ronald Reagan. Others were mentioned—former Tennessee Senator and Watergate committeeman Howard Baker, for one—but by the late 1970s, Reagan was the top contender.

In fact, Reagan's campaign had shifted into gear before 1980 and was operating smoothly and skillfully. Despite a few minor setbacks, Reagan took the convention by storm and won the presidency by a landslide. Carter had been defeated by the economy, the Iran hostage crisis, and by Reagan's patented charm. (*See also* Debates; Elections—Presidential.)

Ronald Reagan was the most popular president since Eisenhower, and perhaps the most popular president in American history. In 1984 he was reelected by one of the greatest margins in elective history and, despite downturns in his popularity caused by a recession during his first term and the Iran-Contra scandal during his second, he continually rebounded in public opinion polls. He was the first president since Eisenhower to leave office at least as popular as when he entered; at the end of Reagan's presidency his approval ratings stood at 56 percent.

Reagan's presidency ended in 1989; after attending George Bush's inauguration, he headed home to California and retirement. Unlike Jimmy Carter, Ronald Reagan, a much older man, did not become an active elder statesman, although he did make a few speaking tours, published his memoirs, and made various other public appearances.

On November 5, 1994, Ronald Reagan announced that he had been diagnosed with Alzheimer's disease. His handwritten announcement in effect was his farewell to the country, delivered in his typically informal and highly personal style. His illness ended his public life, and he lives with his wife in Southern California. (*See also* Anticommunism; Assassination Attempt; Barry Goldwater; Nancy Davis Reagan; Reagan Family.)

REAGAN DOCTRINE

During the mid-1980s, the Reagan administration's goal was to roll back Communist influence in the Third World by attempting to destabilize pro-Soviet or Marxist regimes, such as the Sandinistas in Nicaragua, or by aiding governments against leftist insurgencies, such as in El Salvador, along with other programs of foreign aid, military aid, and so on.

The Reagan Doctrine went beyond the traditional policy of

containment, which sought to contain communism where it already existed by opposing its spread. Containment policy sometimes involved military action, such as in Korea and Vietnam in the 1950s and 1960s. More often, containment was effectuated through diplomacy and foreign aid and the mere threat of military action. The nuclear sword of Damocles always hung over the proceedings.

Containment began in the Truman administration, and the principle produced a series of "doctrines" meant to add each president's individual stamp to the Cold War. The Truman Doctrine held that the United States would aid any nation threatened by communist insurgency; the Eisenhower Doctrine vowed to keep communism out of the Middle East; the Nixon Doctrine pledged to honor all treaty commitments, uphold the Truman Doctrine (but with the caveat that the "threatened" nation must supply the bulk of the manpower), and added the pledge to provide a "shield" if a nuclear power threatened one of America's allies or any other nation that the United States considered vital to American security.

The Carter Doctrine, prompted by the Soviet invasion of Aghanistan, was in some ways a reprise of Eisenhower's, in that it concerned the threat of Soviet adventurism in the Persian Gulf. Carter announced that any Soviet action in the gulf region would be repelled by any means necessary, including military force. Kennedy, Johnson, and Ford seem to have refrained from adding their names to the doctrine pool.

All the doctrines served to enforce containment, but the Reagan Doctrine went beyond that principle in a push to try to win the Cold War outright, rather than maintain a balance of power according to the status quo. By the Reagan years, the fear of nuclear war subsided enough to permit such thinking in high government circles—either that, or the Reagan administration was willing to count nuclear war as a calculated risk. In any case, the administration's foreign policies reflected the Reagan Doctrine in that the United States carried out both overt and covert operations aimed at combating Communist influence all over the Third World, particularly in Central America and the Middle East.

The Reagan Doctrine was not without its critics, some of whom charged that the administration's obsession with rolling back communism led directly to the Iran-Contra affair. Ronald Reagan himself, after his presidency ended, described his doctrine as nothing more than an acknowledgment that the United States understood Soviet plans for world domination and would not stand for them. Reagan meant it as a direct answer to the so-called Brezhnev Doctrine, but it caused trouble in superpower relations, even after Mikhail Gorbachev came to power in the Soviet Union. (*See also* Brezhnev Doctrine; Central America; Cold War; Foreign Policy/ Foreign Relations; Grenada; Middle East; Persian Gulf.)

REAGAN FAMILY

Like those of many first families, Ronald Reagan's relatives, politically speaking, were a mixed blessing. Every president has suffered some public embarrassment because of family members: Mary Todd Lincoln was a compulsive shopper, given to fits of irrational behavior, and was even investigated for alleged confederate sympathies by a congressional committee; some of Franklin Roosevelt's sons got involved in questionable business dealings and had messy domestic problems that included adultery and divorce.

Dwight Eisenhower's brother, Edgar, was a right-wing extremist who liked to denounce the president in public; Lyndon Johnson's brother, Sam Houston Johnson, liked to drink and gamble; Richard Nixon's brothers engaged in questionable business transactions; Jimmy Carter's brother, Billy, was an alcoholic and made business deals with foreign investors who seemed intent on exploiting their relationship with a president's brother. Some of these business associates were Libyan nationals, and Billy Carter answered criticism on this point by noting that there were many more Arabs in the world than Jews. He also made news by urinating on an airport runway.

One thing that sets Ronald Reagan's brood apart from other first families is that three of his children wrote books and so did his wife. So, for that matter, did he. During the late 1940s, Eleanor

Roosevelt wrote two autobiographical volumes, which were surprisingly frank and candid about family matters, considering the times, and both books occasioned some criticism. But Reagan's family, including the first lady, turned out a series of tomes that some readers found utterly alarming, with their accounts of violence, alcoholism, drug abuse, and sexual molestation, among other elements of postwar American family life.

In the spirit of the times, some of the Reagans wrote outright confessionals, notably Michael Reagan and Patti Davis. But even Ronald Reagan's own postpresidential memoir, *An American Life*, and Nancy Reagan's *My Turn*, are rife with anecdotes and revelations of the sort that readers in previous generations would not expect to find in public figures' writings.

Ronald Reagan wrote of his father's excessive drinking; Nancy Reagan wrote of her own traumas, and those of her children, as well as her conflicts with both her own offspring and her stepchildren. She also wrote movingly of her own father's desertion and her loneliness when her actress-mother left her with relatives during touring seasons. (*See also* Nancy Davis Reagan.)

Of the president's four children, three wrote autobiographical books while he was still in office, and the fourth, Ron, wrote numerous articles, although most were not autobiographical. The younger daughter, Patti Davis, caused the most uproar and scandal among both denigraters and supporters of Ronald and Nancy Reagan, although her older half-brother, Michael, managed to contribute his share of controversy to the Reagan years.

Maureen Elizabeth Reagan, born January 4, 1941, was the first child of Ronald Reagan and his first wife, the actress Jane Wyman. She wrote a book; her memoir of life as Ronald Reagan's daughter is probably the least controversial of the brood's chronicles. Even so, Maureen Reagan tells of a first marriage to a terribly abusive husband, and, like her brother Michael, depicts Jane Wyman as a distant and difficult parent. Ronald Reagan, although described in glowing terms, nevertheless emerges as the idealized father who was somehow out of reach—the fact that Maureen went to boarding school as a child probably has something to do with that, along with the fact that her parents divorced, and, as was virtually automatic during the 1940s, her mother was the main custodial parent.

Nicknamed "Mermie," Maureen Reagan was a visible public figure during her father's presidency. She had become a Republican during her teen years, and later pointed out that she had been a Republican longer than her father. She also claims to have told her father in 1961 that he could be president in twenty years.

Married several times, Maureen Reagan revealed in her 1987 memoir that her first husband was physically abusive. After divorcing him, she pursued a career as an actress and had some moderate success in Hollywood. As her father became more political, so did she, and even before Ronald Reagan was governor, Maureen Reagan was active in state Republican politics.

Probably the only thing resembling a public clash between Ronald and Maureen Reagan came when Maureen entered the 1982 Republican senatorial primary in California. Asked his thoughts on his daughter's possible entry into elective politics, the president replied that he hoped she wouldn't do it. This came across to many people, including Maureen Reagan, as a rebuke.

According to Maureen, the president clarified his comment when she talked to him personally; he meant that political life was not easy, and that he would prefer his children not get involved in it. As to his failure to endorse her candidacy, Maureen reminded her readers that, as governor and president, Reagan always maintained a policy of not endorsing candidates in primary elections so as to avoid party division and so he could give credible support to the winner. In any case, Reagan voted for his daughter in the primary.

Michael Edward Reagan wrote a tormented memoir that told of sexual abuse by a trusted camp counselor and being accused by the Secret Service of kleptomania. The Secret Service's charges, according to Michael, led to a serious rift between him and his father and stepmother; by Michael's account, when he tried to tell Ronald Reagan that the Secret Service was mistaken, the president believed the Secret Service.

Ronald Reagan and Jane Wyman adopted the infant John Flaugher in 1946 and renamed him Michael Edward Reagan.

Michael describes his mother as difficult but writes glowingly of his father. In striking contrast to Patti Davis's accounts, he also writes very affectionately, though not entirely uncritically, of his step-mother Nancy Reagan, and of her parents, Dr. Loyal Davis and Edith Luckett Davis.

However, there was trouble ahead for the young Reagan. His parents divorced; he discovered he was adopted at an inopportune moment (his sister, Maureen, told him during a spat, when the two were small children); and then, worst of all, a young adult camp counselor sexually molested him when he was a preteen.

According to Michael, the Secret Service's allegation that he was a kleptomaniac was probably the reason that the Reagans did not see their second grandchild, Michael's daughter, until she was well over a year old. The trouble began, according to Michael, in March 1983, when a high-ranking Secret Service agent told him that the agents assigned to his protective detail observed him steal-ing on several occasions. They concluded that Michael was a klep-tomaniac who did not know what he was doing. Assuring Michael that he understood it was an illness, the agent told him that the Secret Service wanted to help him.

By Michael's account, most of the family believed the Secret Service, including his father, who wanted Michael to see a psychia-trist. No one, including the president, would listen to Michael's side of the story, which was that the report was a mistake. Michael figured that a new agent saw Michael tuck a child's shirt under his own shirt to protect it on a rainy day and had somehow gotten the impression that he was hiding a stolen item. The agent's report led to the Secret Service's "diagnosis" of kleptomania. More than a year later, Michael found out the full extent of the Secret Service's accusations.

It was that long before Michael met his parents face to face. In August 1984, just before the Republican convention, the president and Mrs. Reagan finally invited Michael and his wife, Colleen, to meet them to discuss "the problem." Michael demanded that his father tell him exactly what the Secret Service alleged that he had stolen. When President Reagan insisted that Michael see a psychi-atrist, Michael angrily asked if his father was taking the word of a nonfamily member over that of his own son. According to Michael, the president answered, "Yes, I am." Michael and Colleen left in a huff, but on the way out, Michael told his father that only when the Secret Service produced an itemized list of what he supposedly had stolen would he be interested in talking to his parents again.

Finally, a few weeks after President Reagan was nominated for his second term, a presidential assistant presented Michael with the list of items. According to the Secret Service, Michael had stolen the child's T-shirt that he tucked under his own shirt, a small bottle of bourbon from an airplane in 1982, mouthwash from a drugstore in Century City, a pin from a shop, and candy from a shop in the Intercontinental Hotel in London in 1982.

Michael thought that the list was absurd. The merchandise altogether was worth about fifteen dollars, and, in any case, he did not steal any of it. There was an explanation for each item; for example, in the Century City drugstore, Michael had already purchased one object, then remembered he needed some mouthwash. He told the clerk, paid for it, then picked it up from the shelf on the way out. The Secret Service agent on hand only saw him take the mouthwash, and never thought to ask Michael about it.

The story sounds like an assumption building on itself. Once the Secret Service decided that Michael Reagan was a thief, they interpreted what they saw in terms of their assumption. In any case, Michael Reagan maintains that the accusation was the reason for the much publicized rift between him and his parents during most of Ronald Reagan's presidency. The rift was well known, but not the reason for it.

Peace with the family was not forthcoming, and during one telephone argument with his father, Michael blurted out that he wished Ronald Reagan had never adopted him.

Eventually, Michael told the full story to his pastor, who agreed to speak to his parents. Michael believed he was too angry to tell the story himself. The president, first lady, Michael, his wife, and the pastor all met, and the pastor told Michael's story to Ronald and Nancy Reagan. When the pastor finished, the president apologized to his son and said he guessed the whole thing had been a misunderstanding.

Michael then asked why the president believed the pastor when he would not believe his own son, and why he believed the Secret Service in the first place. President Reagan answered that the Secret Service saved his life in 1981 and he trusted its members completely. On the other hand, the president added, Michael's "history" left "a lot to be desired."

Despite that rather unsatisfactory explanation, Michael made peace with his parents and later told them about the sexual molestation he had suffered as a boy. The breach was healed, at least between Michael Reagan and his parents. Michael remained unsure about other family members, particularly Maureen, who continued to believe the Secret Service even after Ronald and Nancy Reagan changed their minds.

The following year, Michael met his natural brother and through him made contact with his biological family, although his birth mother had died some years before. Michael's brother told him that he had only recently found out that President Reagan's son was his own brother recently, since his mother had told him on her deathbed. That cleared up a mystery for Michael's brother; the mother, who gave up her first baby for adoption because she was poor and unmarried, kept a scrapbook for years, and her second son always thought that it was a documentation of Ronald Reagan's career. The book had photographs of Ronald Reagan and his family at all stages of Reagan's career after 1946, and her son assumed that his mother was simply an avid Ronald Reagan fan.

After she told him that Michael Reagan was her first son, he realized that Michael appeared in every picture in the scrapbook. Michael's birth mother had not put together a record of Ronald Reagan; she had assembled a chronicle of her lost son.

Michael Reagan spent the first few years of his father's presidency trying to make a go of several business ventures, and he admits that he used his father's name to enhance his prospects. He was a professional boat racer (he won a professional championship, in fact), and a boat salesman, and hosted a television game show called *Lingo*.

While one or two members of the Reagan administration later wrote unkindly of Michael (one reports that some members of the

White House press office pejoratively referred to Michael as "Sonny Boy"), the former president and first lady wrote quite kindly of the elder Reagan son in their own books, although Nancy Reagan wrote more candidly and in more detail about Michael than did Ronald Reagan. My Turn relates Michael's revelations of the past sexual abuse, and Nancy Reagan also writes of the various troubles she had with Michael during his teen years, although she omits the klepto-mania accusation. In fact, Mrs. Reagan goes into considerably more detail about Michael's teenage and young adulthood than about the tensions and rifts when Ronald Reagan was president.

Born October 21, 1952, Patricia Ann Reagan, better known as Patti Davis, was Ronald Reagan's third child and his second daughter. She is Nancy Reagan's first child.

The president's rebellious younger daughter published several tell-all books, thinly disguised as fiction, and scandalized her family while angering her father's supporters. She sought work as an actress, reluctantly by her account, in order to make a decent living—and, partly, to support a drug habit of diet pills. She managed to net a few guest-starring roles on several television series, and her acting was competent if not distinguished.

Patti Davis took her mother's maiden name rather than her father's and has not gone by Patti Reagan during her adult life. Both her parents have written that Patti Davis opposed Reagan's entry into politics, and Patti Davis herself has made no secret of her displeasure at her father's career choice and of her opposition to his political views. During Reagan's presidency, Davis embarrassed him by publicly advocating the Equal Rights Amendment and taking up with anti-nuclear activists.

During the second term, the bad feeling between Patti Davis and her parents became public when she published two novels that portrayed people very much like Ronald and Nancy Reagan as dishonest, negligent parents. Openly hurt, Nancy Reagan told reporters that she had tried to be a good mother. The president generally avoided commenting on his daughter's escapades.

Like her two older siblings, Patti Davis wrote an undisguised memoir of her life as a member of the Reagan family; it was published in 1992, after she had already gained notoriety with the two novels. In *As I See It*, Davis depicted a turbulent home life during her childhood and teenage years.

The memoir targets Nancy Reagan and is a bit easier on Ronald Reagan, although neither parent fares well under the daughter's determined pen. She describes her father as essentially passive when it came to child rearing and recounts that he refused to listen to her side of any number of stories, particularly when she told him that Nancy Reagan often physically struck her.

According to Patti Davis, Ronald Reagan was usually puzzled by his daughter's rebelliousness and whenever she told him of Mrs. Reagan's violent behavior, he would accuse her of fabricating. When it came to any sort of complaint against her mother, by Davis's account, Ronald Reagan was always unreceptive and unbelieving.

In this, Patti Davis's accounts are consistent with those of her older brother Michael, who also reported that their father would not listen to criticism of Nancy Reagan. For that matter, both siblings wrote that Ronald Reagan often would not listen to his children's accounts of a great many matters; when they stood accused of various misdeeds, he tended not to let them explain themselves.

Patti Davis also describes her mother's stepfather, Loyal Davis, as a martinet. Her grandmother Edith Luckett Davis consistently blamed Patti Davis herself for the ongoing strife with Nancy Reagan during Patti's teen years. Nancy Reagan, on the other hand, wrote entirely lovingly of her mother and stepfather. The contrasts between the two depictions are striking.

Nancy Reagan receives the most blistering criticism of all. According to her daughter, Mrs. Reagan was addicted to pills and physically abusive, and had no real identity or sense of herself apart from being Mrs. Ronald Reagan. Davis wrote that even when she was a teenager, most of the family rallied behind her mother when word got around that they were having fights. On one occasion, Patti Davis retaliated when her mother struck her, and pushed her mother onto a nearby bed. By Davis's account, her grandfather, Loyal Davis, remonstrated with her for attacking her mother.

Despite areas of agreement and corroboration, Patti Davis's depiction of her parents' personalities does not quite match those in her siblings' books; Michael Reagan, in particular, writes more affectionately, even lovingly, of both Ronald Reagan and Nancy Reagan. But Patti Davis paints an almost completely dark picture of her life with her parents and is none too charitable in detailing her relations with her brothers and sister, either, although in general she treats them more kindly.

For their part, both President Reagan and Nancy Reagan wrote about their respective relationships with Patti in each of their autobiographies. Ronald Reagan wrote sympathetically and diplomatically that it was hard for all of his children to grow up with celebrity parents, and then especially difficult for them, as young adults, to have their parents be president and first lady. Reagan recalled that Patti cried when he first decided to run for governor, and Patti Davis herself wrote of her despair when her father entered politics, describing his elections as governor and president as very unwelcome events in her own life.

Nancy Reagan, in *My Turn*, wrote of her relationship with her daughter at more length than did the former president. Mrs. Reagan commented that her relationship with Patti has been painful and disappointing, and acknowledged that the two have been consistently prone to conflict. Nancy Reagan's book does not address Patti's accusations of physical abuse or drug addiction.

After former president Reagan was diagnosed with Alzheimer's disease in 1994, Patti Davis publicly reconciled with her family and published a book about the reconciliation. Even so, some of Davis's accounts of her mother's personality and conduct accord with the negative accounts published by Donald T. Regan and other former members of the Reagan administration. This does not in and of itself vouch for the accuracy of the accounts, but it has contributed to the controversy about the former first lady.

Thanks to such accounts as Patti Davis's and Donald T. Regan's, Nancy Reagan had to defend herself more frequently and more thoroughly than any first lady since Mary Todd Lincoln. Only Hillary Clinton's difficulties have exceeded Nancy Reagan's. Patti Davis, Michael Reagan, Donald T. Regan, and others have done much to define Ronald and Nancy Reagan's images for a large segment of the American public.

The youngest son, Ronald Prescott Reagan, known as Ron Reagan, was born May 20, 1958, and has somehow managed to resist the public confessional's siren call. After quitting the Joffrey Ballet Company, Ron Reagan pursued a career in journalism. He has practiced real journalism, rather than join in the crusade to describe his family's dysfunction to a bemused world.

Intelligent, quick witted, and well informed, Ron Reagan also has his father's easygoing presence before a camera, and he put these qualities to good use as host of a short-lived public-affairs discussion show on commercial television. The show offered consistently high-quality forums on social and political issues. Young Reagan was as informed and informative as many of his guests and displayed something of a genius for conducting discussions among experts.

Ron Reagan also displayed highly professional writing ability as a journalist and is easily the best writer among the Reagans. He guest-hosted *Saturday Night Live*, appeared in a political satire television show (in which huge, grotesque puppets represented various political figures, including President and Mrs. Reagan), and made a commercial for the American Express Company.

During his father's presidency, he was as publicly visible as his siblings but managed to avoid scandal. Early in his father's White House years, the younger Reagan married his live-in companion, thus negating the potential scandal of unwed domesticity. (*See also* Nancy Davis Reagan; Ronald Wilson Reagan.)

REAGANOMICS

Broadly speaking, Reaganomics—the collective name given to the economic ideas and policies of Ronald Reagan and his administration—was composed of supply-side theory, traditional conservative principles involving largely unregulated business, and reliance on the private sector for meeting the nation's social responsibilities. Along with conservative tax-reform measures, these principles created a national atmosphere generally favorable to business.

In his memoirs, Ronald Reagan wrote that he did not base his economic program on supply-side theory and that those who thought so were mistaken. Reagan wrote that his guiding principle was that which the Laffer curve delineated: Overtaxation dampens incentive to earn. Reagan considered this a common-sense principle, and it was the basis of his economic policies and tax-reform programs.

Despite the former president's disclaimer, many economic analysts consider supply-side theory a vital aspect of Reaganomics. According to Donald T. Regan, who was Reagan's Treasury secretary and White House chief of staff, supply-side theory holds that incentives will stimulate economic growth, and so it is necessary to encourage business to produce and to encourage individuals to save money. Supply-siders advocate lower taxes, deregulation, and other measures to provide incentives to business. In other words, supply-side theory advocates stimulating the suppliers, rather than the consumers. Theoretically, in such an economic environment, with government spending held down, inflation would decline and more capital would be created, which would, in turn, expand government revenues without taxation.

The theory further holds that direct assistance to the poor has an effect opposite to its intention, robbing people of their initiative. Of course, that is an old argument; during the 1930s, President Franklin Roosevelt's opponents often criticized the New Deal on those very grounds. Supply-siders, on the other hand, were accused of advocating a callous disregard for social responsibility, and supply-side economics was seen by its critics as simply a new term for the old trickle-down theory of the Great Depression days during Herbert Hoover's presidency.

In a 1981 article for *The Nation*, for instance, Martin Carnoy and Derek Shearer criticized President Reagan and the supply-siders' notion that lower income taxes would stimulate citizens to work harder and save more. Carnoy and Shearer wrote that a family making an annual income of $25,000 would get a $400 tax refund in 1982 and an $800 refund in 1984 under Reagan's first-term tax plan. But, the two critics pointed out, real wages were at the time declining, so that any savings in taxes would go into maintaining the family's standard of living, rather than elevating financial activity."

Conroy and Shearer also doubted that businesses would put their tax savings into jobs creation; consolidating and monopolizing were more often the goals in the early 1980s, rather than expanding and creating jobs, according to this critique. The article summarized the major contemporary arguments against supply-side economics.

Another critical element of Reaganomics was the free-market theory, most prominently propounded by economist Milton Friedman, that the Federal Reserve should set a fixed rate of growth for the national money supply. Some economists saw the two principles—Friedman's fixed rate of growth and supply-side theory—as incompatible, but others, including Donald T. Regan, saw no essential conflict between the two.

None of this was particularly surprising or radical as a conservative economic policy. But in 1980, Reagan ran for president after several decades of heavy government spending; even conservative presidents, such as Eisenhower and Nixon, had spent considerable federal funds on various social programs in the post–World War II era. Reagan was the first Republican president since Herbert Hoover to commit himself to a genuinely conservative supply-side policy.

Reaganomics, as a policy, was highly controversial, as it involved sharp cuts in social spending that resulted in the end, or at least diminishment, of many long-standing programs. Consequently, many critics see the Reagan years as a time when liberal social policies and programs lost considerable ground, while Reagan supporters still hail the reversal of decades of liberal policies.

Whether Reaganomics succeeded or failed remains a subject of debate among historians, economists, and others, although it certainly is worth noting that, at the end of 1988, the United States was $1.5 trillion deeper in debt than when President Reagan took office. Many critics consider the greatly increased deficit the prime legacy of Reaganomics.

Critics also point to the drastically increased economic disparities between rich and poor, or any number of other economic inequities in American life. But Reagan supporters view

Reaganomics as the policy that revitalized the United States economy in the 1980s.

Still others, such as David Stockman, assert that Federal Reserve chairman Paul Volcker's monetary policies brought about the 1980s economic revival, and not the administration's economic policies at all. The debate will go on forever, if not longer. (*See also* Deficit; Laffer Curve; Reagan Recession/Reagan Recovery; David Stockman; Stock Market Crash of 1987; Tax Reforms; Trade Policies; Paul Volcker and the Fed.)

REAGAN RECESSION/REAGAN RECOVERY

During the early part of Ronald Reagan's first term, the United States suffered its worst recession since the Great Depression of the 1930s. Unemployment hit double digits, and there was speculation that Reagan might be yet another single-term president.

Between 1981 and 1983, unemployment rose to 10.8 percent, more than 11.5 million people lost jobs, about 10 million more had to take lower-paying jobs, and there was a startling increase in homelessness across the nation.

Because the federal government cut social spending in Reagan's first term, many of the traditional safety nets, such as food stamps and housing subsidies, were drastically weakened or nonexistent as more Americans fell below the officially recognized poverty line.

But during the previous year, the administration had backed off a bit from supply-side Reaganomics, and the Federal Reserve had expanded the money supply and lowered interest rates. The stock market responded favorably, and the Reagan recovery was in full swing during 1983. The inflation rate radically declined from about 14 percent in 1980 to less than 2 percent in 1983.

Capitol spending declined, and the federal deficit reached undreamed-of heights—nearly $200 billion by the end of 1983.

President Reagan's standing in the public-opinion polls declined precipitiously during the recession, hitting an approval rating of 35 percent early in 1983. By the campaign season of 1984, unemployment was down and Reagan's popularity was high. The president was not too modest to claim credit for the recovery, pointing to it as evidence of the wisdom of his economic policies.

Whether Reagan's claim was justified or not, the voters were generally satisfied, and the state of the economy very likely contributed heavily to his landslide reelection in 1984. The Democratic presidential nominee, former Vice President Walter Mondale, charged Reagan with mismanaging the economy and reminded the voters of the recession. But the recession had faded from public memory, and recovery was felt throughout the land, thus weakening the challenger and favoring the incumbent. (*See also* Reaganomics; David Stockman; Stock Market Crash of 1987; Unemployment; Paul Volcker and the Fed.)

REAGAN REVOLUTION

Ronald Reagan and his supporters sought to reverse what they saw as the liberal, big-government trends of the previous fifty years. They set about their task with a speed and decisiveness that startled even many of those who voted for Reagan in 1980. The "Reagan Revolution" was as much a departure from the political status quo as Franklin Roosevelt's New Deal was in its day.

The Reagan Revolution heralded the ascension of a newly militant conservatism to the national agenda, and the fading of the old liberal, activist politics that had held sway since the Roosevelt era. Reagan conducted the most avowedly conservative administration since the 1920s; even the Republican administrations of Eisenhower, Nixon, and Ford did not pursue the conservative agenda to the extent that the Reagan administration did. Additionally, the Republicans took the Senate in 1980 and held it for six years.

Although Reagan's 1980 election victory was not a landslide in the popular vote, he still won by a solid majority, and the electoral-vote margin was overwhelming; also, the Republicans made considerable gains in the House of Representatives besides winning the Senate. Consequently, it seemed to many observers in 1980 that the Republican victory would usher in a national realignment in American elective politics, as the old order unraveled.

Millions of voters who were neither doctrinal conservatives nor the movement conservatives of the Christian Right voted for Reagan for reasons more immediate than ideological objections to the New Deal. Many voters were angry and frightened by the economy; inflation and stagnation (stagflation) were the order of the day. Reagan's campaign promises to cut taxes proved very attractive.

Other voters were unnerved by the social changes of the 1960s and 1970s. Some of these voters, though conservative, were not rabidly so, and they hoped that the new administration would restore what they thought of as a "normal" America. Reagan took office with the expectation that he would restore something many voters thought lost, a conservative America that Reagan himself seemed to embody and personify. In this respect, Reagan found a ready audience for his homespun views on morality, patriotism, and religion.

During the first two years of the first term, the Reagan White House showed a legislative mastery and dominance that helped to actualize the new conservative agenda, and thus began the first direct conservative assault on the entrenched liberal social welfare complex. The Reagan Revolution precipitated drastic cuts in public spending, a hard line in international affairs, supply-side economic policies, and an attempt to reduce the social welfare role of the federal government. On the other hand, the Reagan Revolution certainly posited an active role for the federal government on selected moral issues; under Reagan, the government went on an anti-pornography campaign and openly opposed legal abortion.

The Reagan Revolution was not empty rhetoric, as the administration vigorously pursued its policies and had many successes, especially during the first term. Reagan's victory energized the entire conservative movement, and the 1980s saw some of the most divisive political conflicts since the 1960s. The opposition was energized, but the Reagan forces proved very strong, politically, during Reagan's presidency.

It is too early to assess the full historical impact of the Reagan Revolution, but it certainly had wide-ranging effects on the nation. In the 1990s, the Republicans, and not the Democrats, are the majority party; the Democrats have been driven more to the center by the conservative tide that the Republicans represent. Liberalism has fallen out of fashion, and many pundits joke about the *L* word. Since Reagan's time, the conservatives have been setting the terms of the nation's political discourse and have gained considerable success and power by attacking liberalism and Democrats. The Democrats are in the position of having to argue that they, too, stand for law and order and family values.

The Reagan Revolution, while not inventing these conditions, solidified them and carried the Republican party, the federal government, and the entire political arena to the right. (*See also* Christian Right/New Right; Elections—Presidential; New Deal Coalition; Reaganomics; Franklin Delano Roosevelt.)

FRANKLIN DELANO ROOSEVELT

Thirty-third president of the United States (1933–1945), Roosevelt, a Democrat, was elected to the office four times. Between 1933, when he first took office, and 1945, when he died, a few months into his fourth term, he was a major proponent of the liberal, federal activism that conservatives such as Ronald Reagan stood against.

Although Reagan later opposed most of Roosevelt's New Deal philosophies, he many times recalled that the older president was a hero of his youth. In his White House memoirs, Reagan wrote that Roosevelt was still one of his favorite presidents, and he remembered Roosevelt's personality, style, and leadership with respect and affection.

Roosevelt instituted his New Deal programs in order to combat the Great Depression. The New Deal was a haphazard collection of federal programs aimed at stimulating the economy by imposing some amount of regulation on business and using federal funds to create relief programs and jobs. Roosevelt also presided over most of the World War II years, dying just before the war ended. He left a legacy of a federal government active in the nation's social affairs, a variety of federal regulatory agencies, and a large military establishment.

Franklin Roosevelt came to maturity during the Progressive Era in the early twentieth century, when the federal government embarked on a course of active involvement in social welfare, labor relations, and regulation of business and commerce. There was a general trend toward democratization of American political institutions (for instance, in 1914, United States senators were elected by direct vote of the people for the first time ever). Roosevelt absorbed many political principles from his cousin, Theodore Roosevelt, and Woodrow Wilson, in whose administration Franklin Roosevelt served as undersecretary of the Navy.

A basic tenet of classic progressivism is that a liberal democracy must use the instrumentalities of government to ensure equality, progress, and freedom, and this principle was central to Roosevelt's approach to his presidency in the 1930s. He believed workers must be protected from exploitive employers and that business must be regulated in order to rein in tendencies toward avarice and exploitation. Progressivism holds that it is the power and the duty of the federal government to implement such measures, since it oversees the nation as a whole.

At the same time, Roosevelt did not favor mere welfare, for he believed that limitless relief would sap people's initiative and promote permanent dependence on government largesse. Roosevelt preferred to give relief to those who truly could not provide for themselves or their families. For the rest, he favored job-creation programs, such as the Works Progress Administration (WPA), which put the unemployed to work building hospitals, schools, bridges, highways, and other public-works projects. The New Deal was never intended to be a national welfare program, despite what some of its critics charged.

Neither did Roosevelt intend the New Deal as some sort of conversion to socialism or communism, as other critics charged. Roosevelt publicly said many times that he sought to reform capitalism in order to save it. He believed in free enterprise, but he believed corporate behavior needed to be regulated, and the federal government was the only entity capable of doing the regulating.

Roosevelt believed that every American had the right to a certain standard of living, and the nation had to guarantee conditions to make that possible. Again, regulation was necessary, according to this view, because interested parties could not be relied upon to ensure equity on their own. George Bush's "thousand points of light" never would have lit the interest of Roosevelt and the New Dealers.

Ronald Reagan came to maturity during Roosevelt's presidency, and, as a young man, was a solid Roosevelt supporter and New Dealer. In old age, while Reagan professed admiration for FDR, he argued that the old New Deal policies had become outdated. Reagan claimed that Roosevelt never meant to promote or perpetuate popular dependency on federal welfare programs, and he was given to quoting some of Roosevelt's warnings against the danger of causing such dependency through overuse of federal relief programs.

During Reagan's presidency, many commentators proclaimed the end of the Roosevelt era. Reagan's policies greatly curtailed the intense federal social involvement that Roosevelt had instituted and championed. At the same time, many of the constituencies that had supported Roosevelt and later Democrats became bastions of support for Reagan and the Republican Party in a startling partisan realignment. (*See also* New Deal Coalition.)

Since the 1980s, political analysts have often spoken of Roosevelt and Reagan in the same breath. Both left their stamps on the nation, Roosevelt ushering in a new period of social activism for the federal government, and Reagan reversing a long trend of activist government. But in the final analysis, Roosevelt probably had the more lasting social impact, since many of his innovative social programs, such as Social Security, became institutionalized to the point that even many conservative voters oppose abolishing them or even drastically changing them.

President Reagan considered reducing Social Security, among many other measures to curb the New Deal legacy, but he found himself forced by public sentiment to back away from such measures. Even so, Reagan still led the assault that hastened the breakdown of the old New Deal Coalition.

The turn away from social welfare notwithstanding, the presidency has shown no signs of surrendering the power that it has gathered during the twentieth century, and a good deal of that power was gathered and institutionalized by Franklin Roosevelt. While conservative presidents and conservative presidential candidates proclaim their opposition to big government, once in office they continue to use presidential powers extensively. The conservative presidents who have held office since Roosevelt, including Ronald Reagan, have sought to modify the federal government's roles and functions in some respects, but the powerful presidency has remained.

Ronald Reagan, conservative as he was, still exercised considerable executive power as president. The Reagan administration made a point of not consulting Congress on any number of initiatives it took, particularly in foreign policy. In so doing, this conservative president contributed to perpetuating the powerful, modern presidency. No president since Franklin Roosevelt has done otherwise. (*See also* Anticommunism; William Casey and the CIA; Iran-Contra; Reaganomics.)

S

DAVID STOCKMAN

A student radical in the sixties and Ronald Reagan's budget director in the eighties, David Stockman was a crusading supply-sider for a time, and one of the most famous and visible members of the Reagan administration during the first term. In the early days, he carried the gospel of Reaganomics to Congress and the public, and then embarrassed the administration when he told an interviewer that he did not believe in the economic program he was espousing.

Stockman joined the president-elect's prospective team after serving two terms in the House of Representatives as a Republican from Michigan. Stockman believed in an old-time capitalism—that is, he believed that deregulating capitalism almost completely would stimulate the economy and thus achieve the greatest good for the greatest number. He wanted drastic tax cuts, and equally drastic cuts in government spending, except for the military. Stockman called this scheme his Grand Doctrine.

Stockman's idea for liberating the economy involved what he called a "spare and stingy" approach to "minimalist government," which would mean cutting social programs, farm subsidies, foreign aid, Social Security, oil-depletion allowances—you name it, Stockman wanted to cut it. He believed that many people would suffer in the short run but that the long-term effect would be widespread prosperity. Furthermore, Stockman believed social welfare was not the federal government's concern, and he sought a return to

235

the nonregulating, laissez-faire government of a bygone era, in order to set the economy free.

Stockman's laissez-faire approach failed to endear him to many members of the administration. Treasury secretary Donald T. Regan later wrote that the young budget director was "opinionated to the point of zealotry." Regan's interpretation of Stockman's theory was that the federal budget should "run the economy" and, by extension, determine social policy. According to Regan, this position was essentially a philosophical principle that would be effectuated by bureaucratic measures.

Stockman believed, according to Regan, that the Office of Management and Budget (Stockman's domain) should control the money flow into the Cabinet departments; consequently, the budget director would be able to determine de facto cuts by starving designated departments and programs, and funding the ones considered more economically productive. Therefore, the president's budget office could control the spending cuts, which would cause inflation and interest rates to go down and prosperity to return.

Stockman's Office of Management and Budget also played a key role in the Reagan administration's drive to deregulate the economy. Stockman's office subjected federal regulations to cost-benefit analysis and, as journalist Lou Cannon has noted, tried to take executive action on certain issues of deregulation that, under different circumstances in different administrations, might have fallen to Congress to remedy legislatively.

Part of Regan's critique of Stockman's position was that it involved more, not less, centralization of power and thus undermined Stockman's very idea that capitalism should be set free. Regan believed that the country needed less economic centralization, not more, and that Stockman was in effect proposing a highly regulated economy—regulated, that is, by the very government that Stockman argued should stay out of the economy's way. Regan believed he had spotted a critical contradiction in Stockman's thinking.

Whether contradictory or not, Stockman's budget proposal ran into a solid wall of resistance in the Cabinet. Each Cabinet officer balked at having his or her own departmental budget cut, and the

Democrats in Congress, predictably, also proved hostile. Worse, from Stockman's viewpoint, President Reagan himself thought some of Stockman's cuts too severe or at least politically infeasible, such as slashing the hallowed oil-depletion allowances.

Considering that Stockman spent two terms in Congress, it is difficult to understand how or why the politics of the situation caused the former divinity student a crisis of faith. In June 1981, six months into Reagan's presidency, Stockman had the revelation that "maybe we were not all crusaders on the road to Jerusalem." Governance, Stockman wrote later, did not run on "pure reason, analysis, and the clash of ideologies." Stockman now discovered that politics involved force of personalities, "the effrontery of bloated egos," and sheer desire for power. His Grand Doctrine began to seem utopian to him, in his sadder but wiser maturity.

In November 1981, the budget director went public with his crisis of faith. An article appeared in that month's *Atlantic* wherein Stockman was quoted as saying he did not actually believe in the programs he had been trying to get through Congress. He revealed that he essentially cooked figures to please the president; that is, after calculating that Reagan's proposed tax cuts would produce severe budget deficits, he had his computers reprogrammed.

Worse, the *Atlantic* article quoted Stockman as calling the entire supply-side theory a "Trojan horse" that hid a trickle-down economic program to cut taxes for the wealthy. Stockman lowered his stock in the administration even further when he got into a running fight with defense secretary Caspar Weinberger over defense spending. The president intervened and told Stockman that the administration had promised to increase defense spending, and that the Defense Department was to get whatever it needed.

The *Atlantic* article and his resistance to defense spending increases contributed to making Stockman's position in the administration untenable. After 1981, the public heard a lot less from, and about, Stockman, but he stayed on until 1985, when he resigned to take a Wall Street job.

Many commentators, including some members of the Reagan administration, have noted that the sort of shenanigans Stockman indulged in during 1981 would have gotten him fired by many other presidents and surely would have finished his career had he done the same sorts of things in, say, a private corporation. But President Reagan, according to many (including Donald T. Regan), did not like confrontations and disliked firing people. Instead, Stockman lingered on, living with the enmity of his fellows for another four years.

To his conservative critics, Stockman's worst apostasy was his repudiation of the hallowed Laffer curve, reflected in his insistence that the administration needed to raise taxes. Stockman later wrote that as early as November 1981, he believed Reaganomics was not working and that supply-side theory would not ultimately salvage the economy. Rather, Stockman believed there might be some short-term growth, but following supply-side theory would eventually dump the entire economy "into the drink." The Reagan Revolution, he wrote in 1986, would leave economic wreckage in its wake.

Stockman's 1986 memoir, *The Triumph of Politics: Why the Reagan Revolution Failed,* was one of the earliest critiques of the Reagan administration written by a former insider. Stockman severely criticized the still-incumbent president and the administration in blistering terms. At the same time, the book is a vivid look at the legislative and negotiating processes of Washington, with intricate details of the give-and-take in the conference rooms. It is also a fascinating account of personalities and events of Stockman's years in the Reagan administration. (*See also* Deregulation; Laffer Curve; Tax Reform.)

STOCK MARKET CRASH OF 1987

With the Reagan economic recovery, consumer confidence returned and Reagan won a landslide reelection in 1984. A subsequent increase in consumer spending set off a wave of stock market speculation. In August 1982, the bull market took flight, and the Dow Jones average stood at around 777 for the next five years. During the middle 1980s, the national business amosphere remained buoyant, as multimillionaires like Lee Iaccoca of Chrysler and Donald Trump, with his vast financial and real estate empire, became contemporary folk heroes. (*See also* Elections—Presidential; Reagan Recession/Reagan Recovery.)

Starting in 1985, a series of corporate scandals jolted the nation and undermined the optimistic mood. Officials of E.F. Hutton pleaded guilty to charges of manipulating funds and defrauding several hundred banks; the notorious Ivan Boesky went to prison in 1986 for insider trading, and even Trump lost some of his luster as his empire fell on comparatively hard times.

These may have been harbingers of what was to come. During the year previous to the October 1987 crash, some perceptive and worried observers saw signs of trouble ahead, but their voices sounded faint in the still-euphoric investment climate. A few Wall Street investment managers wondered if the 1920s were not in fact replaying themselves and another crash was imminent. One manager advised his clients accordingly. The venerable economist John Kenneth Galbraith, too, published a warning about current trends in speculation creating conditions for an economic crash.

On October 19, 1987, a Monday, almost exactly fifty years after "Black Monday" of 1929, the stock market crashed. As the day approached, the Dow measured 2722.42. Investors anticipated that the next year would see it rise at least another thousand points, if not more. But on the fateful day, the Dow fell 508 points, the largest drop during a single day ever. A fifth of the paper value of all the nation's stocks vanished into thin air, and people all over the nation wondered if Black Monday 1987 would have results similar to Black Monday 1929—would there be another Great Depression?

During that terrible day, banks called in loans, and large corporations found themselves unable to trade their stock, since everyone stopped buying. Banks also refused to extend extra credit to clients caught short in the crash. A general panic took hold, and one partner of a major company later said that he thought the stock market came within one hour of utter collapse.

Almost literally at the last moment, the Federal Reserve Board suspended its tight money and credit policy and pumped cash into the banking system. The Fed also purchased government securities and issued guarantees to banks that it would provide the necessary liquidity for assets to flow.

The effects were immediate. In Chicago, the Board of Trade's Major Market Index rose dramatically, and that reversal of the day's decline inspired enough last-minute confidence for buying to resume in Chicago, the last market of the day still open and doing business. The Fed did its job; with trading revived, many major banks eased their credit restrictions.

As that week went on, the markets rallied. The day after the crash saw a rally of 102.27 on the Dow, which was a record, and the next day there was an even bigger rally, of 186.84 points. Still, the upsurge immediately after the crash did not convince Wall Street, the nation, or the world that there would not be another Great Depression. The weeks after the crash saw widespread worry and finger-pointing, and the general fear and mistrust did not help the Reagan administration's damaged public image.

The crash of 1987, coming on top of the Iran-Contra scandal, added to President Reagan's troubles. Several newsmagazines commented that the president now seemed "irrelevant" to the state of affairs. One magazine solemnly declared the 1980s over and Reagan's presidency moribund.

Reagan puzzled many people during the week of Black Monday when he tried to dismiss the crash and insisted that "the underlying economy remains sound." Financial analysts and writers struck back with a vengeance, blaming the crash entirely on Reagan's economic policies, on his tax cuts combined with increased defense spending. The president, one columnist wrote, created the illusion that the nation could "live beyond its means."

Journalist Haynes Johnson pointedly noted the irony that Wall Street investors and the "yuppie generation," the very people who cheered Reagan and Reaganomics when the boom was on, turned on him when the crash took away their "dream of easy riches and endlessly rising stock prices and profits."

Certainly, Reagan and the Reagan administration encouraged the wave of speculation that triggered the crash of 1987, and then the president refused to acknowledge the situation's seriousness when the crash came. But it is also an abdication of responsibility to attribute the crash solely to the administration, when the investors' behavior itself fueled both the bull market and the panic that set in when the market faltered.

The Federal Reserve's quick and decisive action likely averted a depression, or at least made a critical contribution to avoiding general disaster. Although the administration had little to do with the solution, in time Reagan regained his standing in the public-opinion polls, as both the crash of 1987 and the Iran-Contra scandal faded from memory.

In his memoir, Reagan gave a terse explanation of the stock market crash. Only a couple of days before the crash, he wrote, he worried about the money supply and wondered if the Federal Reserve Board was being too tight in circulating money. In retrospect, however, he believed the market crashed mainly because stocks were overpriced and investors suddenly realized it. (*See also* Paul Volcker and the Fed.)

STRATEGIC DEFENSE INITIATIVE

Popularly known as Star Wars, the Strategic Defense Initiative for a time held center stage in the controversies between the United States and the Soviet Union. SDI was a plan for an elaborate, space-age antimissile system. Theoretically, antimissile devices orbiting the earth in outer space would be able to destroy incoming missiles before they could reach the United States. The program, if workable, would give the United States a definitive strategic advantage over the Soviet Union, and over everyone else as well.

The Soviets took the SDI plan to mean that the United States sought a foolproof strategic defense so as to guarantee a first-strike advantage over the Soviet Union—at least the Soviets took that stance as a negotiating position.

SDI's eventual workability remained debatable, as the technology for such a system did not exist during Ronald Reagan's presidency, nor does it exist in the middle 1990s. Some analysts commented that for Reagan to support SDI, in light of 1980s technology, would be something like President Woodrow Wilson wanting to begin research on sending astronauts to the moon, in the context of 1918 technology.

Still, Reagan's commitment to SDI worried the Soviets and helped intensify the president's renewal of Cold War hostility in American foreign policy. Whether workable or not, SDI at the very least suggested America's intentions of attaining nuclear strategic superiority, making it incompatible with arms control, or with any sort of détente, for that matter.

By Reagan's own account, SDI was not originally conceived by scientists. Reagan did not like the "mutual assured destruction" arrangement that pertained prior to his presidency; he described "MAD" as a tacit nuclear balance of power in that the two super-powers unofficially sought to maintain nuclear parity, and Reagan wanted to ensure American superiority in military matters.

Accordingly, Reagan and the Pentagon developed the idea of a defensive shield for the United States. The scheme took various forms over the years, usually involving devices orbiting the earth, capable of launching antimissile missiles or other sorts of destructive, high-tech weapons that could destroy airborne nuclear missiles. Despite Reagan's stated commitment to military superiority, he publicly offered to share the technology (once it was developed) with the Soviets and others, if they would agree to strategic arms limitations.

Whether or not scientists originally dreamed up SDI, a number of scientists liked the idea and encouraged the president to pursue it. The most prominent was Edward Teller, who worked on the original Manhattan Project that developed the atomic bomb and was known as the "father" of the hydrogen bomb. Teller insisted that a workable space-defense system was possible, and he became one of SDI's most vocal and public supporters.

The problems with SDI, however, went beyond mere feasibility and Soviet discomfort, for a critical question arose as to whether such a space shield for the United States would violate the ABM Treaty, by which the United States and the Soviet Union had agreed not to test or deploy any new antimissile systems. Further,

SDI might have violated the 1967 Outer Space Treaty, which prohibited deploying weapons of mass destruction, or testing weapons, in outer space.

Whether or not Reagan meant SDI as a bargaining chip, the Soviets quickly saw it as one, and Mikhail Gorbachev made SDI a centerpiece of Soviet arms negotiating. The Soviet leader wanted the United States to forgo developing SDI, and accused Reagan of seeking definitive strategic nuclear advantage—and, of course, first-strike capacity.

Critics speculated as to whether the Reagan administration really believed the system could work or was actually playing yet another card in its efforts to keep the Soviet Union competing in an arms race that would eventually bankrupt the Soviet economy. Whatever the administration's motive, President Reagan always maintained that he believed the Strategic Defense Initiative could work, and that it could break the "mutually assured destruction" of the nuclear arms race. He continued to maintain that this was his belief long after he left the White House. (*See also* Arms Control/Arms Race; Foreign Policy/Foreign Relations; Mikhail Gorbachev.)

SUPREME COURT AND FEDERAL JUDICIARY

Ronald Reagan came to the presidency following a long period of activism by the Supreme Court and the federal judiciary in general. Even though Republican presidents Richard Nixon and Gerald Ford had appointed Supreme Court justices and federal judges, the liberal justices still held a thin majority on the Court, and a large percentage of federal judges had sat since the days of Kennedy and Johnson. The Democratic presidents left a liberal legacy in the nation's federal courts, and Republicans—mainstream conservatives as well as New Right activists—hailed the Reagan presidency as an opportunity to shift the focus of the national judiciary toward conservatism.

They were not incorrect in this assumption, for many of the federal judges were getting older and looking to retire, and the liberal Supreme Court justices were aging, too. Consequently, in his eight years in office, President Reagan named 78 appeals court judges and 290 district court judges,   all confirmed by the Senate. Thus, the Reagan administration left its mark by replacing over half of the sitting federal judiciary.

The Supreme Court later proved to be the supreme battleground, but things went smoothly enough at first. When the first vacancy of his presidency arose in 1981, Reagan remembered his campaign promise to appoint a woman to the Supreme Court. Later that year, Sandra Day O'Connor became the first woman associate justice, and added a conservative vote to the Court.

There was not another Supreme Court vacancy for nearly five years after Justice O'Connor's confirmation, but when it came it afforded Reagan the chance to leave one of the most enduring stamps on the Court available to a president. In 1986, Chief Justice Warren Burger retired, leaving it to President Reagan to nominate a successor. Reagan chose the conservative Nixon appointee William Renquist, who was confirmed by the Senate. There now sat a reliably conservative chief justice of the United States, and the impending retirements or deaths among the aging senior justices would afford greater opportunities for a Republican judiciary.

Altogether, besides making Renquist chief justice Reagan appointed three associate justices. After O'Connor, the next vacancy for an associate justice came up in 1986, and the administration had an easy time getting Antonin E. Scalia confirmed. But the Senate made up for its compliance when Reagan nominated the controversial Robert H. Bork; the Senate Democrats mounted a ferocious campaign against Bork's confirmation in 1987, and Reagan was forced to accept a very public, very bitter defeat.

After Bork's rejection, Reagan nominated U.S. appeals court judge Douglas Ginsburg, a young former Harvard law professor. Ginsburg seemed fairly moderate, and the administration expected he would be more acceptable to the Senate Judiciary Committee, but things went wrong anyway. The antichoice Republican right found him unacceptable when it came out that his physician wife performed abortions in the past. Worse, Ginsburg was involved in a possible conflict of interest when he helped the Justice Department in a cable television First Amendment case while he was an investor in a cable company. But worst of all, from a public relations standpoint, the press got wind of the fact that Ginsburg, while a law professor, used marijuana.

The administration in effect just said no, and Ginsburg withdrew from consideration under pressure from the White House. Later in 1987, the Senate confirmed Anthony M. Kennedy as President Reagan's final addition to the Supreme Court.

As a result of the normal attrition of resignations and retirements, by the time Reagan left office he had appointed nearly four hundred federal judges in all. In 1989, that made up a majority of the federal judiciary. Since federal judicial appointments are for life, the political orientation of the federal judiciary is one of the most lasting impressions a president can leave on the country.

The obverse of this is that, since the appointments are for life and federal judges can only be gotten off the bench voluntarily or by congressional impeachment, a president's judicial appointees have a way of acting independently and often do not conduct themselves, nor rule, the way their appointing presidents and those presidents' supporters anticipated. The Reagan Court did not repeal *Roe v. Wade,* nor did it throw out any major civil-rights legislation or repeal standing Court rulings on such things as busing.

On the other hand, the newly conservative Supreme Court did restrict certain rights of criminal suspects and defendants and allowed states more leeway in regulating such things as pornography standards and the legality of various sexual activities.

The federal judiciary after Reagan has proven more conservative but not radically so. The judiciary, true to form, continues to go its own way. It is never entirely indifferent to the mood of the voters, but neither does it always, as the great political satirist Finley Peter Dunne put it, follow the election returns. (*See also* Robert Bork; Sandra Day O'Connor.)

TAX REFORM

One of Ronald Reagan's principal campaign pledges, and central to his entire conservative philosophy, was the promise of major tax cuts. As Reagan maintained that "government was not the solution, but the problem," he also asserted that the old "tax-and-spend" habits of his liberal opponents had swollen the government and made it intrusive, overregulatory, and bureaucratic.

Taxation, according to the American conservative political credo, is the tool of regulatory tyranny and a threat to private property. Reagan and other conservatives were fond of quoting John Marshall's famous maxim, "The power to tax is the power to destroy."

In his presidential memoirs, Ronald Reagan wrote that he believed the tax cuts of 1981 and the Tax Reform Act of 1986 were among his most important achievements as president. Reagan claimed that during his presidency, despite lower tax rates, the government gained a $375 million increase in tax revenues, which, he further claimed, was more than sufficient to pay for the massive military buildup of the 1980s. These claims are highly controversial.

In the early days of Reaganomics, the administration set about implementing new measures based on its belief that capitalism would benefit from less taxation and less government regulation. In his first budget, the president proposed a plan to cut taxes over a five-year period by about $750 billion. Reagan suggested a 30 percent income-tax reduction over three years; Congress accepted a 25 percent income-tax cut over three years.

Such a major tax cut had to be offset by major reductions in federal spending. The Reagan administration therefore proposed large cuts in school lunch programs, student loans, job-training programs, and funding for urban mass transit. In Congress, many of these cuts, with some modifications, passed with the support of conservative Republicans and Boll Weevil Democrats.

Tax reform figured as a major theme in Reagan's 1984 reelection campaign. At the beginning of the year, the president's state-of-the-union message called for a simplification of the tax code, and the administration promoted the idea up to and through the campaign season. Even so, Reagan did not present a specific program until after the November election.

During 1984, before and after the election, members of the administration, sometimes led by Treasury Secretary and White House Chief of Staff Donald T. Regan, put together the series of plans and proposals that eventually came together in the Tax Reform Act of 1986. The act, in its final form, decreased the number of personal income-tax brackets from fourteen to three and lowered the highest personal tax bracket to 28 percent. The top bracket had been up to 70 percent, and Reagan claimed the new rate was the lowest since 1931, in Herbert Hoover's day.

Reagan further claimed that, under the 1986 act, 80 percent of Americans either paid the lowest tax rate (15 percent) or no taxes at all, and that the 1 percent of Americans who earned the most money paid increased taxes. More than 80 percent of increased personal income-tax revenues between 1981 and 1987, Reagan asserted, came from taxpayers who earned over $100,000 per year, while taxpayers who earned under $50,000 per year paid billions of dollars less taxes.

According to Reagan, his tax policies significantly stimulated the economy, resulting in widespread jobs creation and a 27 percent increase in real gross national product (that is, the overall value of all goods and services, with adjustment for inflation) during his presidency. Further, Reagan pointed to a 12 percent increase in median income for American families during the years 1981 to 1987, as compared to a 10.5 percent decrease during the 1970s.

As explained by Donald T. Regan, the maximum tax rate for individuals was reduced from 50 percent to 28 percent, and the standard deduction both for couples and individuals was increased to, respectively, $5,000 and $3,000. Interest on mortgages remained deductible, but interest on such items as car loans, credit cards, and insurance was no longer deductible. Tax shelters and investment tax credits were drastically cut or abolished. Most of these reforms had been contained in Regan's proposal, which was known as "Treasury I" in the White House, and then found their way into the 1986 Tax Reform Act.

Many commentators considered the 1986 act the most significant change in the American tax system since the 1930s. There is a good deal of argument about the results of the tax reforms. As early as the 1980 campaign, David Stockman, who would become Reagan's budget director in 1981, believed that large tax cuts without massive spending reductions would cause deficits of more than $100 billion a year.

Reagan had promised to increase defense spending and try to balance the budget; Stockman had his doubts that both goals could be accomplished simultaneously, and wondered if the threat of cutting taxes and raising defense spending might be a political ploy to scare Congress into cutting social spending. According to historian Michael Schaller, Reagan himself never confirmed Stockman's suspicions. (*See also* Deficit; Reaganomics; David Stockman.)

TRADE POLICIES

Ronald Reagan identified himself as a free trader. He opposed import quotas and favored competition. To support his free-trade philosophy, Reagan often cited the example of the Smoot-Hawley Tariff Act, passed during the Great Depression. According to Reagan's analysis, the law imposed a rigid tariff on imports in order to protect American farmers. But, Reagan wrote in his memoirs, Smoot-Hawley backfired, harming not only farmers but also much of the rest of the American economy, because it provoked stiff tariffs in other nations, with the result that American farmers and manufacturers sold fewer products in foreign markets.

Even with this history lesson in mind, Reagan's trade policy still ended up a mixture of free trade and protectionism. During his first months in office, Reagan's administration opted to impose import controls on Japanese automobiles. According to budget director David Stockman, Reagan's cabinet and some other economic advisers favored the restrictions, despite the president's stated commitment to free trade.

Reagan later explained that, while he and his administration believed in free trade, excessive government regulation in the past had restricted the American automobile industry, and the automakers were losing money by installing government-mandated air bags, pollution-control devices, and other safety equipment. Consequently, according to Reagan, Detroit was less competitive with the Japanese, so some measure of what in effect was protectionism was warranted.

The Japan restrictions were the first examples of the Reagan administration's mixed trade policies, and they occasioned a feud between the free traders and the protectionists within the administration itself. Treasury Secretary (and later White House chief of staff) Donald T. Regan, White House Chief of Staff (and later Treasury secretary) James Baker, and Stockman led the free-trade faction.

Free trade, Stockman later wrote in his hostile White House memoirs, is actually a simple extension of free enterprise itself. Free competition, wrote Stockman, does not stop at national boundaries. Stockman also argued that government regulation had nothing to do with making Detroit less competitive; after all, Japanese automakers had to obey the same safety and environmental requirements in order to sell their products in the United States. Whatever it was that made Japanese vehicles outsell many American vehicles, it had little if anything to do with government regulation.

But protectionism, at least in this instance, became the White House line. Among its most vigorous champions were Transportation Secretary Drew Lewis, Agriculture Secretary Malcolm Baldridge, and Labor Secretary Raymond Donovan. Reagan tended to listen to them, and other cabinet officers, rather than to Regan, Baker, and Stockman, on the issue of Japanese automobile imports.

Reagan originally intended to veto any quota on Japanese cars that Congress might send to him. But then he considered the evidence that the protectionists in Congress (his account does not mention the protectionists in his cabinet) had on their side. The Japanese, for instance, forbade American farmers to sell agricultural products in Japan, and they often sabotaged many American products with subtle but obnoxious regulations. American cigarette companies, for instance, could only advertise in Japan in English.

Consequently, Reagan concluded, protectionist measures in this instance would ultimately promote free and fair trade. By imposing quotas on Japanese automakers, the United States would exert pressure on Japan to open itself up to genuine free trade with the United States. One nation cannot say to the other nation, wrote Reagan, that "we want to sell you something that we make, but don't send us your products."

The free market could work, Reagan maintained, only if everyone competed on equal terms. That left the natural economic laws of supply and demand, and competition, to take their course. When governments attempt to fix or control prices and impose quotas, or otherwise restrict free market trade, then the whole system will not work. But in this case, he thoguht protectionist measures appropriate.

America's problems with international trade, however, went beyond arguments with Japan over automobile import quotas. The United States' position in the balance of trade slipped dramatically in approximately half a decade. According to Reagan biographer Haynes Johnson, only a few years before President Reagan took office, 95 percent of telephones and 80 percent of television sets sold and used in the United States were manufactured in the United States. By Reagan's first term, only one out of every four telephones and one out of every ten televison sets in America were American made.

Johnson also reported that America's share of automotive manufactures fell to 23 percent by the end of the Reagan years, from 52 percent in the early 1960s. In other words, according to Johnson, in the late 1980s, one of every four cars in use in the United States was foreign made. Also, from about 1960 to the end of the 1980s, America's portion of the world's steel output fell to 11 percent from 26 percent. Johnson wrote that other industrial powers—notably Japan, West Germany, France, and Canada—were catching up with American industry in many markets, and by the late 1980s dominated some of them. (*See also* Economic Summits; Japan.)

TWENTY-FIFTH AMENDMENT

The Twenty-fifth Amendment to the Constitution was adopted in 1967. The need for it was highlighted by the death of John F. Kennedy; from November 22, 1963, until January 20, 1965, the United States had no vice president, and the next in line for the presidency, House Speaker John McCormack, was in his seventies. The second in line, Senate president pro tempore Carl Hayden, was in his eighties.

Of course, such conditions had existed before, but in the age of mass media, widespread alarm over the deficiencies of existing law prompted the drive for the amendment. In the nineteenth century, no one seemed to care much if the nation lacked a vice president for a while. But in more modern times, the situation caused greater concern.

Gerald Ford was the first vice president chosen under the amendment. In 1974, Spiro Agnew resigned after pleading no contest to a criminal charge, and President Nixon nominated Ford to take Agnew's place. The Senate confirmed Nixon's choice, and Gerald Ford was on the way to his own presidency. When Nixon resigned that August, Ford moved into the Oval Office and chose Nelson Rockefeller as his vice president under the same procedures of the amendment.

George Bush was the first vice president to become acting president under the amendment, when President Reagan turned over his authority before undergoing cancer surgery (see below).

The Twenty-fifth Amendment follows in near entirety:

"Section One: In case of the removal of the President from office or of his death or resignation, the Vice President shall become President.

"Section Two: Whenever there is a vacancy in the office of the Vice President, the President shall nominate a Vice President who shall take office upon confirmation by a majority vote of both Houses of Congress.

"Section Three: Whenever the President transmits to the President pro tempore of the Senate and the Speaker of the House of Representatives his written declaration that he is unable to discharge the powers and duties of his office, and until he transmits to them a written declaration to the contrary, such powers and duties shall be discharged by the Vice President as Acting President.

"Section Four: Whenever the Vice President and a majority of either the principal officers of the executive departments or of such other body as Congress may by law provide, transmit to the President pro tempore of the Senate and the Speaker of the House of Representatives their written declaration that the President is unable to discharge the powers and duties of his office, the Vice President shall immediately assume the powers and duties of the office as Acting President.

"Thereafter, when the President transmits to the President pro tempore . . . and the Speaker of the House . . . his written declaration that no inability exists, he shall resume the powers and duties of his office unless the Vice President and a majority of either the principal officers of the executive department[s] or of such other body as Congress may by law provide, transmit within four days to the President pro tempore . . . and the Speaker of the House . . . their written declaration that the President is unable to discharge the powers and duties of his office. Thereupon Congress shall decide the issue, assembling within forty-eight hours for that purpose if not in session. If the Congress, within twenty-one days after receipt of the latter written declaration, or, if Congress is not in session, within twenty-one days after Congress is required to assemble, determines by two-thirds vote of both Houses that the President is unable to discharge the powers and duties of his office, the Vice President shall continue to discharge the same as Acting President; otherwise, the President shall resume the powers and duties of his office."

The first section, stating that the vice president will actually become president, was necessary because, amazingly, the Constitution did not specify the succession. The original clause stated, "In case of the removal of the President from office or of his death, resignation, or inability to discharge the powers and duties of the said office, the same shall devolve on the Vice President. . . ."

That was quite vague. When William Henry Harrison died in 1841 after only one month in office, Vice President John Tyler made his own decision to take the oath of office as president of the United States. His inauguration occasioned much criticism in Congress, but he nevertheless set the precedent that, upon a president's death, the vice president becomes president.

As for the rest of the amendment, it became pertinent when President Reagan was shot in 1981, and during the times that Reagan underwent cancer surgery. On the first occasion, there was a good deal of confusion in the White House over who was in control of what, and a nasty argument broke out between the secretary of state and the secretary of defense in the vice president's absence. Upon the vice president's arrival, the situation quieted down, and George Bush assumed a caretaker role unofficially. (*See also* Assassination Attempt.)

Contrary to what many people believe, Bush did not invoke the amendment when President Reagan was shot in 1981; as Reagan underwent treatment for his wound, he was in full possession of the powers of his office. The first invocation of the temporary transfer of power clause was on July 13, 1985. Before undergoing cancer surgery, Ronald Reagan signed the required letter transferring the "constitutional duties and powers" of the presidency to Vice President Bush, which took effect at 11:30 A.M., when the president went under anesthesia. The letters were delivered to House Speaker Tip O'Neill and Senate president pro tempore Strom Thurmond. The president reclaimed his authority and power at 7:22 P.M. that same day, by signing the paper attesting to his capability to resume his office.

Probably the most controversial section is number four. There have been persistent rumors that, during the Iran-Contra scandal, several White House officials investigated the possibility and advisability of invoking the amendment's fourth section to set President Reagan aside in favor of Vice President Bush.

In their 1988 book, *Landslide,* journalists Jane Mayer and Doyle McManus claimed that, in March 1987, James Cannon, assistant to newly appointed White House Chief of Staff Howard Baker, specifically recommended that Baker consider applying the amendment's set-aside provision. According to the two journalists, Baker took the idea seriously, but did not act upon it, once he determined that the president was capable of fulfilling his duties.

Mayer and McManus cite an interview with Cannon as the sole source for the story; the authors of this book have not encountered any evidence that Baker actually considered approaching Vice President Bush with the proposal, nor that Bush would have been receptive.

After the Iran-Contra scandal broke in the news, rumors circulated that Howard Baker, or George Bush, or other administration officials had considered invoking the amendment to set President Reagan aside. But substantial evidence for the rumors has not, to the author's knowledge, turned up.

TWENTY-YEAR CURSE

Also known as the Zero-Year Curse, the Twenty-Year Curse has haunted the American presidency since someone noticed that every twenty years or so (superstitions never are terribly precise), a president who has been elected to a term ending in the year zero dies in office.

Believers point to the fact that the first president to die in office, William Henry Harrison, died four weeks after his 1841 inauguration, having been elected in 1840. Twenty years later, in 1860, Abraham Lincoln was elected president, and John Wilkes Booth shot him in 1865, at the beginning of his second term. One president died out of sequence: Zachary Taylor was elected in 1848. However, he died in 1850.

Except for Taylor, every other president who died in office did so after winning a term in a zero-year election: Besides Harrison and Lincoln, James A. Garfield, elected in 1880, was assassinated in 1881; William McKinley, elected to a second term in 1900, was assassinated in 1901; Warren G. Harding, elected in 1920, died of a stroke or heart attack in 1923 (there is no reliable evidence that his wife poisoned him, although a lot of people like to believe she did); Franklin D. Roosevelt, elected to a third term in 1940, died in 1945, at the beginning of his fourth term; and John F. Kennedy, elected in 1960, was murdered in 1963.

In 1980, as it grew clear that Ronald Reagan would win, some expected the curse to hold only because Reagan was nearly seventy years old. When Reagan was shot, in 1981, thoughts of the curse gave many people an ugly jolt. The author of this book recalls hearing his coworkers in an Oakland, California, real estate office speculate about the curse on the day that John Hinckley shot Reagan. The curse definitely has a grip on the public's imagination, even if most people do not literally believe in it.

Of course, Ronald Reagan did not die in office. Not only did he not die, but he became the one and only American president ever to survive a direct assassination attempt. Andrew Jackson, Franklin Roosevelt, Harry Truman, and Gerald Ford all were targets of botched attempts, but Reagan is the only president to survive wounds inflicted by a would-be assassin.

The Twenty-Year Curse should have been laid to rest by Reagan's eight full years in office, but, human nature being what it is, belief in the curse no doubt will persist. Some dedicated believers have probably rationalized Reagan's exception and anxiously await the election of 2000.

U

UNEMPLOYMENT

During 1982 and 1983, unemployment hit its highest levels since the Great Depression of the 1930s, and there followed a much-publicized recovery. The unemployment figures declined, but changes in the American work environment and a persistent lack of employment among certain groups, along with the literal disappearance of many kinds of jobs, made unemployment the other side of the coin during the recovery period.

A key to understanding the economy of the Reagan years is that, according to most analyses, during the 1980s the disparity between rich and poor increased greatly, thus creating a cavernous gulf between the haves and have-nots of American society. The growth and entrenchment of a huge urban underclass, the rise of a "new poor," and an alarming increase in the rate of homelessness reinforced class distinction that tended to divide along rigid racial and ethnic lines. The poor became poorer as the rich became richer, and it was largely the traditionally poverty-stricken groups that suffered all the more severely. The wealthier groups rode a euphoric wave of investment growth and consumer confidence as the Reagan recovery got underway in 1983 and 1984.

During Reagan's first term, the recession set in during 1981, and that year unemployment hit double digits for the first time in nearly fifty years. National unemployment figures rose to 10.8 percent in 1981; by November of 1982, 11.5 million Americans filled the ranks of the unemployed (additionally, nearly 10 million employed people had to take lower-paying jobs, some drastically so). Since people usually vote their wallets, the Republicans ran into trouble in the 1982 elections, and President Reagan had trouble in the polls.

The official unemployment figures always underestimate the real numbers of the unemployed, in any era, recession or not. Unemployment statistics reflect the numbers of people who have filed unemployment claims or answered various surveys, census reports, or whatever. The figures usually do not take into account the long-term unemployed who have dropped off the unemployment rolls, nor do they necessarily estimate how many unemployed people simply do not show up at a county unemployment office. All that can make unemployment figures all the more alarming, since we can always assume there are more jobless than indicated.

When Reagan first took office in January 1981, the unemployment rate was 7.5 percent, but by November 1982, in the depths of the recession, it hit the 10.8 percent figure that still stands as the post–Great Depression record. During the Great Depression, incidentally, the unemployment rate went as high as 30 percent.

Reagan biographer Lou Cannon noted that the Teflon effect that marked much of Reagan's presidency did not pertain during the recession, and his administration had to withstand the grumblings of national discontent. In February 1982, in Minneapolis, Reagan was picketed by unemployed protesters at a fund-raiser; one banner addressed him as "President Hoover," on whose watch the stock market crashed in 1929. That spring, in Washington, activists erected a tent city of homeless people near the White House and set up other tent cities in several locations around the country; the activists dubbed their communities "Reagan ranches."

Shantytowns of homeless appeared all over the nation, on riverbanks, beneath freeway overpasses, in back alleys. Similar places in the early 1930s were called Hoovervilles; many people called these new shantytowns Reaganvilles. Cannon reported that Reagan's approval ratings fell to 41 percent by the end of 1982.

During 1983 the economy began to recover, and the unemployment rate declined. Over the next few years, 18 million jobs were created, and yet a stubborn strain of unemployment persisted amid the rapturous confidence of the recovery. According to journalist Haynes Johnson, despite the 1983 economic rebound, another 10 million Americans lost their jobs because of layoffs and plant closings between 1983 and 1988. Of those 10 million, about 2.5 million were experienced workers who had held their jobs for three years or more and had to take lower-paying jobs.

The decline of the American steel industry provided another chronic source of unemployment and underemployment during the Reagan years, and many steel-producing areas stayed trapped in perenniel regional depressions; the media named these areas the "Rust Belt." In Minnesota, Illinois, Pennsylvania, and other places that once supplied the workers and sites for the burgeoning steel industry, towns withered into boarded-up wastelands as Japan and other nations overtook America in steel production. These conditions helped create a population of hard-core unemployed in many of the nation's industrial towns.

The end of the Reagan era saw a permanently depressed urban underclass that was largely black and Latino. The smaller cities and towns of the Rust Belt, and those that had been mining towns and oil towns, remained mired in hard times, and remained impervious to the Reagan recovery, even though, according to many economic analysts, the recovery ushered in the longest sustained economic boom in American history. (*See also* Elections—Congressional; Reagan Recession/Reagan Recovery.)

V

Former Treasury Secretary and White House Chief of Staff Donald T. Regan described Federal Reserve Board chairman Paul Volcker as brilliant, dedicated, enigmatic, and stern. He was, according to Regan, the only person in Washington who could "stand up with impunity" to President Reagan's remarkable popularity. Volcker was an independent figure who often locked horns with some members of the Reagan administration.

As head of the governors of the Fed, Volcker technically had more to do with monetary policy than the president or the Treasury secretary. The Federal Reserve Board is designed to stand independently of the executive branch, and monetary policy is its own preserve, though rare is the president who can simply leave the Fed and its board of six governors alone. Volcker, a strong and determined sort, understood his role and exercised the power inherent in his position, which was to see that the economy had sufficient cash and credit for growth.

An imposing presence at six feet seven inches tall, Volcker literally towered over his critics, as well as his supporters. President Jimmy Carter appointed Volcker the Fed's chairman in 1979. Carter and Volcker believed that following a "tight-money" policy—that is, contracting the circulating money supply—would produce high interest rates that would reign in the rampant inflation then plaguing the nation.

President Reagan and others in his administration tended to approve of the tight-money approach but had reservations about Volcker's policies, especially since Volcker was not receptive to supply-side theory. The administration's money men, such as Treasury Secretary Regan and budget director David Stockman, worried about Volcker for another reason: They suspected that his tight-money policy was having bad effects.

Part of the money-supply theory is that interest rates rise if there is less money in circulation, but if there is a lot of money circulating, inflation results. The Fed sought a balance, since the 1970s had seen drastic inflation. But by 1982, the economy became so pinched that interest-sensitive businesses suffered. The housing industry slowed to a crawl, Detroit had its fewest car sales since the early 1960s, and American industry as a whole felt the high-interest pinch. Regan and other supply-siders maintained that Volcker's actions stalled recovery.

Even though Reagan, shortly after taking office in 1981, personally asked Volcker why we needed the Federal Reserve at all, he tended to support Volcker in the tight money controversy, thus going against his own top economic advisers.

The Republican president and the Democratic Fed chairman were not very far apart in some matters. When the country was in the depths of the worst recession since the 1930s, Reagan believed that his spending cuts dovetailed nicely with Volcker's tight-money crusade against inflation. Reagan believed that some belt-tightening would force a disciplined correction in the nation's economy; he often said that the country had been living beyond its means since the heady spending days of Lyndon Johnson's Great Society. Now Keynesian economic liberalism would have to give way to what Reagan and the administration considered solidly grounded thinking.

However, Reagan would not raise taxes, though some in his administration wanted him to do so. David Stockman and others argued that they could not achieve further spending cuts without a tax increase. Even some Senate Republicans, including Robert Dole, said that there would have to be a tax increase if the economy did not show significant signs of improvement within a few months.

Stockman and his cohorts further argued that Volcker needed

to ease up on the tight-money policy because the higher interest rates were damaging the economy. Secretary Regan, for one, told Reagan that the first quarter of 1982 was going to be even worse than anyone predicted because of the high interest rates.

Regan added that Volcker personally told him that he would try to compromise with the White House by easing the money contraction and then seeing if the interest rates might ease as well. But Volcker also told Regan that he feared declining interest rates might bring inflation back, and he wanted to see some solid administration action on the mounting deficits.

During 1981 inflation declined to 5 percent, but interest rates rose sharply, which, according to Donald Regan and others, made a 1982 recovery impossible. Regan's Treasury Department blamed the Fed for keeping the money supply reduced. Some suspected that Volcker was willing to see the economy stall on a short-term basis, since he believed with nearly religious fervor that inflation must be banished.

Other Republicans contemplated drastic action. In the House of Representatives, Jack Kemp portrayed Volcker as the enemy of recovery, demanded that he resign, and threatened congressional action to force the Fed into lowering interest rates. So Volcker had an unexpected ally in Ronald Reagan.

Stockman called Reagan's support of the Fed chairman "unwavering." That no doubt accurately describes it, since 1982 was a terrible year of recession, low approval ratings for the president, fights within the Republican party over monetary and fiscal policies, and widespread frustration over the economy's erratic performance.

Even after the dark days of 1982, Reagan renominated Volcker as chairman of the Fed in 1983, much to the dismay of Secretary Regan. Shortly afterward, Volcker did ease the Fed's restrictions on the money supply. That summer Mexico threatened to default on its loans, which in turn raised the threat of a worldwide banking collapse. Volcker believed that, in 1929, the Federal Reserve had imposed a tight money policy at the precise moment the supply should have been eased, and he decided to take a lesson from history.

The Fed therefore allowed new bills to flow hither and yon, and the money in circulation increased. That same year, the recovery finally set in, and, of course, many would argue that Volcker's actions contributed heavily to the economy's rebound. Unemployment fell from 7.1 percent to 5.5 percent, and inflation continued to decline.

The Fed still liked its tight-money policies, but the governors showed intelligent flexibility when necessary. When the stock market crashed in 1987, the Fed's timely action may have saved the day. The new chairman, Alan Greenspan, and the governors released the money supply and guaranteed credit, thereby allowing cash and credit flow to alleviate the panic that set in after the crash.

David Stockman credits Paul Volcker for the recovery from the recession of the early 1980s, and praises Reagan for supporting the man whom Stockman believes the greatest chairman the Federal Reserve had ever had. Others, including Donald Regan, remained unconvinced and still claim that Reaganomics was the salvation of the American economy in the 1980s.

Whatever the answer, Paul Volcker (who left the Fed toward the end of the Reagan years) was the first Federal Reserve chairman whose name became a household word in America. He was, in his time, in the news as frequently and as prominently as any famous politician or other public official and many have praised him for active, independent leadership that steered the country out of a severe recession and into a recovery. (*See also* Stock Market Crash of 1987.)

W

WEDTECH SCANDAL

The Wedtech scandal was a major embarrassment for the Reagan administration. It involved fraud, influence buying, and any number of other misdeeds on the part of crooked businessmen who were publicly praised by President Reagan and enjoyed the support of White House contacts before the scandal broke. Wedtech took down several public figures with it, and Attorney General Edwin Meese was very nearly one of them.

The scandal began with the Welbilt Electronic Die Corporation, renamed Wedtech in the early 1980s. The company began in the blighted South Bronx of New York City, and through the business smarts of its founder, John Mariotta, Wedtech became a military contractor, albeit on a limited scale. Mariotta claimed to employ welfare recipients (thus getting them off the welfare rolls), and, he said, if more companies followed his example, they would save the government millions of dollars and generate even more millions in new business.

Wedtech grew, began to sell stock, and then abruptly filed bankruptcy at the end of 1986. Its executives (including Mariotta) and many of its Washington supporters found themselves under criminal investigation. What unfolded was a tale of scamming, bribery, influence buying, and influence peddling.

In 1981 Welbilt (not yet Wedtech) was barely making it in the South Bronx. It had been there for ten years and was losing money—about a million dollars during 1981. Since Mariotta was the son of Puerto Ricans, the company had managed to win a couple of small government contracts under the federal set-aside program for minority businesses, but it had not gotten much. In 1981 Welbilt was trying to get a five-year contract to build small engines for the army. It lost out by overbidding.

During that same year Wedtech's fortunes changed. The company somehow managed to hire a San Francisco attorney named E. Bob Wallach, a close friend and professional associate of Attorney General Edwin Meese. Wallach immediately started lobbying Meese on Wedtech's behalf.

In 1982 Lyn Nofziger, President Reagan's political director, quit his job in the White House, opened a public relations firm, and took on Wedtech as a client. Wedtech paid Nofziger in stock and fees that totaled about a million dollars; Wallach, too, profited to the tune of over a million dollars for his efforts on behalf of Wedtech, which entailed interesting the attorney general in the company.

One of Nofziger's White House contacts set about pressuring the army to award a gasoline engine contract to Wedtech. Nofziger's contact went so far as to attend the negotiations between Wedtech, the army, and the Small Business Administration. When the SBA head denied Wedtech the army contract, he was fired within weeks.

That April, Nofziger directly asked Meese to intervene in the Wedtech-Army-SBA situation. The apparent result of this was a very unusual meeting in the White House itself between representatives of Wedtech, the army, and the new head of the SBA. One of the attorney general's deputies presided over the meeting; the deputy said that Meese had ordered that the Wedtech negotiation be resumed. The deputy allegedly made it known during the meeting that Wedtech was to get the army contract.

Wedtech signed a $27.7 million deal with the army for the gasoline engines and collected a $3 million grant from the SBA—an unusually high amount, even for a grant, as opposed to a loan. SBA's policy was to limit such grants to $100,000, but Wedtech proved a special case. As a result of the White House's largesse, Wedtech became a major success, its profits shot up, and John Mariotta and others connected to Wedtech became millionaires and multimillionaires in short order.

Things began falling apart in the wake of a stock deal. Several of Wedtech's officers and some of its consultants, including Nofziger, sold their shares for at least $10 million, prompting the Securities and Exchange Commission to look into the deal. The SBA revoked Wedtech's minority business status shortly after the transaction, and that led to suspicions of illegal insider trading. Not long after that, in 1986, Wedtech declared bankruptcy. The company already was under criminal investigation.

What followed was a nightmare for the Reagan administration. Wallach and another consultant were indicted for racketeering, fraud, and conspiracy. Attorney General Meese also came under investigation. Less than two years before, during the 1984 presidential campaign, Ronald Reagan had publicly praised both Mariotta and Wedtech, calling the erstwhile businessman a "hero for the eighties." Between 1982 and 1986, Wedtech had gotten about $250 million in no-bid minority contracts from the Pentagon, deals that included contracts with the army and the navy. The company fell far quickly, and the administration was singed by scandal.

The subsequent investigations turned up some interesting transgressions. For one thing, Wedtech never actually qualified for the minority set-asides, since Mariotta, of Puerto Rican parentage, did not own a majority of the company. Another partner, not a minority-group member, owned a full 50 percent of Wedtech, so the partners simply lied about Mariotta's share of ownership, which they reported as two-thirds.

But Wedtech's misdeeds weren't confined to the White House deals. It turned out that the company had hired a law firm owned by New York congressman Mario Biaggi as consultants, and Biaggi proceeded to persuade federal agencies to award Wedtech contracts. While lobbying on Wedtech's behalf, Biaggi neglected to identify himself as a hired consultant, or lobbyist, for the company.

On other occasions, when the company's minority status became suspect, Wedtech bribed a federal official, who in turn confirmed Wedtech's entitlement to the minority set-aside and thus saved a profitable navy contract for Mariotta and partners. When Wedtech failed to deliver on the navy order, the navy nevertheless renewed the contract and paid cash advances, and Wedtech sold $75 million in a public bond offering. At this point, Wedtech was on the verge of collapse and insolvency, and the company officers knew it.

Ultimately, Wallach and Nofziger, along with some other less famous parties to the misadventure, were convicted for their parts in the Wedtech scandal. Nofziger's conviction was overturned on appeal. Attorney General Edwin Meese admitted exerting some influence on Wedtech's behalf but was not indicted, and this prompted several of his Justice Department aides to resign in protest.

Wedtech itself failed, and its stocks and bonds turned worthless. The bankruptcy ended up costing millions of dollars for both the federal government and Wedtech's private investors.

President Reagan escaped major public censure for the scandal, and his popularity remained intact, at least until the major revelations of the Iran-Contra scandal. (*See also* Cabinet; Iran-Contra.)

WHITE HOUSE CHIEFS OF STAFF

James Baker III began in the Reagan administration as the White House chief of staff, then switched jobs with Treasury Secretary Donald T. Regan during the second term. Baker later served as George Bush's secretary of state, and Regan eventually resigned from the White House after drawing the first lady's enmity and being censured by the Tower Board for his alleged failure to avert the Iran-Contra scandal.

Regan's successor, Howard Baker, helped the president restore stability to his administration and recapture his standing in the public-opinion polls. After Howard Baker left in 1988, Kenneth Duberstein saw the administration through its final year as Ronald Reagan's last White House chief of staff.

James Baker belonged to one of the founding families of Houston, Texas. He served as George Bush's campaign manager in the 1980 race for the Republican presidential nomination, then helped to secure Bush's vice-presidential nomination. Though not an extreme conservative, Baker fit comfortably into the Reagan White House, and later settled into the Treasury Department. A good "insider" politician, Baker flourished as a cabinet officer, presidential adviser, and campaign manager—although his last campaign effort in 1992 ended in defeat for George Bush.

As a relative moderate in his politics, Baker endured the mistrust and hostility of Reagan's more conservative staffers and advisers, and he was widely mistrusted among the ranks of the Republican right wing. But he was capable and savvy, and soon formed a solid working relationship with Ronald Reagan's two most intimate and trusted advisers, Edwin Meese and Michael Deaver (Deaver was Baker's deputy on paper, but not in reality).

The archconservative Meese and Deaver never liked Baker. Recognizing his capabilities, however, they set aside their differences with him, and the three men built a solid wall around the president as they ran the White House's day-to-day business. Others in the administration nicknamed this unlikely team the "troika," after the famous Russian sleigh that had a team of three horses.

Baker was pragmatic rather than ideological, but he was an accomplished negotiator and a skilled political operative. Folksy but sophisticated, Baker won many people over during Reagan's first term and served as an important stabilizing figure. Baker, Meese, and Deaver ran the White House and, to some extent, insulated the president from ultraconservative influences and political miscalculations.

Some analysts of the Reagan years have wondered if Baker's continued presence, with or without Deaver and Meese, would have saved the Reagan White House a good deal of trouble, as many believe Baker alone would have had the good sense to steer the administration clear of the arms-for-hostages deals and that he probably would have kept John Poindexter and Oliver North from acting so freely and foolishly.

Keeping a cool head when others are losing theirs can antagonize associates, and Baker's moderation may have had something to do with the reshuffling that occurred early in Reagan's second term. Before that, late in 1983, National Security Adviser William Clark wanted to move into the cabinet as secretary of the interior to replace the departing and unlamented James Watt. According to the president's account, when James Baker heard of Clark's request, he asked to be appointed national security adviser and recommended that Michael Deaver take over as White House chief of staff.

Reagan wrote that he found the idea agreeable, but Meese, Casey, and Defense Secretary Caspar Weinberger did not. They disliked the idea of Deaver as chief of staff, and they were not pleased with the prospect of their ideological adversary, James Baker, presiding over the National Security Council. Reagan decided to avoid friction among the White House staff and did not make the appointments.

In due course, Reagan gave the NSC job to Robert McFarlane, and then, just after the 1984 election, James Baker and Treasury Secretary Donald T. Regan suggested to the president that he switch their jobs between them. Reagan later wrote that appointing Baker to Treasury shortly before his second term began was a turning point in the administration, although Reagan did not realize it at the time.

Baker's departure to Treasury removed him from a position in which he might have headed off Iran-Contra by keeping North, Poindexter, and, for that matter, CIA Director William Casey, under control; perhaps this is what Reagan meant by calling Baker's cabinet appointment a turning point. Baker's successor in the White House, Donald T. Regan, had neither the diplomatic nature nor the manipulative skill to deal successfully with other administration officials—or with the president's wife, who disliked and opposed Regan early on.

As Treasury secretary during the first term, Regan came into conflict with budget director David Stockman and other presidential advisers. Even so, Regan had a lot to do with Reagan's tax reform bills and strongly advocated that mixture of supply-side theory and fixed-rate growth monetarism that constituted Reaganomics.

Regan's switch from cabinet to White House staff was unusual, and he exercised unusual power in the position. After Meese left the White House to become attorney general and Deaver left the administration altogether, Regan alone tried to fill the shoes of three, and his performance drew very mixed reviews.

Regan managed to incur Nancy Reagan's wrath and nearly everyone else's. He got embroiled in the fallout from the Iran-Contra scandal. Regan wrote one of the more famous and revealing memoirs of the Reagan administration, which he published after leaving the White House but while President Reagan was still in office. It was Regan who broke the story that Nancy Reagan consulted an astrologer, thus embarrassing the first lady and the administration. He wrote blistering criticisms of Nancy Reagan, and his onetime close relationship with the president soured in the wake of Regan's public revelations.

The Tower report later noted that Regan "asserted personal control over the White House staff" and even involved himself in national security affairs. He was present, according to the report, at all the "relevant meetings regarding the Iran initiative" and should have insisted "that an orderly process be observed."

Regan claimed to be ignorant of much of the doings of those responsible for Iran-Contra and denied the report's claim that he was at least culpable for letting such things occur while he was chief of staff, even if he engaged in no actual wrongdoing. He was never charged with any crime. At most, the report implies he committed a sin of omission—no small matter for someone in a position of public trust.

Many staffers thought that Regan considered himself a "deputy president," empowered to make administrative decisions. Some believed he limited or granted access to the president to punish his opponents or reward his supporters. The first lady often clashed with him, sometimes over his control of the president's schedule. He ended at least one telephone argument with Nancy Reagan by hanging up on her.

Regan resigned his post under considerable pressure from the administration, and, apparently, from Nancy Reagan. Both Reagans wrote unfavorably of Regan in their autobiographies. Ronald Reagan wrote that he allowed Baker and Regan to switch jobs "not realizing how much it would enlarge Regan's powers at the expense of others on the staff, restrict access to me, and lead to problems later on."

Nancy Reagan wrote that she advised her husband to fire Regan when the chief of staff became a "serious liability." Both Reagans stated publicly that they resented Regan's White House memoir; Regan portrayed the president as a passive cypher for aides like Meese and Deaver, and the first lady as a willful harridan.

Regan described the president as a sort of anchorman who acted the role of president, and he referred to Nancy Reagan as the president's actual chief of staff. Regan claimed not to be guilty of peremptory attitudes attributed to him, and he explained some of the perks he enjoyed (such as use of the presidential helicopter) as efficiency measures.

A few other members of the administration, such as former press spokesmen Larry Speakes and Marlin Fitzwater, have spoken on Regan's behalf, and deny the persistent rumors that Regan insisted on being addressed as "chief," or that he forced the resignation of National Security Adviser Robert McFarlane. But Nancy Reagan made her dislike of Regan abundantly clear in her memoirs, and vigorously sought to confirm the worst rumors about him.

Regan's successor, Howard Baker, former United States senator from Tennessee, achieved national prominence as the ranking Republican on the special Senate Watergate Committee in 1973 and 1974. He tried, unsuccessfully, for the Republican presidential nomination in 1980; when the Republicans won the Senate in 1980, he served as majority leader. He left the Senate in 1985 (Robert Dole replaced him as Senate majority leader), and in 1987, just before Regan resigned under pressure, President Reagan called him out of retirement to take the chief-of-staff position.

Howard Baker faced a White House in chaos, an administration in disrepute, a number of senior presidential aides under investigation, and a president in trouble with the public. The new chief of staff enjoyed considerable prestige with the public because of his stint on the Watergate Committee, and Reagan relied on him to bring some measure of respectability and stability back to the White House. Baker had the public image of being a "clean" Republican, and many in the administration believed his presence would combat what the press called the "sleaze factor."

Baker, an experienced politician, still had good relations and close ties with Capitol Hill, and a firm grasp on the workings of the federal government in both the legislative and executive branches. He would stand in stark contrast to Regan in that he was not peremptory, didn't alienate the cabinet or Congress, and got along well with National Security Adviser Frank Carlucci and Carlucci's successor, Colin Powell (Regan and McFarlane were barely on speaking terms a good deal of the time). In short, Baker didn't consider himself a sort of White House CEO, or deputy president, as some alleged Regan had.

Baker's successor, Kenneth Duberstein, previously served in the Reagan White House in other capacities. He was an experienced operative who had ties and connections in Washington that proved useful when he became chief of staff. Duberstein did not become a pervasive public figure, as nearly all his predecessors in the Reagan White House had, but that may attest to his quiet competence as he saw the administration out, during 1988 and 1989. (See also Astrology; Bitburg; Cabinet; Iran-Contra; Laffer Curve; Nancy Davis Reagan; Reaganomics; Reagan Recession/Reagan Recovery.)

Z

ZERO-ZERO OPTION

In an address to the National Press Club in Washington on November 18, 1981, President Reagan proposed that the Soviet Union and the United States reduce the threat of nuclear war by eliminating both sides' intermediate-range nuclear weapons in Europe.

That was the basic proposal that Reagan himself called the Zero-Zero Option, a name sometimes shortened to "Zero Option." Reagan put it forth as a basis for the INF Treaty and for the ongoing arms reduction dialogues between the United States and the Soviet Union.

The Zero-Zero Option was a big hit at home. Both houses of Congress endorsed it; the Senate vote was unanimous. The NATO allies liked it, too, and it received ringing endorsements from British prime minister Margaret Thatcher and West German Chancellor Helmut Kohl. It played well in the press, and in the following days many newspaper editorials praised it.

Reagan invited the Soviet Union to enter into negotiations to reduce both sides' arsenals of long-range strategic nuclear weapons at equal levels. Reagan also proposed bringing conventional military forces in Europe to parity between NATO and the Warsaw Pact countries.

The Soviets were not impressed. Leonid Brezhnev reigned in Moscow, and U.S.-Soviet relations were in a poor state. Brezhnev made it known that the Soviet Union would not agree to any such proposal, and the Soviet press questioned American motives.

Reagan's own rhetoric no doubt helped fuel Soviet suspicions, as the president revived many Cold War themes in his speeches and was still conducting the massive military buildup that the Soviets realized they had no hope of matching. To the Soviets, it seemed that Reagan tried to have it both ways; he wanted to appear both tough and reasonable.

At the actual arms-control negotiations, representatives of both superpowers found themselves working around their respective leaders' public statements; American negotiator Paul Nitze could not seriously propose the Zero-Zero Option, and Soviet negotiator Yuli Kvitsinsky tried to steer a more moderate course than Brezhnev's bellicose tone suggested. The two came up with a compromise, which pleased neither government, as it would have left both nations with some deployed missiles. America wanted Zero-Zero, and Brezhnev was not in a compliant mood. The Soviet leader feared America's Pershing II intermediate missiles, but was unwilling to meet a removal of the Pershings with a matching stand-down of Soviet missiles.

The Zero-Zero Option did not become a viable negotiating tool until Mikhail Gorbachev took power in Moscow in 1985. A loosening of U.S.-Soviet relations followed, and Reagan's Zero-Zero Option figured into the renewed arms-control dialogue between the two nuclear superpowers. It became the central element of the 1988 Intermediate Range/Nuclear Forces under which the United States and the Soviet Union agreed to withdraw their intermediate-range nuclear missiles from Europe.

In keeping with the spirit of Zero-Zero, the treaty provided that each side destroy the missiles it withdrew. (*See also* Arms Control/ Arms Race; Leonid Brezhnev; Cold War; Foreign Policy/Foreign Relations; Mikhail Gorbachev.)

Selected Bibliography

Ambrose, Stephen E. *Rise to Globalism*. New York: Penguin, 1985.

Anderson, Martin. *Revolution: The Reagan Legacy*. Stanford, Calif.: Hoover Institution Press, 1990.

Bell, Terrel H. *The Thirteenth Man: A Reagan Cabinet Memoir*. New York: The Free Press, 1988.

Beschloss, Michael R., and Strobe Talbott. *At The Highest Levels*. Boston: Little, Brown, 1993.

Boaz, David. *Assessing the Reagan Years*. Washington, D.C.: Cato Institute, 1988.

Boyer, Paul, ed. *Reagan as President*. Chicago: Ivan R. Dee, 1990.

Cannon, Lou. *President Reagan, The Role of a Lifetime*. New York: Simon & Schuster, 1991.

Carter, Hodding. *The Reagan Years*. New York: Braziller, 1988.

Carter, Jimmy. *Keeping Faith: The Memoirs of a President*. New York: Bantam, 1982.

———. *The Blood of Abraham*. Boston: Houghton Mifflin, 1985.

Dallek, Robert. *Ronald Reagan: The Politics of Symbolism*. Cambridge, Mass.: Harvard University Press, 1984.

Daniloff, Nicholas. *Two Lives, One Russia*. London: Bodley Head, 1989.

Davis, Patti. *The Way I See It*. New York: G.P. Putnam's Sons, 1992.

Deaver, Michael, with Mickey Herskowitz. *Behind the Scenes*. New York: Morrow, 1987.

Duffy, Michael, and Dan Goodgame. *Marching in Place: The Status Quo Presidency of George Bush*. New York: Simon & Schuster, 1992.

Fitzwater, Marlin. *Call the Briefing!* New York: Times Books, 1995.

Friedman, George, and Meredith LeBard. *The Coming War with Japan*. New York: St. Martin's Press, 1991.

Gaddis, John Lewis. *Strategies of Containment*. New York: Oxford University Press, 1982.

Johnson, Haynes. *Sleepwalking Through History: America in the Reagan Years*. New York: W.W. Norton, 1991.

Kissinger, Henry. *Diplomacy*. New York: Simon & Schuster, 1994.

Kurz, Kenneth Franklin. *Franklin Roosevelt and the Gospel of Fear*. University of California, Los Angeles Dissertation, 1995.

LaFeber, Walter. *America, Russia, and the Cold War, 1945–1984*. Fifth edition. New York: Alfred A. Knopf, 1985.

Mayer, Jane, and Doyle McManus. *Landslide*. Boston: Houghton Mifflin, 1988.

McClellan, Woodford. *Russia: A History of the Soviet Period*. Englewood Cliffs, N.J.: Prentice-Hall, 1986.

McFarlane, Robert C., with Zofia Smardz. *Special Trust*. New York: Cadell & Davies, 1994.

Meese, Edwin III. *With Reagan: The Inside Story*. Washington, D.C.: National Book Network, 1992.

Morely, Morris H., ed. *Crisis and Confrontation: Ronald Reagan's Foreign Policy*. Totowa, N. J.: Rowman and Littlefield, 1988.

Nelson, Michael, ed. *The Elections of 1984*. Washington, D.C.: Congressional Quarterly Press, 1985.

Nofziger, Franklyn. *Nofziger*. Washington, D.C.: National Book Network, 1992.

Noonan, Peggy. *What I Saw at the Revolution*. New York: Ballantine Books, 1990.

O'Neill, Thomas P., with William Novak. *Man of the House*. New York: St. Martin's Press, 1987.

Reagan, Maureen. *First Father, First Daughter*. Boston: Little, Brown, 1989.

Reagan, Michael, with Joe Hyams. *On the Outside Looking In*. New York: Zebra Books, 1988.

Reagan, Nancy, with William Novak. *My Turn*. New York: Random House, 1989.

Reagan, Ronald. *An American Life*. New York: Simon & Schuster, 1990.

————, with Helene Von Damm. *Sincerely, Ronald Reagan*. New York: Green Hill, 1976.

————. *Speaking My Mind*. New York: Simon & Schuster, 1989.

————. *The Creative Society*. New York: Devin-Adair, 1968.

————. *Where's the Rest of Me?* New York: Dell, 1965.

Regan, Donald T. *For the Record*. San Diego: Harcourt Brace Jovanovich, 1988.

Schaller, Michael. *Reckoning with Reagan*. New York: Oxford University Press, 1992.

Schwarz, Bernard. *A History of the Supreme Court*. New York: Oxford University Press, 1993.

Schwarzkopf, H. Norman, with Peter Petre. *It Doesn't Take a Hero*. New York: Bantam Books, 1992.

Shultz, George P. *Turmoil and Triumph*. New York: Charles Scribner's Sons, 1993.

Smith, William French. *Law and Justice in the Reagan Administration*. Stanford, Calif.: Hoover Institution Press, 1991.

Speakes, Larry, with Robert Pack. *Speaking Out*. New York: Charles Scribner's Sons, 1988.

Stockman, David A. *The Triumph of Politics*. New York: Harper & Row, 1986.

Thatcher, Margaret. *Margaret Thatcher: The Downing Street Years, 1979–1990*. New York: HarperCollins, 1993.

Walsh, Lawrence E. *Iran-Contra: The Final Report*. New York: Times Books, 1994.

Wills, Gary. *Reagan's America*. New York: Penguin, 1988.

Index

Page numbers in **boldface** indicate main entries.